Dance in a World of Change

Reflections on Globalization and Cultural Difference

Sherry B. Shapiro, EdD
Professor of Dance
Director of Women's Studies
Meredith College
Raleigh, North Carolina

Human Kinetics

Library of Congress Cataloging-in-Publication Data

Dance in a world of change : reflections on globalization and cultural difference / [edited by] Sherry B. Shapiro.
  p. cm.
Includes bibliographical references and index.
ISBN-13: 978-0-7360-6943-4 (hard covcr)
ISBN-10: 0-7360-6943-7 (hard cover)
  1. Dance--Social aspects. 2. Dance--Anthropological aspects. I. Shapiro, Sherry B., 1952-
GV1588.6.D374 2008
306.4'84--dc22

                              2007050891

ISBN-10: 0-7360-6943-7
ISBN-13: 978-0-7360-6943-4

Acquisitions Editor: Judy Patterson Wright, PhD; **Developmental Editor:** Amanda Eastin-Allen; **Assistant Editors:** Laura Koritz and Christine Horger; **Copyeditor:** Jocelyn Engman; **Proofreader:** Kim Thoren; **Indexer:** Dan Connolly; **Permission Manager:** Carly Breeding; **Graphic Designer:** Fred Starbird; **Graphic Artist:** Tara Welsch; **Cover Designer:** Keith Blomberg; **Photographer (cover):** Nada Dogan; **Photo Office Assistant:** Jason Allen; **Art Manager:** Kelly Hendren; **Associate Art Manager:** Alan L. Wilborn; **Illustrator:** Denise Lowry; **Printer:** Sheridan Books

Photos in chapter 9 courtesy of Shu-Ying Liu

Printed in the United States of America   10 9 8 7 6 5 4 3 2 1

Human Kinetics
Web site: www.HumanKinetics.com

United States: Human Kinetics
P.O. Box 5076
Champaign, IL 61825-5076
800-747-4457
e-mail: humank@hkusa.com

Canada: Human Kinetics
475 Devonshire Road Unit 100
Windsor, ON N8Y 2L5
800-465-7301 (in Canada only)
e-mail: info@hkcanada.com

Europe: Human Kinetics
107 Bradford Road
Stanningley
Leeds LS28 6AT, United Kingdom
+44 (0) 113 255 5665
e-mail: hk@hkeurope.com

Australia: Human Kinetics
57A Price Avenue
Lower Mitcham, South Australia 5062
08 8372 0999
e-mail: info@hkaustralia.com

New Zealand: Human Kinetics
Division of Sports Distributors NZ Ltd.
P.O. Box 300 226 Albany
North Shore City
Auckland
0064 9 448 1207
e-mail: info@humankinetics.co.nz

For those who seek to create peace, love, and justice,
and, of course, for those who just dance.

contents

preface

Dance, like just about every other human experience today, is affected by globalization. We are all being globalized—and being 'globalized', as Zygmunt Bauman (1998, 1) tells us, "means much the same to all who are 'globalized'. Globalization is the intractable fate of the world, an irreversible process." The human migration across borders, the shrinking of distance and time through technology, and the growing connections between diverse communities are creating a world that is transforming our sensibilities and understanding of others. These transformations are not always easy, since they disrupt our assumptions about what are good and bad, beautiful and ugly, and rational and irrational. Traditional forms of belief and expression are undermined by the influx of alternative visions and values. Yet at the same time, these changes are generative; they produce new and sometimes startling forms of art, they help to create new identities formed from disparate histories and experiences, and they help us rethink how we value one dance form over another. Nowhere is this clearer than in dance itself, in which globalization has opened new possibilities for appreciating and recognizing the amazing range of human embodied expression. More than this, globalization is creating new forms of dance expression that join the modern to the traditional, the urban to the indigenous, and the secular to the spiritual. This exciting expansion of the meaning of dance demands that educators understand these changes and have the knowledge that enables them to illustrate to their students what these changes might mean.

Multiculturalism, or cultural diversity, has been at the forefront of our recent concerns in dance and pedagogy in our attempt to address why we value one cultural dance form while belittling or even silencing other cultural dance forms. Though our work in multiculturalism has been relevant and necessary, it is now time to turn a critical lens to dance in an emerging global culture. As we cross borders and learn and take from each other, questions concerning the meaning of tradition itself begin to surface. An example of this cultural borrowing is the explosion of African dance in our colleges, universities, schools, and community dance programs. Questions that emerge are those such as "What is African dance?" and "Is it African dance if it is taught by a non-African?" or "Does it remain cultural dance if it is performed simply as a dance and no longer as a story of the people?" When traditional forms, such as Irish step dance, develop into new forms, as demonstrated in *Riverdance*, we are asked to consider whether these changes represent the fluid dialogue between the country's history and the country's changing social, economic, and political makeup. As dance educators, can we continue to celebrate cultural traditions and at the same time recognize the forces and forms that bridge our common experiences?

In my travels across the globe I have had the opportunity to learn about the ways in which countries have begun to celebrate their own forms of dance and about the importance of people "telling their own stories" through dance. For example, in South Africa they have challenged the dominant tradition that has valued Western dance forms over their own indigenous cultural forms. Today we find African dance courses being taught alongside ballet and modern dance in colleges and universities, as well as the blending of African and modern dance to create new dance forms. In the Middle East and South America, dance has been used as a healing process for Palestinian and Brazilian children as they learn to express their experiences of oppression and poverty through dance. In Australia, New Zealand, and the United States, people have drawn upon the traditions of the indigenous cultures to rethink their relationship to the land and environment. Across the globe, the effect of MTV or hip-hop culture has become evident in the behavior of youths, whether through fashion, language, music, or dance. Popular culture in the United States has become a dominating force in shaping youths across the globe. The time is over when we can claim to live in a world unaffected by the "other." Today, more than ever before, we are constantly influencing each other's world.

My interest in this book, *Dance in a World of Change: Reflections on Globalization and Cultural Difference*, goes beyond deconstructing dance traditions, a practice that has focused on cultural differences. I am not alone in this interest. Throughout the international dance community, scholars, educators, choreographers, historians, performers, researchers, and critics are increasingly examining the possibilities of art and embodied expression in this dynamic, tumultuous, and often conflicted time of social global change. Therefore, this book draws upon the contributions of current dance educators, choreographers, critics, and scholars, each of whom has a distinguished record of scholarship and practice in the field of dance education. They represent a spectrum of international perspectives on pedagogy, the body, performance, dance, and culture. Their diverse backgrounds, which include areas of South Africa, Brazil, Croatia, Ireland, Canada, Taiwan, New Zealand, the United Kingdom, Holland, Jamaica, and the United States, ensure a rich and generative set of experiences through which the themes of globalization are pursued. The authors speak from their own cultural, historical, and geographical location to the experiential dimensions of dance and dance education as they are understood through a critical social lens. At the center of this work is the desire to provide those engaged in dance education with a text that expands the discourse and curriculum of dance to connect it to the critical, political, moral, and aesthetic dimensions of our contemporary social situation. These dimensions include the following:

- Dance as a form of human empowerment or cultural resistance
- Dance as a means of recognizing diverse cultural experience *and* communicating our common humanity
- Dance as an expression of social conflict, injustice, violence, or marginalization
- Dance as a process of education approaching questions of identity, cultural and global awareness that has the possibility of transcending the particular, and encompassing commonality

The authors write about their own teaching, research, or programmatic experiences in issues of cultural affirmation and questions of difference. The breadth of issues has enabled the writers to connect their work to the larger context of this book: dance as a way of affirming specific cultural traditions and experiences and as a means of expressing the universality of our humanity.

Part I introduces themes that have recently developed regarding traditional dance forms and how they are being influenced by the global dance environment as well as how they are helping to shape new forms of popular dance. What is discovered in these chapters is the fluid dialogue that has developed between the historical and the new. Questions are raised concerning dance in relationship to preserving the past and moving into the future. Each chapter speaks from a specific location (Ireland, Croatia, and Jamaica) and addresses these issues by examining cultural history, colonial oppression, cultural infusion, and assimilation.

In Part II, the focus moves to a discourse on the body. Each of the three chapters explores what "different bodies," whether gay, Black, or differently abled, have experienced under a narrow definition of what is normal. As prejudice against sexual orientation, race, and disability is considered, a deeper appreciation of the meaning of community and inclusion emerges. Readers become sensitive to concepts of difference as they are challenged to question taken-for-granted assumptions of what is normal, and gain a better understanding of representations and visual images as these have become fixed within dance.

Part III engages the reader in conversations about dance pedagogy. These chapters are about teaching dance in three different locations: Canada, Finland, and Taiwan. The writers discuss their own teaching situations and life experiences and how they have come to develop pedagogies that recognize and value different cultures, utilize multisensory and multidisciplinary forms of pedagogy based on exploration and collaboration, and integrate within their pedagogy a global perspective of the world as a unity of individuals and interacting cultures.

Part IV brings the reader back to questions of dance and the body as primary vehicles for holding cultural memory and experience. The emphasis here is on the moving body and on the way dance expresses our embodied experiences. Dance also touches those things that transcend our social spaces, and it connects us to the universality of human life. In this sense, dance is not only an expression of our time and space but also a means through which we can perceive our commonalities with others. Dance offers a powerful cultural form to help us become more aware and more empathic to the diverse yet increasingly connected world.

There are a number of professionals in dance education who have been thinking about how to understand all that we teach our students in the studio, in the audience, or in the classroom both explicitly and implicitly. Many have written about, and developed curriculum and choreography around, issues of the self, others, and our larger world. In so doing, a critical lens is utilized to examine issues of dance, power, difference, and gender. It is not possible, of course, for this book to include all of the issues, projects, and ideas that are ongoing in the field of dance. This book does not attempt that feat; rather, it attempts to extend the conversations and show that there is more to the phenomenon of globalization that is shaping the future of dance.

Many of us are engaged with dance and dancing as a way of life. We have chosen to experience, teach, and create with and through our bodies and embodied memories. It has been our work as artists to mirror the world we experience and, at times, to imagine something different. In this book you will find voices of those who know something about the world of dance; you will find that you are not alone. It is your choice to travel with us as we come to know something particular about our lives. We hope that with this knowledge you are able to find the connections that join us as a global community that is shaping the world in which we share.

acknowledgments

It would have been impossible for me to develop this book without Dance and the Child International (daCi). Because of the opportunities that daCi provided me, I was able to journey across the globe to meet and dance with others who are in the field of dance. It was from the daCi international conference held in Australia that I found and engaged other dance educators to write about dance, the results from which my first dance text, *Dance, Power and Difference: Critical and Feminist Perspectives on Dance Education*, was published. I also met many of the writers in this book at daCi international conferences. So, I wish to thank all of those in daCi who have shared their struggles, joys, creations, and imaginations with me as we met, conversed, argued, and danced in countries across the world.

I must, of course, acknowledge the many students with whom I was granted the opportunity to learn in classrooms, in studios, onstage, and in research. They always came with openness and trust. Thank you.

Many people have taught me as they wrote about, presented, discussed, and created choreography that challenged my assumptions and nurtured my imagination. Your work is what makes mine possible. Thank you.

My personal editor, theorist, dialogue companion, and avid supporter, my husband Svi, challenges my ideas, corrects my grammar, and tells me I am brilliant. Thank you—it is your hand I hold as I journey onto the edge.

Every question possesses a power that does not lie in the answer.

—Elie Wiesel

We may have different religions, different languages, different colored skin, but we all belong to one human race.

—Kofi Annan

Imagination is more important than knowledge.
Knowledge is limited. Imagination encircles the world.

—Albert Einstein

In every community, there is work to be done. In every nation, there are wounds to heal. In every heart, there is the power to do it.

—Marianne Williamson

Dance as Cultural Memory:

Challenging Globalization

one

Stepping Into Footprints: Tradition and the Globalization of Irish Dance

Michael Seaver
The Irish Times
Dublin, Ireland

Riverdance and its spin-offs brought globalization to Irish dance. Themes that prolonged postcolonial victimhood and techniques that homogenized regional styles became the international face of Irish dance. In Ireland, training programs are promoting diversity of style, both in genre and geography. Rather than rigidly preserve the past, these programs allow a more fluid dialogue between history and the present and interrogate notions of preservation. The cultural statements that emerge have a special resonance within the country's changing social, economic, and political makeup. In a climate that still grapples with national identity and globalization, Irish dance is comfortable with its past and confident in its present.

Celtic Tiger: Dance and Economy of Ireland

Celtic Tiger is the most expensive Irish dance production ever, reportedly costing $18 million U.S. Its creator, Michael Flatley (the world's wealthiest dancer, whose legs are insured for $20 million U.S. each), has described it as his most satisfying production. "I've got the biggest TV screen in the world—72 tons—at the back of the stage," he says. "Imagine being at the premiere of a new movie—except in front of the screen you've got arguably the best dance troupe on earth, a lighting show that rivals [that of] Pink Floyd, $3 million worth of costumes, the best sound effects and a musical score by Ronan Hardiman that's like an Irish rock concert" (McManis

2005, p.TK19). Extensive touring to international venues and sales of merchandising, including a DVD, will mean that *Celtic Tiger*—the latest in a series of Irish dance shows—meets the criteria for a global cultural product. As *Celtic Tiger* toured in the fall of 2006, so too did *Riverdance* (two shows), *Gaelforce Dance, Lord of the Dance, Magic of the Dance, Spirit of the Dance,* and *Ragús.* A largely participatory and competitive dance form has been transformed into multimillion-dollar cultural enterprises.

Similarly, Ireland has transformed from a small nation striving for self-sufficiency to the most globalized country in the world.[1] This resurgent economy was dubbed the "Celtic Tiger" in a Morgan Stanley report (Gardiner 1994)[2] and Michael Flatley has appropriated the economic metaphor for his latest dance spectacular, claiming that *Celtic Tiger* "portrays the oppression of a people and the tiger symbolizes the awakening of their spirit and their struggle for freedom" (Celtic Tiger Live n.d.). But the Celtic Tiger economy has affected Irish society, just as shows like *Celtic Tiger* have influenced Irish dance. Similar questions confront both: Does globalization allow Ireland to independently manage its economy and society? Do large-scale Irish dance spectaculars stifle local practices and homogenize regional styles and voices?

Globalization:
The State of Dance or Dance and the State

> On the eve of the storm, the world economy was, to an extent never seen before, truly global. It was linked together by new technologies that made it possible to ship products cheaply from one side of the globe to the other, to communicate virtually instantaneously over huge distances. [It led] to unprecedented transfers of Western capital and technology to emerging economies—transfers facilitated by the fact that everyone knew that any country that strayed from the path would be punished by financial crisis, and would soon be obliged to accept the harsh austerity prescribed by teams of Western technocrats. The year, of course, was 1913. (Krugman 1998, 18)

Globalization is thought of as a recent phenomenon, but the first wave of globalization is considered to have taken place from 1870 to 1913 as commodity markets integrated, communications improved, and transport costs fell dramatically. As Keynes wrote in 1919, "The inhabitant of London could order by telephone, sipping his morning tea in bed, the various products of the whole earth, in such quantity as he might see fit, and reasonably expect their early delivery upon his doorstep" (4). Although Britain was a major trading power, Ireland's economy was underdeveloped with little industry, so it benefited little from this time of globalization.

Instead, within a time of fluid transference of goods and people, Irish republicanism embarked on a more immediate separatist mission to gain independence from Britain. Part of this political assertion was a cultural nationalism that sought to establish what was perceived as an authentic Irish culture free from foreign, particularly English, influence. The de-Anglicanization of Irish culture became organized with the establishment of the Conradh na Gaeilge (Gaelic League) in 1893, which not only advocated the Irish language at the expense of English but also popularized Irish music, poetry, and dancing.

When Ireland gained independence from Britain in 1921, there remained a postcolonial desire to forefront "Irishness" within society. In a September 25, 1928, review of one of Ninette de Valois' first ballets for the Abbey, *Faun, The Irish Times* claimed it as the first Irish ballet: "Mr. White's music is built on Irish airs, and the choreography is the work of an Irish woman for all her French name; the dancers are Irish; the orchestra is Irish. . . . There could be no mistaking the verdict of the audience who saw the first Irish Ballet" (The Irish Times 1928, 5). The belief was that if theater dance was unmistakably Irish, then its place in the cultural landscape could be more secure. But dance continued to face political and moral pressure from church and state. In 1929 one of the first ballet companies to visit Ireland, an offshoot of Anna Pavlova's company, was denounced by several priests when it visited Cork. The performances at the Cork Opera House were poorly attended and the company had money sent from London to pay for the return trip to England.

Social dance was also perceived as a corrupting influence, and it was necessary to mold bodies to reflect the body politic of the new state. According to Barbara O'Connor, "The state's interest in dance can also be seen as part of a broader concern with the moral state of the nation and with the conduct of its youth in particular. So the combined anxieties resulted in public social dancing becoming an object of scrutiny and a site of struggle over identity politics" (Mulrooney 2006, 39)

Coimisiún le Rincí Gaelacha (Irish Dancing Commission) was established by Conradh na Gaeilge in the late 1920s to oversee the organization of Irish dancing through competitions. This was a nationalization of the dance form that preceded competition leading to stylistic homogenization within the genre. Distinguishing this instructional Irish dancing from other social dancing became a crucial issue. Conradh na Gaeilge took an active part in the antijazz movement that grew in the 1920s, as did other culturally nationalist organizations and the clergy. Cardinal Logue wrote in a pastoral letter in 1924, "While it is not our business to condemn any dance, Irish dances . . . [should not be excluded from] any educational establishment under our care . . . Irish dances do not make degenerates" (O'Toole 1997, 134). In other words, Irish dancing under the eyes of the church was acceptable, but the practice of unsupervised dances in private houses or other meeting places was a threat to morality and had the power to corrupt. Taoiseach (Prime Minister) Eamon DeValera, in an effort to assuage the church's anxieties, introduced the Public Halls Act of 1935, which required that all dances be licensed and operated under strict supervision, thereby ending informal dances in houses or crossroads.

Assertion of a National Dance

As dance writer Randy Martin (1998, 42) claims, "Once the definition of culture as a common content that defines a population is accepted as credible, the result is likely to be a conception of identity that is as rigidly homogenous." These protectionist cultural policies were mirrored by protectionist economic policies. Ireland remained politically neutral through World War II, and trade from the 1930s to 1960s was encumbered by high tariffs and practices that pursued self-sufficiency. The economy gradually became internationalized through the Anglo-Irish Trade Agreement in 1965 and entry to the European Economic Community (EEC) in 1973, which also led to the openness to cultural influences from abroad. But the assertion of Irish dance over other forms continued until the 1990s, and policy makers such as An Chomhairle Ealaíon (Irish Arts Council) (1995) constantly yearned for the creation of a distinctive Irish theater dance style that interacted with traditional dance. Successive reports (Brinson 1986; An Chomhairle Ealaíon 1994) yearned for contemporary dance and ballet practitioners to evolve a national dance style that interacted with traditional practice. Although some practitioners did use traditional steps (most notably Mary Nunan's *Territorial Claims* for Daghdha Dance Company in 1993), most dance artists aligned themselves to European and American styles rather than Irish styles. To paraphrase composer Aaron Copland talking about jazz, they didn't set out to make an Irish dance style, but they also didn't set out *not* to make an Irish dance style.

   Riverdance satisfied the desire for theatrical values to be applied to a traditionally nonperformance genre. Statements advocating the formation of a "national style" disappeared after its first performance at the Eurovision Song Contest, an annual European competition that reaches a potential television audience of more than 300 million.[3] The interval act of this contest takes place after the competing songs have been performed, to allow each country to collect and tabulate its votes, before all votes are

A scene from *Riverdance*, produced by Moya Doherty, directed by John McColgan.

Photo: Jack Hartin. By kind permission of Abhann Productions.

added together. Like the halftime act during the Super Bowl, the interval act reaches a huge audience and offers a chance for cultural promotion for the host country. Ireland has won the contest seven times and, since the winner hosts the following year's competition, those victories have been used to broadcast aspects of Irish culture to a wide audience.

Riverdance seemed an accurate expression of Ireland in 1994. According to O'Reilly (2004, 53), it was "an international statement of joie de vivre, self-confidence on the Euro[pean] state despite size, and demise of colonial/neo-colonial complexes." This cultural confidence had its roots in Ireland's economic success: That same year Ireland had the fastest-growing economy in the European Community (OECD 1994) and the phrase *Celtic Tiger* was used for the first time. The economic boom was in full swing because of a combination of low corporation tax, investment in education, and European Union subsidies as high as 7 percent of GDP. If the phrase *Celtic Tiger* helped to define the newfound confidence, then *Riverdance* embodied it.

But the fast-growing economy also produced inequality. In 2005 Irish people were the second wealthiest in the world after Luxembourg, according to the United Nations 2005 Human Development Report (Watkins

2005). But the same study revealed that 15.3 percent of Irish people still live in poverty and the richest 10 percent of Irish people are 9.7 times wealthier than the poorest 10 percent. Inequality in Ireland is higher than it is in any other Western country apart from the United States. Critics have pointed out that Ireland's economic success wasn't a means to an end, like a better society. Rather, the success became everything, resulting in a society that is subservient to the economy not for the sake of progress, but to sustain the high tide. Kirby (2002, p. 159) points out that "values such as individualism, materialism, intolerance of dissent, lack of concern for the environment and a failure to value caring are identified as characterising life under the Celtic Tiger."

Riverdance: **Challenging Tradition**

In the 1990s *Riverdance* met a need that people didn't quite know was there: the need for reassurance at a time of rapid and sometimes confusing change. According to Fintan O'Toole (2005, p. 110), they wanted to believe that *Riverdance* wouldn't destroy what was distinctive in Irish culture, "but would, rather, refurbish it." *Riverdance's* refurbishment of Irish dance was seen as infusing what was a largely competitive genre with some showbiz values, maintaining cultural reassurance by turning what was a recognizable folk tradition into a commercially successful spectacle. *Riverdance* was a more urban and modern depiction of Irish dance and, with the Eurovision set providing a backdrop of megalithic stones blending with skyscrapers, the performance both challenged and upheld tradition.

Even without this social and political backdrop, the performance can be read as outside influences confronting tradition. As hooded singers from the choral group Anúna sing about uisce beatha (the water of life), Jean Butler enters from the side of the stage with her red hair in ringlets like that of a competition dancer and dressed in a short black dress. The dance vocabulary—notably arms straight down by her sides—is traditional, although she twice reaches her hands behind her head and flicks them forward through her hair, hinting at a later metaphoric letting down of her hair. In spite of her short dress, she seems like a traditional dancer with her silent steps to a lilting slip jig (in 9/8 time). In contrast, Michael Flatley is introduced by thundering drums, and his entrance is on hard shoes as the music changes to a faster tempo. He careens across the stage with uncharacteristic high kicks and jetés, a powder-blue satin shirt billowing. Arms outstretched with palms facing forward, he invites our gaze and his call and response with the drummers underpinning his challenge. For the finale, the stable 9/8 rhythms are replaced by more driving Bulgarian rhythms (alternating bars of 6/8 and 4/4), and the show ends with a presentational chorus line of dancers with hard shoes moving in unison.

This challenge to tradition was also taking place in the world of commerce, as private enterprise challenged state monopolies in the economic shake-up. A small company such as Ryanair, the low-cost airline, was successfully competing with the state airline Aer Lingus on its most lucrative routes.[4] Ryanair livery included a harp on the planes' tail wings, a constant reminder of its Irishness. Ryanair wasn't seen as a threat from outside but rather as a local enterprise fueled by *Celtic Tiger* confidence. Similarly, as *Riverdance* became increasingly successful in London and on Broadway, the achievements of producers John McColgan and Moya Doherty reflected the entrepreneurial chic that had pervaded at home.

Like Ryanair, *Riverdance* was able to badge its nationality, but to compete in the global market it needed to repackage this Irishness. The self-confidence of the seven-minute original disappeared in the expanded evening-length show as a narrative was introduced that depicted Irish people leaving a land ravaged with famine to find prosperity in the United States. This postcolonial victimhood, absent in the original, was at odds with a forward-thinking *Celtic Tiger* Ireland, and people were sensitive to noncontemporaneous depictions of the country.[5] But it appealed to international audiences in a similar way that Frank McCourt's book *Angela's Ashes* won the 1996 National Book Critics Circle Award and the 1997 Pulitzer Prize for biography or autobiography. Yet it was pilloried in Ireland. Actor Richard Harris, who knew the McCourt family in the 1950s, claimed that McCourt's "anger and his opportunism blinded him into distortion" and that his book was based on a theme of self-pity and relied on "fabrication and lies" (Cunningham 2000, p. 6). Both *Riverdance* and McCourt were capitalizing on a rags-to-riches story and a sense of Ireland that had little to do with reality but instead suggested a green, rainy land populated by amiable drunks.

Furthermore, to meet touring demands, *Riverdance* created carbon copies of itself; at the height of its popularity, it produced three shows simultaneously with a flying squad of dancers for cover. The *Riverdance* Web site now boasts that more than 9 million *Riverdance* videos and DVDs have been sold, the *Riverdance* companies have traveled more than 800,000 kilometers (500,000 miles, or "to the moon and back!"), and the show has been seen live by more than 18 million people in 250 venues worldwide, throughout 30 countries across four continents. In the words of O'Toole (2005, p. 110), "If what we wanted from *Riverdance* was a souped-up version of traditional culture which could protect us from marketing and globalization, the show isn't just a failure, it's a betrayal."

Globalizaton: Cultural Borrowing

So how has Irish dance coped with this betrayal, and how has the global cultural product influenced practice at a local level? O'Toole (2005) sees globalization by *Riverdance* as undermining traditional dance forms and, presumably, leading to homogenization and a dominant monoculture assimilating local forms. Catherine Foley (2001) applies world system theory and the nation-state theory of globalization to Irish dance to argue how global products have actually brought attention to local practice. She sees the center as being represented by the Coimisiún le Rincí Gaelacha and the periphery as being represented by local practice, such as the noncompetitive sean-nós dancing.[6] Similarly, *Riverdance* and other large-scale shows are the global, the Coimisiún le Rincí Gaelacha is the national, and sean-nós dancing is the local. Within these strands of practice ideas are transferred, which reflects the theory of glocalization. The term *glocalization* emerged in the 1980s from the Japanese word *dochkuka*, literally, global-localization. Debunking the common assumption of the global overriding the local, the theory of globalization proposes that the local (or periphery) absorbs ideas from the global (or center). Also there is a flow of ideas and practices from the periphery to the center. Foley (2001) finds no obvious evidence of the global affecting the local, but former *Riverdance* star Jean Butler identifies how competitions organized by Coimisiún le Rincí Gaelacha have been affected by the global shows like *Riverdance*. Similarly, the global products have helped promote local practice by making Irish dance transnational so that it is now as identifiable as flamenco. But *Riverdance* presented a one-dimensional view of Irish dance. As Foley (2001) points out, "When people came, they didn't see *Riverdance* danced in pubs. They found set-dancing and, in some parts of the west, sean-nós dancing" (Seaver 2005, para. 8). Comparisons are made with the effect of Paul Simon's *Graceland* on South African music. Neither *Riverdance* nor *Graceland* was an unadulterated reflection of the culture, but both acted as a bridge between the pure form and what was required to survive commercially.

The flow of ideas from core to periphery reflects ideas on hybridity. Dance has engaged in this practice for centuries, and although Western dance in this time has constantly looked to the "other," non-Western dance cultures to enrich its language, this cultural borrowing has worked two ways. Anna Pavlova and Ruth St. Denis both inspired Indian dance not only through the growth of state-sponsored dance schools but also, more cogently, in the changing language of Indian temple dancing at the time of the Indian revolution. When *Riverdance* grew from the original Eurovision interval filler, it added American tap, Russian folk ballet, and flamenco dance with Irish step dance, embodying the principle articulated in the program:

> We are one kind. We are one people now, our voices blended, our music, a great world in which we can feel everywhere at home.

Foley (2001, p. 41) states, "In reaction to the global representation of Irish dance in the form of *Riverdance*, through its hybridity and 'inclusiveness,' the margins have become represented. The step dance practices in the margins of Ireland are those that have survived the process of modernisation."

Local practice has received a profile indirectly through *Riverdance*, but it hasn't been changed or absorbed by the global. That isn't to say it is inflexible or resistant to change: Many sean-nós dancers have styles that are constantly changing. Its curiosity and self-interrogation have led it into academia. Within this climate of hybridity and exchange, education programs such as the postgraduate degrees at the Irish World Music Centre at the University of Limerick have allowed traditional and contemporary styles to be taught together. Ex-*Riverdance* dancers Colin Dunne and Jean Butler have been artists in residence, and both are adamant that the results of their explorations aren't fusion. Butler claims that fusion is like an excuse, an apology for one or other of the art forms being joined up. "It suggests insufficiency. I'm looking for something that's quite pure and unique" (Seaver 2005, para. 7). Dunne has collaborated with contemporary choreographer Yoshiko Chuma in creating *The Yellow Room*, and both dancers have been influenced by the release technique, changing from the rigid and upright competitive dance style to more fluid movement. Dunne has claimed the following:

> Whereas before my style was very muscular and lifting out of the floor, now it's more released into the floor. It's like thinking of the body hanging down as opposed to being held up. It's a subtle difference to look at, but a huge shift to find physically. (Seaver 2005, para. 6)

The looser sean-nós style of traditional dance has been blended with contemporary movement. Siamsa Tire is the national folk theater company; it has also collaborated with ballet and contemporary choreographers. The most successful production was *Clann Lir*, based on the story of children who are transformed into swans. Contemporary choreographer Mary Nunan's movement vocabulary is based on release technique and minimizes physical tension in the search for clarity and fluidity and the efficient use of energy and breath. This vocabulary matched Siamsa's fluid

North Kerry sean-nós style as well as the depiction of swans. In *Oileán (Island)*, American choreographer Cindy Cummings deconstructs the traditional vocabulary by underpinning and driving the action with the pulse of heel taps, whether by stationary standing figures or by schoolchildren seated at their desks. This one ingredient of Irish dancing technique becomes a thread through *Oileán* that is both visual and rhythmic. Sean-nós practitioners are also keen to see traditional steps evolve rather than become petrified. Risteard Mac Aodha is a sean-nós dancer and organizes what he calls "conventions" around certain dances. In reality, these are gatherings in a pub where a historian first outlines the history of the dance and then encourages people to dance individual versions and debate the merits of each. The original purpose of storytelling and commemoration behind some of these dances has been lost mainly because of the pressures of competitive dancing. Mac Aodha's conventions don't seek a definitive interpretation but rather celebrate difference.

Risteard Mac Aodha's get-togethers in small pubs are far from Michael Flatley's stadium-scale *Celtic Tiger*. Yet they push the boundaries of Irish dance more than Flatley's boasts do. *Celtic Tiger* and other spectaculars may have popularized Irish dance to the point where it has become recognizable worldwide, but they are formulaic. Little variation in movement vocabulary, common themes (beginning with a pre-Christian awakening leading to a presentational depiction of Irish dance as a Broadway-like success story), and mimed foot taps in the various shows have led to homogenization within that genre. Driven by commerce, they are also feeding stereotypes of the Irish as victims of oppression whose only escape route is emigration. Although they have given Irish dance confidence to take to the stage, they have done little to develop the form.

Conclusion

The interaction between local and global can be seen through the lens of what theorist Pierre Bourdieu (1993) refers to as "cultural banking." The cultural banker collects symbolic capital and then redistributes it. In the case of *Riverdance*-type spectaculars, the banker borrowed symbolic capital from Irish dance as a traditional form and redistributed it to the world market. The product was aligned to a preexisting genre that, although it wasn't recognized internationally, contained cultural value in the uniqueness of its form. As Jean Butler points out, competitive Irish dancing has in turn taken symbolic capital from shows such as *Riverdance* to borrow legitimacy (Seaver 2005). This is visible not just in the borrowed steps and sequences but also in the borrowed costume styles and colors.

Irish dance at the local level has been robust in surviving homogenizing influences, whether these influences are coming from the Irish Dancing Commission or *Riverdance*-type spectaculars. This is largely because of a strong local tradition, where one dance style might be completely different from another practiced 50 kilometers (30 miles) away. Away from institutions, Irish dance has absorbed influences ranging from the French quadrilles in the 18th century to jazz syncopations in the 20th century.

Riverdance and its ilk are now repaying their cultural capital by bringing attention to the local. Colin Dunne and Jean Butler were trained in the competitive dance world, both becoming world champions before appearing in *Riverdance*. At the University of Limerick their virtuosity and willingness to engage with local and contemporary forms add legitimacy to their acceptance in the cultural landscape.

Some writers have predicted that *Celtic Tiger* will be the last Irish dance spectacular (Taylor 2006), so it would seem that any threat from local to global practice has now passed. Similarly, there is also evidence that the economic globalization of Ireland has gone as far as it will go. O'Sullivan (2006) argues that the side effects of globalization on Irish society, like social inequality, mean that there needs to be state intervention. Could this disillusionment with globalization result in a return of the kind of Irish nationalism that demands that dance constantly affirm its Irishness? Is the real threat to local not the global but the national? In spite of the political globalization of Europe through the European Union, nationalism has intensified in many countries. The United Kingdom granted devolved governments in Scotland, Wales, and Northern Ireland in 1997, while in Spain the Basques, Catalans, and Galicians are increasing their demands for autonomy.

Currently in Ireland, cultural purity has no currency in cultural policy making or in local practices. This situation is unlikely to change. Gone are the days of policy documents demanding interaction between contemporary and traditional dance forms, and traditional dances continue to evolve. There is fluid interaction among the local, national, and global. Local practice continues to acknowledge otherness, an important statement to make in contemporary Irish society, which has seen an increase in racism as immigration has replaced emigration for the first time in Irish history. While there is evidence that *Riverdance* and similar shows have brought attention to marginalized forms, they haven't been a homogenizing force, and they haven't stifled evolution. What keeps the tradition alive is the richness of practice in all strands of participation and performance. This richness allows Irish dance to acknowledge its past and dream its future.

REFLECTIONS

We have learned in dance history that choreographers have often borrowed from and been inspired by other cultures. In a global world, fast
access to a variety of cultural dance forms, including popular expression,
has greatly influenced the development of cross-cultural dance and
music. World music has emerged on the global scene and has become
common terminology used for music that expresses merged forms.
Dance has been less clear about the separation of its traditional forms
and those forms that have been shaped by other influences. Performance dance, for example, has been created for national recognition
but also functions as a vehicle for capitalistic gain.

Michael Seaver helps us to understand how some dance forms in
Ireland, such as *Riverdance*, were developed out of traditional forms
and were influenced by the desire for national recognition on the global
stage. Several important themes emerge in this discussion. One is the
way that shows such as *Riverdance, Celtic Tiger, Gaelforce Dance, Lord
of the Dance, Magic of the Dance, Spirit of the Dance*, and *Ragús* have
become an expression of national resurgence and the emergence of
a dynamic Irish society liberated from its colonization by England
and from a rural economy that kept much of its inhabitants poor and
oppressed. At the same time, dance, like *Celtic Tiger*, expresses *both*
the freedom of expression and the sexuality of modern society, while it
draws on themes of oppression and suffering rooted in the history of
the Irish people. With the recent phenomenon of people moving into
rather than out of Ireland (for the first time in Irish history), there has
also been a move away from insular national politics. This fluidity of
movement of people as well as influences between the local and the
global has opened Irish society to a multiplicity of influences. Challenges to our notions of what is traditional, authentic, or even aesthetic
dance are raised as the boundaries between the differences in dance
or in dances are erased or redrawn. In a postmodern world, there are
no longer clear boundaries that mark us from the "other," or what
characterizes a dance as specifically belonging to a particular people,
ethnicity, or nation. As notions of cultural purity erode, we see more
clearly how our lives and our culture reflect an interconnected world
in which we are all shaped by one another.

Notes

1. According to the annual A.T. Kearney *Foreign Policy Magazine* Globalization Index in 2002, 2003, and 2004 Ireland was the most globalized country from 2002 to 2004. (www.atkearney.com)

2. The phrase is based on the East Asian Tigers (principally South Korea, Singapore, Hong Kong, and Taiwan) that experienced rapid economic growth in the 1980s and early 1990s.

3. Various sources quote audience figures of 100 to 600 million. It is also broadcast in nonparticipating countries such as Australia, Canada, Egypt, Jordan, Hong Kong, India, Korea, New Zealand, and the United States. Winning performers have included Abba and Céline Dion, and winning songs have included "Volare."

4. Aer Lingus was privatized by the Irish government in 2006, and Ryanair purchased a 20 percent shareholding.

5. This narrative of emigration as survival prevails in the Irish dance spectacular: Flatley's *Celtic Tiger* has many self-pitying depictions of atrocities by outsiders at the expense of historical accuracy. The Romans never invaded Ireland as shown in *Celtic Tiger*.

6. A form that predates competitive dancing. It has a looser form with hunched shoulders and swinging arms, as opposed to the rigid back and straight arms of competitive dance.

two

The Quest for Preserving and Representing National Identity

Ivančica Janković

Ana Maletić School of Contemporary Dance
Zagreb, Croatia

As a dance educator and choreographer, rather than a dance historian, theorist, sociologist, or critic, I believe that the social and historical contextualization of dance as an art form is of great relevance for countries occupying only a small segment of the world map. As Croatia seems to be lacking in systematic research of the field of dance, the question arises about whether such contextualization should outgrow the usual models of analytic discourse—that is, whether it should be broadened by a detailed questioning of one's own merit in relation to the standards existing outside that framework and requiring an outside evaluation as the only relevant criterion of such a practice. We might claim that a potential feeling of national inferiority can be manifested in two divergent points:

1. Asserting national affiliation by incorporating artistic interpretations of folklore elements into the existing dance forms, or attempting to infiltrate the new influences with the elements of the national

2. Uncritical receptiveness of foreign influences and the degree of assimilation of these influences into the existing national framework, which might encourage an exodus of dance artists from their native countries

In this chapter I focus on the first point, which includes the conditioning of the motives and modalities of incorporating folklore elements based on the changes of the historical and political contexts, either by emphasizing the national heritage as an expression of patriotism or by consciously applying national elements aimed at creating an (exotic) export product.[1]

Preserving and Exposing National Identity

Croatian history has been characterized by a continual struggle for preserving and exposing its national, and consequently its cultural, identity—an identity that geography marks as a focal meeting point of Western and Eastern cultures and civilizations. Jane Desmond (1997) discusses this kind of marking, which can be used to read the discourse or code of dance both as a particular social identity and as a manifestation of a cultural identity (182). Following Desmond, Govedić (2002) discusses corporeal communication of a dancing body which is "coded by numerous distinctive marks" (310). We might make a conclusion that a conscious and thinking body in dance is a genuine manifestation of the human essence, primarily its need for communicating meaning. This corporeal communication is enabled by the decoding of a number of coded marks, placing a certain dance discourse into the frame of a particular social identity.

Walter Sorell (1967) reminded us early on that dance, such as folk dance, strengthens the feeling of collective identity which surpasses individual participation to the group (75). Thus we might claim that the folk dance with its kinesthetic and auditive message represents a strong manifestation of both collective and national identities, among other reasons, for the almost ritualistic feeling of group identification which the dancing of folk dances awakens in the individual.

We examine the history of ballet and dance in Croatia[2] based on the research of historic sources oriented primarily to its capital, Zagreb. As early as 1898 the Croatian National Theatre in Zagreb staged a national, authentic ballet, titled *Towards the Plitvice Lakes*, with local characters, local musical motifs, and a national setting. This was followed by a general withdrawal of ballet as an independent art form until the 1920s. In 1921 Margareta Froman, former member of Diaghilev's dance troupe, revitalized the ballet repertoire by introducing the fresh touch of the Russian ballet and creating a national repertoire. During that time Europe was between the two world wars, a time characterized by the fall of the Austro-Hungarian monarchy, the Russian Revolution, the forming of new national borders, economic crisis, the strengthening of the communist grasp, and the awakening of national consciousness as well as the expansion of nationalist movements.[3] In this context of huge social and political changes occurring within a relatively short time, the works created by Croatian composers reflected the spirit of national identity. Parallel with the onset of the Russian ballet repertoire, national ballets inspired by national themes became an integral part of the Croatian dance scene and became a desirable export article.[4] The most famous Croatian ballets, *The Gingerbread Heart* (music by Krešimir Baranović, choreography by Margareta Froman) and *The Devil in the Village* (music by Fran Lhotka, choreography by Pia and Pino Mlakar), are still part of the current Croatian repertoire.

Along with the ballet revival and the presence of artistic interpretations of folklore elements that enriched the standard vocabulary of classical ballet, several other strong influences marked the years between 1920 and 1930 in Croatia. These included the new dance aesthetics advocated by Isadora Duncan, the new thoughts on movement and dance introduced by Rudolf Laban, and the new approach to music theory through movement advocated by E.J. Dalcroze.

Laban's influence[5] can be traced to various sources. Interestingly, the Croatian dancer Vera Milčinović Tashamira, who was a member of Laban's Tanzbühne, initiated the 1924 visit of Laban's Chamber Dance Theatre to Zagreb as part of its tour. Apart from that, the choreographies of Laban's former students Pia and Pino Mlakar, who joined the Croatian National Ballet, reflected the great influence of Ausdruckstanz. The influence that Laban exerted on dance education in Croatia is covered in more detail later in this chapter.

Collective Construct of Dance

The 1920s to 1930s were a rich and creative time in the field of dance not only in its performance but also in its educational aspects. A great number of Croatian dance artists, upon completing their education abroad, returned to their homeland and opened private studios and dance schools. Perhaps it would not be too bold to claim that such an intense migration of dance influences among the countries of Western Europe, the Balkans, the former USSR, and the United States could be viewed as an onset of a future globalization or internationalization of dance arts. Viewed from the contemporary context of globalism, the time of Diaghilev's vision of modern ballet, of Fokin's innovations, and of the birth of American and European modern dance can perhaps be seen as the representation of cultural differences with an aim of creating a "collective construct" (Slunjski 2005)—an issue to be investigated by historians and dance theorists.

When we view the 1920s to 1930s from the position of the contemporary globalization processes characterized by the dynamics of interaction between representation and preservation of authenticity within a framework of homogeneity, we can certainly welcome the time's emphasis on the ethnic concepts as a statement of national identity, regardless of the fact that its occurrence could be linked to the historical and political context. However, one should bear in mind a certain one-way interaction in the case of Croatia, since the foreign influences of the "greats" did not at that time remain at the level of exchanged information but instead became permanently assimilated (with all the necessary changes that such cultural assimilations entail). On the other hand, the reciprocity of Croatian national influences was harder to ascertain. Was it because folk elements in ballet and dance of that time were aimed at promoting Croatian national identity? Most likely these could not find a common semantic code with the narratives produced by dance artists abroad in order to be "transformed into symbols of Croatian national identity."[6] However, is assimilation a necessary requirement, or can the pure act of recognition pose as a satisfaction? Can the inspiration by national elements be viewed only as a trend? Or is it in fact a reflection of national consciousness and ultimately a reflection of a person's acquaintance (or lack of acquaintance) with the country's folk heritage?

It could also be questioned to what extent such fruitful times in the history of the dance art of a small nation (as in 1930s Croatia) counter or support the claim about the symptomatic inferiority complex of small nations. And to what extent did the lack of society's interest in the promotion of its national identity via various aspects of dance art contribute to its (lack of) knowledge, (un)recognition, and (non)evaluation on the part of both the foreign and the local populations?

It is revealing how Ivana Slunjski (2005), representative of the younger generation of dance theorists, in an attempt at tracing the lineage of Croatian elements in Croatian contemporary dance, omits the ethnoconcept as its potentially distinctive element, claiming that the "Croatian dancer is not characterised by his/her citizenship or nationality, but rather by a continual process of individual awareness in the field of their own personal experience in . . . the creative polygon of expressing the social construct within which the author operates" (123). The answers to such questions should form the basis for more thorough research that also includes political, social, economic, cultural, and national contexts, examining all aspects of dance art in Croatia: the working space, formation and application of a high-quality dance education, professional development of dance artists, production, performance, marketing, decentralization, and defining of the social status of dance art and dance artists (which unfortunately comprise the burning issues in Croatian dance art).

Ana Maletić and the Zagreb School of Contemporary Dance: An Educational Frame for Representing Identity

The deepest permanent trace of Laban's influence in Croatia can be recognized in the artistic thinking and overall professional orientation of Ana Maletić (1904-1986), dance artist, choreographer, writer, choreologist, and pedagogue and founder of the only Croatian school of contemporary dance based on the teachings of Laban and Dalcroze. Maletić's professional dance education started in Belgrade in the school of Dalcroze's student Maga Magazinović (1882-1968). She received further education at Laban's school in Paris, directed by Dusia Bereska. Ana Maletić completed her education by graduating at Laban's Institute of Choreography in Berlin. Obtaining the highest degree possible enabled Maletić to educate professionals in the field of movement and dance upon her return to Zagreb. Her School of Dance Art, founded in 1932, remained active until the onset of World War II. After the war, Ana Maletić began her struggle to convince the authorities of the new sociopolitical system on the importance of reopening an integral school of contemporary art of movement that would educate future generations of professional teachers, choreographers, and performers. She succeeded in her attempt and in 1954 founded the School of Rhythmics and Dance (today the Ana Maletić School of Contemporary Dance), which is still active as the unique Croatian blend and brand in its original methodological synthesis of European teachings transformed by the author's personal artistic vision.

Ana Maletić's affinity for themes from the national folklore is best displayed in her choreographies, which she created in cooperation with Croatian composers. Among several international performances of her choreographies incorporating elements of folklore, her 1938 Rotterdam (the Netherlands) performance with her dance studio achieved tremendous success. As Maletić's daughter Vera notes, "That was the first European performance of a dance ensemble basing its programme on the national folk themes" (Maletić 2003, 334). Among her post–World War II folklore-inspired choreographies, the biggest success on international scenes was the *Šiptarska suita* performance, created to the music of Croatian composer Emil Cossetto and performed by a professional national folklore ensemble.

For dance teachers basing their teachings on her pedagogical methods, as well as for numerous generations of her students, Ana Maletić was a great artist and teacher, bursting with energy and displaying great persistence in her continual emphasis on the need for a new approach to dance education. Today we could term it an *interdisciplinary approach*. Her persistence in proving the value of the "new" dance education aimed at the holistic development of the child was absolutely fascinating, as the great number of official pleas that she addressed to the communist government bear witness, all with the single purpose of reopening the school. A person certainly had to have courage, ability, and wisdom to keep modern dance alive and to construct the basis of its development. That was during the turbulent era of the postwar 1950s, a time ruled by fear, mistrust, and self-censorship (Đurinović 2003), a time during which the World War II heroes, after only a brief glimpse of fame (1945-48), were found "missing" or "guilty of collaboration."[7] The list of pros and cons in her struggle can be easily imagined if only we remember that Maletić's program originated in the enemy camps in Germany (Laban). Yet, at the same time, outgrowing the former elitist concept of ballet art with her democratic and integrated approach, her vision of incorporating dance education in the school curriculum could easily be fitted into the communist ideological frame, which viewed culture as a product for the masses. It was indeed very fortunate that someone within the communist ranks had enough wisdom and civic sensibility to recognize the value of a program advocating a vision of a new or an integral human being as a distinctive feature of modern educational dance.

Viewed from today's perspective, the almost simultaneous opening of two institutions for dance education—the School of Classical Ballet and the School of Rhythmics and Dance, bearing respectively the traditions of Eastern and Western influences, with two distinct aims and programs—was a typical example of the Croatian post–World War II geopolitical context. Ana Maletić remains the synonym of Croatian identity in the contemporary dance education or, rather, of the modern educational dance, as she used to emphasize this authentic syntagma coined by Rudolf Laban, pointing to the distinction between the two terms (Maletić 1983).

The Croatian example of the development of dance education is good fodder for tracing the dynamics of absorbing and creative reshaping of the Dalcroze-Laban influence via the transmission of their teachings to Croatia, its reinscribing in the new social context as a result of Ana Maletić's methodological elaboration, and the forming and displaying of an identity of a new cultural context that marked the Zagreb school of contemporary dance.[8]

The starting point of Ana Maletić's approach was, as in the case of her teachers Dalcroze and Laban, to make the kinesthetic, cognitive, and aesthetic experience of music and movement available to everyone, with the ultimate aim of introducing modern educational dance as part of the public school curriculum.[9] Unfortunately, her final aim did not receive adequate reception among Croatian educational authorities and still has not received adequate reception to this day.

Rhythmics and Dance Education:
Specific Characteristics of Croatian Dance Pedagogy

The specific characteristics of the School of Rhythmics and Dance, as the title suggests, primarily have been in the juxtaposing and the mutual interaction of the rhythmics and music education[10] and Laban's educational dance. Such a manifestation of synchronicity of music and dance art, unified under the term of *rhythmics and dance education*, is a result of Ana Maletić's precise application of methodological approaches that aimed at inviting a kinesthetic experience of the musical elements; evoking a mental and bodily awareness, recognition, and interpretation of the experienced elements; and leading to a final acquisition of these elements via movement.

It is interesting to compare Maletić's approach with that of Louis Horst, who also advocated and illustrated by numerous examples such a cognitive synthesis of dance and music as well as a synthesis with other art forms. Taking structure as his basis, Horst analyzes compatible elements of music and dance, such as space design and the rhythm of movements, as well as music harmony in relation to the quality and the texture of movement.[11] Thus, apart from dance and theoretical courses related to the dance profession, Maleti 's educational concepts also include rhythmics, music theory, and the actual playing of an instrument as part of the curriculum. Such complementing of dance with musical education is the distinguishing trait of Croatian dance pedagogy, and to our knowledge, it cannot be traced in other countries of the region. Ever since Ana Maletić created the model of a dance school founded on a wide basis, the main advantage of this concept has been, and still remains, its multifunctionality. Nowadays it is unified and best defined with the term *integrated education*, which certainly achieved its concrete realization within the four-year primary curriculum established at Ana Maletić's dance institution.

Along with dance, rhythmics[12] has always been the foundation of the profession, and in the case of Ana Maletić's vision, it became regarded as a distinctive feature in the process of educating professionals in the field of dance pedagogy, choreography, and performance. For the purposes of this text, I offer a brief presentation of the advantages of mastering the course in rhythmics as a valuable springboard toward future professional specialization, as exemplified by the students graduating from Ana Maletić's school. The experience of the Ana Maletić's school teachers has shown that a detailed methodological approach to the cognitive and empirical perception of musical elements via movement (metrics, rhythm, dynamics, tempo, melodic line, and form) not only improves the general musicality of dancers but also guides them in the development of their sensibility

Domesticus vulgaris 1.
Photo courtesy of Renato Brandolica.

for all four Laban movement factors—space, time, weight, and flow. In a discussion related to this enhancement of movement through music education, I describe the basic contents of the rhythmics curriculum as well as the advantages such a program yields to the education of students in the later years of a secondary school program.

Mastering metrics and regular accentuation via movement at a very early stage of dance education enhances the exploration of the relationship between meter and rhythm within the body, enabling students to recognize and express more creatively complex examples of polyrhythmics and polymetrics. Therefore the rhythmics curriculum greatly contributes to achieving coordination of movements, a crucial factor for a professional dancer. This methodological approach, which includes the creation of musical accompaniment to movements, is very significant. Children themselves create the musical accompaniment by using the Orff instrumentary or by creating their own instruments, by using a variety of props, by using their voices, or by using their own bodies to make sounds through the contact between parts of the body. This aspect is particularly important in the case of very young dancers because it activates their kinesthetic, tactile, and auditory sensors. Such an exploration of rhythm through games and free play with numerous surrounding objects transforms the students into an authentic Stomp troupe. The children's enthusiasm for the rhythmics classes thus is no surprise. Lucija, 10 years old, said "I love the rhythmics classes because then I can play with different instruments (rhythm sticks, rattles, drums) and create my own rhythms."

Any person working with movement and dance knows the importance of developing a good sense of a movement phrase as well as of the phrasing of movements.[13] The rhythmics classes, as part of the primary dance education, also help develop a sense of a movement phrase, primarily via recognition and accompaniment of a musical phrase and melody. This will aid secondary school students in mastering the skill in order to stray from the objective elements in music and in perceiving the phrasing of movements as a manifestation of the subjective experience linked to the inner "music" of breathing.

Equally important is the development of "creativity through simplicity," which is influenced greatly by a good sense of movement motifs. Lower-grade students acquire this sense by practicing the recognition of motifs in music, most frequently via dance improvisations of a shorter musical sentence structured as motif-motif-phrase. Furthermore, the skills of recognizing, experiencing, and creating musical forms via movements are advantageous in developing a sense for the structure of an entire dance piece in the process of mastering the basics of choreography at later stages in secondary school. We introduce the concepts of motif, phrase, sentence, period, and canon at the primary school level in order to reach, via an introduction to the AB and ABA forms, the more complex forms such as rondo and theme with variations, as well as the first movement of sonata and finally fugue (dealt with during the last year of the secondary school program).

While teaching dance composition at the final level of secondary school, I have observed that my students have developed a good sense of form, which greatly aids them in concept structuring. I clearly remember the task aimed at exploring the possibilities of motif development[14] during which students skillfully and consciously manipulated the motif, developing it creatively while at the same time constructing a clearly structured dance composition. Although such a task of dance creation largely outgrows the frame of music and rhythmics, I would suggest that the students' way of accomplishing the task reflects the solid base that the students had a chance to acquire during the course of our rhythmics program.

As my personal experience as a dancer and a dance teacher at the school has shown, the advantages of a versatile dance-rhythmics-music educational concept are clearly discernible, particularly in the case of future dance pedagogues. These advantages include music and rhythm memory, musicality, a well-developed sense of rhythm and structure, acquaintance with a variety of musical styles, an ability to understand

the specifics of a particular music score at a quick glance, good cooperation with the music accompanist, and the skill of illustrating a particular
dance composition by piano accompaniment or even creating a musical
or sound background when required.

The school acts as the highest possible institution in the field of dance
education in Croatia. Thus a high-quality educational background seems
a prerequisite of dance educators. (There are also four primary dance
schools in Croatia, all of them based on Maletić's program.)

The constant presence of the Laban-Maletić concept can be traced not
only in the inclusion of the rhythmics and dance curriculum as part of
the institutionalized dance education but also in its application in various forms of informal dance education, starting with kindergarten and
continuing all the way to a variety of dance courses. Moreover, it has
been included in the rehabilitation, education, and integration of hear-
ing- and speech-impaired children at the SUVAG Polyclinic in Zagreb.
Such a widespread application of the program is due to a meticulous
methodological analysis of its contents, inviting every dance teacher to
develop a personal approach to the postulates of dance pedagogy, which
include age adjustment and the encouragement of creativity.

Numerous dance instructors, with or without a degree obtained at
Maletić's school, often advertise their programs under the tried and tested
syntagma of rhythmics and dance since it is not only a distinctive category
in relation to other dance styles but also a certain automatic guarantee
of the quality of the offered dance course. The recent tendencies and
pressures from the educational authorities to minimize the amount of
music and rhythmics input in the dance curriculum offered at the school
therefore seem rather alarming. Although reducing music and rhythmics
courses to the level of partial knowledge may seem an advantage in terms
of decreasing the workload imposed on students, such a demand reflects
a lack of deeper understanding of the integral educational aspects of the
Ana Maletić concept and the well-grounded character of its curricular
upward-oriented hierarchy.[15]

Laban's Teachings: A Necessity and Modality for Preserving the Identity of the Zagreb School

Our secondary school curriculum is deeply endowed with Laban's teachings of space harmony (choreutics) and expressiveness of movement
(eukinetics), a feature which, along with the concept of rhythmics and
dance education, presents another specific and long-lasting characteristic
of the school's identity. It is thus logically acknowledged as yet another
aspect shaping the school's final product. Therefore, it is necessary that

the final product in our region remain educated in the tradition of Laban's teachings as it is a way of preserving the identity of the school. However, over the years of teaching, I have witnessed the Maletić school gradually closing in on the issues of perception, comprehension, and teaching Laban's concepts of space and effort. Two main factors seem responsible for such a counterproductive and (un)conscious isolation:

1. The Maletić school is the only dance institution in Croatia, and in that part of Europe, that bases its program on Laban's heritage. This limits the possibilities for professional exchange and further education of instructors in this method of teaching.

2. There is a general lack of proper public perception of dance art; the public, in fact, perceives of dance as only an attractive performance rather than a highly significant educational component in the development of children. It is not surprising that the need for promoting dance pedagogy, as well as the need for founding a dance pedagogy department at the higher education level, has been largely ignored. Consequently, it has been disregarded that trained teachers from such a department would represent human resources for the implementation of dance education as part of the general education curriculum.

The isolation of the school[16] has resulted in a long phase of status quo, which has led to the unavoidable stagnation in the professional development of Laban-oriented teachers. Thus, despite the teachers' individual creativity, the consequences of a codified pattern in teaching Laban's concepts have become obvious.

The Laban scales had been viewed for too long as the only available module of teaching dance technique in Maletić's school. Such an approach resulted in the overall misperception of technical achievements evaluated solely on the physical criteria of strength and flexibility of the body in its physical mastering of space. The weary insistence on the creation of etudes aimed at increasing the skills of reaching and retaining space direction resulted in generations of students with a limited perception of space, "perforated like Swiss cheese," and thus narrowed down to the core of the system that could be daringly dubbed *Laban ballet*. How wrong and how far this is removed from Laban's concept of body and space as a dynamic relationship of two living matters in the permanent state of transformation (Sanchez-Colberg 1998; Janković 2004).

With the performer's awareness directed solely toward the exterior, toward the general physical space and the space of the kinesphere, the concept of the body's inner space and the proprioceptive experience that results from a refined kinesthetic sensibility have been neglected, imposing the external experience of the physical body action in space. When and why did such a radical break with the original Laban concept occur? Could it be because Laban does not offer a fixed system or method (Maletic 1987), and teachers generally like to rely on such clear sets of directions in their practice? Or is it perhaps because of years of the school's isolation that Laban remained perceived and experienced mainly via German modern dance vocabulary? I would suggest that, within the context of general public disinterest in dance education in Croatia, the school's application of Laban was unable to follow in the footsteps of more recent approaches and applications of Laban's concepts in the development of dance art (Maletic 1987).[17] It is therefore not surprising that such a situation resulted in a dance product that has for years been the target of criticism.

This issue over the past few years set me on a quest to thoroughly reevaluate the possible approaches to Laban, resulting in my permanent preoccupation with discovering the modalities that would make the Laban classification of movement and dance more useful to a contemporary student, and not only in theory. In other words, my question was: How can we make the choreutic and eukinetic contents of our secondary school program more eligible to our students today, who, quite frankly, see no possibilities for the application of or further education in Laban's concepts in the Croatian dance market?[18]

Analyzing my teaching experience and questioning my corporeal memories of knowledge acquisition, the cognition and perception of Laban's teachings, I realized that the solution does not lie in the reduction of contents or, worse still, in their overall exclusion. It is the teaching method that requires a thorough revision, a different thinking, and—the most difficult step of all—a change in the approach to teaching Laban. I must emphasize that Laban's framework in our school has never been viewed only as a concept, theory, and analysis but rather as a predominant basis for dance creation that has been mirrored in the recognizable body language (i.e., in the corporeal sign) as one of the specific traits of the school's identity. With an increasing intrusion of foreign influences as insignia of a different identity, the basic Laban vocabulary of German modern dance later brought the image of an old-fashioned and outlived school, leaving students with a certain feeling of lack of purpose.

Lacking an academic background in dance pedagogy, I base my claims solely on attentive listening to my own body, on years of teaching experience, on my intuition, and on a number of conversations with my students during my ongoing self-education and research. Thus I have recognized two key problems regarding the students' perception of Laban's teachings:

1. Students have a lack of integrated insights (difficulties in comprehending the entire concept caused by a selection and separation of contents within the curriculum, partly due to a codified pattern of teaching).
2. Students perceive Laban's teachings solely from the aspect of the physical experience of the highly demanding technical requirements (on the verge of danger) for acquiring a Laban-like vocabulary instead of viewing his teachings as a permanent and universal concept inviting the engagement of mental and physical perception and its reception and application.

In searching for an appropriate solution, one that would be far more than a mere enforcement of Laban-like vocabulary, I suggest an application of his movement classification that is tailored to fit the dance vocabulary of contemporary students and that is primarily articulated via the most recent dance techniques. I am thus trying to integrate the body–mind awareness characteristic of modern techniques available to students (thanks to former students educated at academies abroad and now returning to teach at our school) with the Laban inner intention, the mental engagement required for a conscious, intentional interaction of inner-body space and the space that surrounds the body and that is in turn reified by that body.

The Choreutic Concept

In my methodological approach to choreutic contents, I often rely on the method of deduction. I start with a free movement sequence, the emphasis remaining on the student achieving a complete and conscious experience of himself or herself and the body, which should feel comfortable while creating its space via movement. I insist on a natural experience of the body in its every movement, often ignoring the canon of dance aesthetics. Thus I frequently remark to my students on the importance of listening to our own bodies, which, I argue, are often more intelligent than we are.

During the second phase, the same sequence is repeated with clarity of space intention. This will depend on the type of the choreutic task, which may range from the recognition of moments of diagonal orientation (emphasizing the unstable character of that moment) or the recognition and emphasis of the dominant space plane to the establishment of central, peripheral, or transversal links between diametral directions. This phase, due to its focus on a given task, often loses the spontaneity and freshness of the first free phase, the issue in turn calling for a conscious verbal analysis. To retrieve the spontaneity and expressiveness of the first phase, enriched with the clarity of space intention, a great deal of training is required in the third phase.

I want my students to experience the true and pulsating presence of Laban's space concept, to view it as logical and natural rather than as learned and externally enforced. I want them to understand that getting acquainted with, for instance, the space scales is not just an end in itself but an alphabet of theoretical concept of Laban's space harmony leading to an all-embracing body–mind reception of the innate logic of the body–space interaction. Having established such an interaction of body and space, a person is no longer restricted with a single choice between "where to?" and "why?" Answers to these questions become interrelated, making the theoretical concept more easily grasped.

Since the free sequence from the onset of the task reflects the individual effort pattern of the performer, excluding the possibility of perceiving the body solely as an instrument, a more natural integration of choreutic and eukinetic experience is achieved. The result is the experience of one's own dancing body, a body that is creating within a given space pattern and feeling natural. Here, I aim at raising my students to the point of experiencing the pleasure of conscious dancing, exclaiming as Ina (18 years of age) did, "Only now have I come to feel what it is like to actually dance Laban!"

The Eukinetic Concept

I believe in practicing the motto "to see, rather than just look; to hear, rather than just listen" aimed at awakening in students the sensibility toward all that surrounds them in order to create movements that truly reflect their individual approaches to life. In the beginning, it suffices to perceive the space of the studio where they practice each day, or to discover the view offered in one glimpse through the window, or to look other participants straight in the eyes in order to become fully aware of their presence. All these components play a role in building a relationship with oneself and one's own body, with others, and with the space where the interaction occurs. (I keep saying to my students, "Just don't dance as if you were acting it!")

While teaching the eukinetic contents, I question the exclusionary choice of the eight basic effort actions as the only possible combination of the motion factors prescribed by the existing curriculum. In my opinion this choice results in a narrow and stereotyped perception of the dynamics of movement and dance.[19] Bearing in mind the rich and diverse shades of inner states that materialize through movement, to be observed, analyzed, and verbalized later, I encourage my students to search for the dominant combinations of movement factors in particular movements in order to discover a variety of verbal equivalents for the respective inner attitudes and states. I emphasize here that conversations with my students play an important role in my teaching process,[20] along with responses and discussions, which greatly sharpen the perception of the body–mind experience, simultaneously enhancing their verbal skills and resulting in an overall feeling of freedom.

I also believe that in teaching the eukinetic concept, the instructor should aim at activating the awareness of one's personal effort pattern as, despite the freedom and idiosyncrasy this pattern yields to the dancer, the unconscious surrender to a prescribed effort pattern may result in stereotypes and monotony in movement phrasing.[21] The recognition of the personal pattern opens the possibilities for the conscious changing of the pattern, thus varying the corporeal sign and message and allowing the body to express itself in a new language.

Can it be claimed, then, that the educational plane, rather than just the artistic one, may indeed have a synergy of verbal and corporeal communication aimed at intensifying the recognition, identification, and reception of meaning between two subjects? The notion becomes clearer if we substitute the performer–spectator dichotomy of performing arts with that of our everyday teaching context, where the dichotomy consists of student and teacher or student and student subjecthood. In turn, the usual discourse of observation and analysis is replaced by the forming of interrelations resulting from experiencing, recognizing, and accepting a certain something offered by the dancing subject in a given moment.

I conclude my exploration of contemporizing Laban in dance education, the exploration of the possibilities of "integrating the past and projecting it into the future" (Maletić 1987, 149), by quoting the school's former student Marjana Krajač.[22] In the context of future visions for the school's development and following our "joined thinking, valuable dialogues and creative frictions in searching for possible approaches to Laban's concepts, and the ways of applying them within the contemporary dance framework," Krajač concludes that "Laban's opus . . . is a complex and fertile concept which fits the fresh saplings of choreographic and spatial thinking." Therefore, "dance pedagogues are expected to reach out for creative innovations rather than producing worn-out copies and weakened patterns," along with a "close cooperation and dialogue with teachers of dance techniques in order to work together on finding the solutions for contemporizing the complex technical requirements of Laban, often obsolete in terms of today's requirements."

Croatian Folk Dances and the Curriculum

I began this chapter with a historical contextualization of the promotion and presentation of various aspects of Croatian dance art throughout the past century, wherein the stage application and inspiration of the elements of Croatian folk dances played a significant role. Apart from the work of Ana Maletić, the remnants of positive evaluation of folk art as a source of continual inspiration of the contemporary dance vocabulary can be traced to the end of the 1970s, particularly in the work of Lela Gluhak-Buneta. A student of Ana Maletić and a former teacher at the school, later a founder and an art director of Zagrebački plesni ansambl (Zagreb Dance Ensemble), she was deeply and permanently inspired by the expressive force of Croatian folklore. With her creative symbiosis of costumes, dancers' vocal articulations, and the resounding rhythm of movement, her work outgrew the national code of identity and reached the global message. Only in 1999 did ethnopoetics manage to regain its place on the Croatian dance scene in the exquisite artistic interpretation by Croatian choreographer Rajko Pavlić titled *And There Stood the Sun, Gazing at the Miracle,* which represented Croatia at the Expo 2000. Pavlić's inspiration by Croatian folklore continued and in 2005 was realized in his choreography *Domesticus vulgaris.*

Domesticus vulgaris 2.
Photo courtesy of Renato Brandolica.

The emphasis on folk dances in the school's curriculum varied only slightly over the past 50 years. Today, despite the positive attitude toward the importance of introducing students to the stunning richness of rhythmic and melodic patterns and space formations of Croatian folk dances (stunning, considering the minuscule size of the country), I have to admit with a slight regret that, because of the inadequate number of folk dance classes, the students' knowledge remains at the level of basic information. (I hope this will change in the future with the possible opening of a folk dance department at our school.)

Because of a domination of folk-kitsch aesthetics in Croatian popular culture, inflating the value of traditional elements, the majority of urban youth readily dismiss the authentic folklore, degrading it to the derogatory context of peasantry. These current trends restrain me from predicting the possibilities of younger generations of students contributing to the integration of authentic elements in contemporary dance projects.

Identity and the Final Product

Although the current needs in Croatia primarily support the professional profile of a competent dance educator for youths and that of a trained dancer, author, and choreographer, the professional nomenclature and the actual practice acknowledge and respect only the school's final product of a "dancer." That product is judged primarily with regard to technical skills.

Over the years, with the formation of a growing number of professional dance ensembles, more pressure has been placed on the school to aim at even greater achievements in mastering the dance technique during the course of studies. Those requirements are naturally also reflected in the requirements placed before the younger students attending the primary school, since integral and complete results can be achieved only via a thorough progression of the education process. Yet, one should also keep in mind the meaning behind Maletić's concept of the rhythmics and dance education: the enabling of each child to express himself or herself creatively via movement and dance.

As the possibility of continuing dance education in Croatia is lacking, the pressure placed on the school to produce a student who is well (in)formed in various dance techniques and in accord with the innovations that come as a result of the dance art development should not be questioned. However, I question the limits of such an evaluation of students because many of their other qualities that have already been mentioned in this text remain overlooked.

Upon completing the program at Maletić's School in 1993 and entering the dance academy in Berlin, my advantages in comparison with
other students included: a) a systematic music education, b) creativity that enabled the smooth conversion/overlap from the role of a
dance performer towards that of an author, c) mastering the space,
both in practice and in concept. . . . The skill that I lacked, however,
was the technique of the body in its widest sense. . . . (personal correspondence by Marjana Krajač)

The increase in the number of dance classes in our curriculum, resulting
from a necessary introduction of new dance techniques, certainly allows
students today to enter the dance market of Croatia, and it ensures their
entry to a number of dance academies abroad. However, it also further
complicates the Gordian knot: The emphasis on the number of dance
technique classes creates a work overload on our students, while at the
same time it also unsettles the balance by threatening the original identity of the school, which had for years been recognized and valued for its
production of dance professionals with, I would say, a versatile Maletić
profile.

Within the previously mentioned context, and with many years of personal experience as a teacher at the school, I am deeply preoccupied with
how to combine the (im)possible, the Laban–Maletić vision of presenting
the concept of educational dance to every child, with a secondary school
education where students would be trained to continue their education
in the field. A student trained in this way might then become:

- A well-educated contemporary dancer
- A daring, free, and thinking author and choreographer
- A future teacher trained in the basics of teaching the Laban and
  Maletić program

As long as the school remains the only and final institution for dance
education in Croatia, the teachers at the School are forced to seek a solution in the forming of a new secondary school curriculum that offers a
specialization directed toward two separate educational modules. I see
them as thus:

1. An emphasis on the final product of dancer-performer
2. The final product seen in terms of dance educator qualified for the
   continuation of his or hers training at a (future) higher school for
   dance pedagogues

This raises an important question: Would this split of the curriculum
into two separate modules automatically result in a distinction between

our students, categorizing them as dancers and lesser dancers? Through informal conversations with my students, I learned that a number of our secondary school students with less adequate physical predispositions for achieving the expected technical skills remain the strongest advocates of such an approach, while at the same time remaining aware of the wide applicability of the existing concept of the school within which they certainly can find their own space. Therefore module 2 would reflect their abilities more realistically, respecting the limits of their physical bodies (Fortin 1998), clearing away the existing frustrations, and enabling them to experience dance education as a free and relaxed expression of themselves and their bodies. Thus we would succeed in tracing the full circle in a logical manner, starting from every child being able to enter the school to the completion of every student's education without changing the identity of the institution and its principles.

However, in writing these words, I become aware of the contradiction in terms. Actually, all these years the school has based its identity on a type of integrated program (Marques 1998), to the point that being forced to make a distinction between the technically skilled dancer and the less skilled dancer, dancer and teacher, or author (choreographer) and dance pedagogue is antithetical to the program's vision. Although I think that such a step (could it be a step in the wrong direction?) should be discussed among both the Croatian dance scene and the dance pedagogues, I fear that the term *dancer* will remain a synonym for a technician (of what kind?), thus remaining trapped in the limited aspect of evaluating the school's final product.

Conclusion

Written from the perspective of my own professional experience, and in an attempt to introduce my country to a wider reading audience, this chapter illuminates the historical circumstances of the founding of the only secondary dance school in Croatia, its activities, and the influences it exerted on the overall dance education and dance art in Croatia. The chapter is also my personal contribution to the inscription and preserving of the school's identity as the central institution of contemporary dance in its historical, social, and educational contexts, both in Croatia and in this part of Europe. It is also my intimate way of dealing with those who refuse to create and share the future of this school, as well as with those whose lack of skill and knowledge disables them from supporting our quest for new approaches to Laban's opus despite the plenitude of the material.

This chapter is a message to the entire Croatian dance scene. This scene seems to be unaware of the efforts that should be invested in preserving the identity of the school in its process of opening toward the professional requirements as well as opening toward foreign influences, especially in the light of the current adjustments of its curriculum to fit the standards of European integrations and the requirements of globalization trends.

REFLECTIONS

The complexity of the role of dance as a form of cultural and national expression, how we may accept or challenge outside influences that may change traditional cultural expressions, and the ways in which we transmit cultural attitudes, values, and beliefs through our art and schools inter-act in the questions posed by Ivančica Janković in this chapter. Noting the significance of both Laban and Dalcroze's frameworks for dance and music in the work of the famous teacher and artist Ana Maletić, Janković provides us with a window through which to view some of the difficulties that art and education encounter with changing political and social forces. Historically, as countries are challenged to determine their national identity, such as during recent changes in South Africa and Ireland (for different reasons), there has been a twofold reaction: to hold on to tradition and to look to other countries (often in the West) to reshape tradition in ways that will connect, or even imitate, what is considered successful. Those are the contexts and the challenges faced by Croatia. As with other countries undergoing fundamental change, Croatia must address questions of the role of arts and arts education within a national culture and decide the dominant aesthetic used in judging what is a good dancer and what is good dance. Formulating a different aesthetic is no easy task. What criteria are used? What values and processes are used? Who should teach? Who should learn? What is to be learned? How is it assessed? These questions inevitably return us to questions involving the role of art and art education in a society. Listening to our students; valuing our own experiences as artists, teach-ers, and mentors; and envisioning a global society and the role of art within it create the context in which the search for Croatian identity, or any national identity, can be engaged. Asking who we are now compels us to ask who we collectively want to be and how we want to be. This process for becoming "someone" demands awareness, perception, imagination, synthesis, connection, vision, and creation. Here is the place that, as Ivančica asked, "Where to?" and "Why?" we can begin to respond with both the artist's sensitivity and the educator's sensibility that together allow us to explore possibilities for "integrating the past and projecting it into the future" (Maletic 1987, 149). Whether it is folk dance that helps us understand our past or new choreography that helps us understand our present, it is always the arts that facilitate the aesthetic challenge of imagining our future. Herbert Marcuse (The Aesthetic Dimension, 1979) gave us permission to claim the arts as that part of humanity that allows us to see reality as more than real, a process that stimulates our capacity to transcend the immediate and the everyday. And, with this in mind, the role of the arts can become the indispensable transformational human experience.

Here, I bring to our attention the issues that Janković has also discussed in reference to Rudolph Laban's movement framework. Much like the notion of a "fixed" identity of a nation, culture, or state, Laban's framework has been maintained in the dance world as something that is fixed, unchangeable. But, as with any identity, fixation is not possible. Reifying any idea, thought, object, or nation as something that cannot be influenced, reinterpreted, or changed creates tensions among what has been, what is, and what might be—past, present, and future. In this chapter we are asked to examine or add to the ways in which we think and use Laban's framework. I am reminded of a time when Isabel Marques, a Brazilian dance educator and choreographer, brought to our attention the importance of her Brazilian dancers' hair as a "body part" when dancing—not something that was included in the original Laban framework. Whether it is in regard to national identity or any other form of identification, we must give attention to the ways in which we construct meaning through forms that are either rigid or flexible, open or closed, or done with humility or done with an uncompromising certainty.

Notes

1. In multinational and thus also multicultural societies of the West, due to a general interaction of various influences within the national boundaries of a single country, all of the previously mentioned motives are likely to be found, which verifies the claim that "identity manifests itself in an interaction with others" (Slunjski 2005, 121).

2. The data were collected by Maja Đurinović, who embarked on the project of researching and publishing data on the history of Croatian dance and ballet.

3. After the fall of the Austro-Hungarian monarchy, Croatia joined the Kingdom of Yugoslavia, and then after World War II became a republic of Socialist Yugoslavia, finally winning its independence in the course of the 1991-95 war for independence.

4. Records show an amazing performance of Mia Čorak Slavenska, at that time already an international ballet star, as well as that of Mercedes Goritz-Pavelić with the Croatian National Ballet and the Association of Theatre Volunteers at the 1936 Dance Olympics held in Berlin, particularly for the program that structured its core on the elements of folklore. Goritz-Pavelić was even offered the position of a lecturer in Yugoslav dance forms at the Berlin Dance Art High School in 1939 (Đurinović 2000; Đurinović and Podkovac 2004).

5. Cf. Huxley's (1994) view on the types of influence, especially on the doubtful quality of Laban's influence on followers who had only a short encounter with his teachings.

6. From an informal conversation with Stjepan Sremac, an ethnologist and a renowned expert for Croatian folklore, as well as a former teacher of folk dances at the Ana Maletić School of Contemporary Dance, Zagreb.

7. The phase of political purges within the context of the historical split between Yugoslav president Tito and Russian leader Stalin.

8. Cf. Desmond 1997, 186.

9. This way of thinking and experiencing dance education certainly brought Croatia nearer to the Dance and the Child International (daCi), from the organization's founding until today.

10. Cf. Dalcroze 1919/1988, 28-30.

11. Cf. Horst and Russel 1961, 30.

12. Until recently the students and graduates of the school referred to it as the school of *rhythmics* rather than the school of *dance*, which should be viewed not only in the context of its original name (which was to be changed later) but also within the context of the importance and emphasis Ana Maletić placed on the rhythmics classes. Unfortunately, the lay observers always associated the term *rhythmics* with the term *rhythmic gymnastics*, which is one of the reasons why *rhythmics* has been removed from the school's original name.

13. I refer to the phrase as an organization of movement in time and the phrasing defined as a dance dynamics pattern. Cf. Maletic 2005.

14. Cf. Blom and Chaplin 1994.

15. In her letter dated February 1, 2006, Marjana Krajač, the former student of the A. Maletić School of Contemporary Dance who later completed her academic dance education in Berlin, Germany, emphasized the advantages of such a systematic music education in the development of a dance artist.

16. The situation changed significantly in 2000 with the election of a new school headmistress (a former student), whose vision of the school's future development includes its opening the door to young pedagogues educated at various dance academies abroad.

17. Various applications of Laban's concepts, as well as the variations of the existing ones or the developments of new ones, unfortunately still remain unavailable in Croatia.

18. This does not refer to the pedagogical aspects of rhythmics and dance education of preschool children, an area in which our former students remain in great demand, but unfortunately not many of them show sufficient interest. A similar topic has been explored by Marques (1998, 172-173, 183).

19. See note 13.

20. Cf. Marques (1998, 177).

21. See note 13.

22. See note 15.

three

Dance Inna Dancehall: Roots of Jamaica's Popular Dance Expressions

Christopher A. Walker

Dancer and choreographer with the National Dance Theatre Company of Jamaica

Visiting lecturer at the University of Wisconsin at Madison

In the Jamaican popular dance space, the dancehall, dances are created to represent an event, to pay tribute, to ridicule, and to celebrate. Sometimes they are created just for the pure exhilaration and exercise of one's creativity. Most of these "new" dances display parallel elements with many traditional Jamaican dance forms. Similar to the Jonkonnu festival, from where some of its traditions are derived, dancehall offers contemporary Jamaicans the medium through which they can make topical commentary on politics, society, and religion, among many other discourses—as did Jonkonnu for the enslaved and the colonized in Jamaica.

The Jonkonnu masquerade is one of the earliest recorded forms of dance in Jamaica, and it is a repository of a rich Jamaican cultural history manifested in the diverse range of parading Jonkonnu characters that represent the multifarious cultural fusions and inclusions common throughout the Caribbean. Jamaican dancehall is a musical style, a dance style, and a subculture. As a secular ritual, it is the outlet for artistic and political expressions embodying resistance by Jamaicans, who are empowered under the mask and by the transformation. This discussion focuses on the physical language and characteristics of Jamaican dance expressions, from the earliest to the most recent. In it, I explore the traditional dance forms, the direct derivatives found in the contemporary dancehall dances, and the further manifestations of these ideas in the Jamaican Dance Theatre and concert dance art expressions.

To understand any of this, we must first recognize that Jamaica, like much of the Caribbean, is creolized, and creolized expressions are iconic of a Caribbean identity formed out of a history of cultural collisions, forced migrations, enslavement, and years of colonial oppression and cultural denigration. Through the lens of the Jamaican dancing body, this document highlights stories, double entendres, and contemporary issues that are asserted in movement that are Africanist in aesthetic and totally Jamaican.

Dance in Jamaica

While still a research fellow at the African Caribbean Institute of Jamaica, Cheryl Ryman (1980) published *The Jamaican Heritage in Dance: Developing a Traditional Typology*. Of the seven core-type dances outlined, five were listed as religious, including myal, maroon, kumina, revival, and rastafari, all of which are African or neo-African in form. The other two are secular, including hosay of East Indian origin and Jonkonnu, an African-Jamaican masquerade form. There are 39 dances that are related to the seven core type dances. Under the secular heading, seven dances (wake, bele, calimbe, comobolo, dinki mini, ring games, gerreh) are related to funeral and death rites, two (quadrille and maypole) are set dances of European origin, four (buru, brukin party, queen party, brag) were listed as variants deriving directly from Jonkonnu and relate to some form of procession, and four (mento, shay shay, yanga, bram) were recreational.

Social dances in Jamaica today fall under the secular headings just listed; however, creators of these popular social expressions have unintentionally drawn upon the traditional forms, both religious and secular, for movement inspiration. As such, the popular movement expressions in today's dancehall display characteristics synonymous with Jamaican traditional dance aesthetics. These include the traditional religious movement dances.

This crossover of movement from religious to secular and from secular to religious is demonstrated in the secular buru form, from which the religious rastafarian form derived, and in the religious pukumina, which was undoubtedly the movement source for the popular ska dances of the 1960s and 70s. The religious forms contribute greatly to the social dance expressions, and while it is possible to trace many dancehall steps to various African-Jamaican religious dances, dancehall is a secular form and has its roots primarily in the secular traditional forms. Stolzoff (2000, 3) contends that

dancehall has been a space of cultural creation since the slavery era, even though the name given to this constellation of oppositional practices has changed over time. This is not to deny the significant disjuncture and radical reformulations in both the form and content of the dancehall performance over time, but it is to recognize that the current set of practices known as dancehall can be traced back to earlier forms from which they derive.

This early set of practices to which Stolzoff refers comprises the social expressions of slaves dancing in 17th-, 18th-, and 19th-century Jamaica, brought to light by the writings of British slaveholders. Some of these practices or social rituals are consistent with dancehall today. Like Stolzoff, I turn to *After Africa: Extracts From British Travel Accounts and Journals of the Seventeenth, Eighteenth, and Nineteenth Centuries Concerning the Slaves, Their Manners, and Customs in the British West Indies,* edited by Roger Abrahams and John Szwed (1983), which presents documentation of recreational practices on the island during slavery. The descriptions of movement are sparse and are Eurocentric in perspective, but these writings provide aesthetic commonalities that substantiate Jamaican dancehall as a form steeped in ancestry and not just a dance of the 1980s. This background creates a historical platform for early movement investigation. I quote the following references to slaves' social behavior from this source.

William Beckford (1790) witnessed and wrote *A Descriptive Account of the Island of Jamaica:*

> Notwithstanding all their hardships, they are fond of play and merriment; and if not prevented by whites, according to a law of the island, they will meet on Saturday nights, hundreds of them in gangs, and dance and sing till morning; nay, sometimes they continue their balls without intermission till Monday morning. . . . (Abrahams and Szwed 1983, 291)

In the article "Characteristic Traits of the Creolian and African Negroes in Jamaica" printed in *Columbiam Magazine* in April-October 1797, an anonymous author adds to the description:

> The song and dance are always united when they associate to amuse themselves. . . . Excellence in dancing is thought to depend on a due performance of certain gestures peculiar to each class. All who please dance in succession, without any formality, introduction, or invitation. (Abrahams and Szwed 1983, 293)

And James Stewart (1823, 269-273) in *A View of the Past and Present State of the Island of Jamaica* wrote the following:

> Plays, or dances, very frequently take place on Saturday nights, when the slaves on the neighbouring plantations assemble together to

enjoy this amusement. It is contrary to the law for the slaves to beat their drums after ten o'clock at night; but this law they pay little regard to. (Abrahams and Szwed 1983, 300-201)

H.T. De La Beche (1825, 40-41) notes how the dance time fits into the week's schedule for the slaves in *Notes on the Present Conditions of the Negroes in Jamaica:*

> When a negro wishes to give a dance, he applies for leave to the overseer, who as a matter of course grants it; the day fixed upon is almost always Saturday, in order that they may keep it up during the night and the next day; the dance, or play, as it is sometimes called, commences about eight o'clock in the evening, and although contrary to law, continues to day-break with scarcely any intermission, those of the old school preferring the goombay and African dances, and those of the new, fiddles, reels, &c. (Abrahams and Szwed 1983, 302)

These recordings are testament to the social dancing dynamics and the importance of dancing to the enslaved in Jamaica. According to Nettleford (1985), the dance was a fierce instrument of survival and the body was a weapon of cultural self-defense. The enslaved body, strengthened as property, was not financially practical to destroy. That the act of dancing was enjoyed is unmistakable, and the dancehall space or the creation thereof was undoubtedly a necessity for practicing this type of social recreation. Though they adapted and practiced European dance forms like the maypole and quadrille, it was in the African-based movements that the enslaved in Jamaica found the most enjoyment. This was consistently demonstrated during Saturday night gatherings, which were the antecedent of today's dancehall.

Another point to consider when investigating the early dancehall dances is the early social music forms. Mento is the earliest social Jamaican music form. It came out of a fusion of African and European musical expressions, both in instrumentation and in sound. The lyrics in mento music, like those of today's dancehall, generally comment on social issues and often have sexual overtones and double entendres. The associated dance movements for mento music included the fifth figure in the camp-style quadrille, which was added by the enslaved as a Jamaican adaptation of the European form. On a purely movement level, mento dancing is closely linked to the dance expressions found in dinki mini and gerreh ring play of the Jamaican wake complex, traditional African-Jamaican dance steps including dinki mini, shay shay, and a ball and flat inching action of the feet commonly referred to as the *conga step.*

Early accounts describe movements that could easily be descriptions of rural ring play dances that are found in the Jamaican wake complex today. William Beckford (1790) wrote the following:

> The dance consists of stamping of the feet, twistings of the body, and a number of strange indecent attitudes. It is a severe bodily exertion—more bodily indeed than you can well imagine, for the limbs have little to do in it. The head is held erect, or, occasionally, inclined a little forward—the hands nearly meet before—the elbows are fixed, the whole person is moved without lifting the feet from the ground. Making the head and limbs fixed points, they writhe and turn the body upon its own axis, slowly advancing towards each other, or retreating to the outer parts of the ring. (Abrahams and Szwed 1983, 294)

George Pinckard (1806, 263-68), in *Notes on the West Indies,* wrote the following:

> It is very amazing to think with what agility they twist and move their joints: I sometimes imagined they were on springs or hinges from the hips downwards; whoever is most active and expert at wriggling is reputed the best dancer. . . . (Abrahams and Szwed 1983, 290-291)

It is not far fetched to assume that many of the dances performed for ritual practices also served social purposes. Even today, many religious traditional dance steps make their way into the social dance arena, the most recent being the pukumina movements that are done to dancehall artist Elephant Man's hit song, "Yu Too Badmine."

The Emergence of Jonkonnu

Cheryl Ryman (1984a, 1984b) contends that Jonkonnu is a neo-African cultural form. Though Jonkonnu demonstrates strong roots in African masquerades, the masquerade took its shape from Jamaican experiences, identifying the form as more Jamaican than African, European, or Asian. Jamaican Jonkonnu is a rainbow of cultures and cultural expressions dominated by an African-Jamaican understanding of self and of how the self copes in varying situations. As many influences as there may have been on this form, the dominant projection was and remains Jamaican, which is consistent with the aesthetics and development of popular and con-temporary dance expressions in Jamaica. The diverse range of Jonkonnu characters is a true representation of Jamaica's cultural complexion, which is also captured in Jamaica's motto "out of many, one people." It was one of the earliest recorded music-dance forms and was the first form of dance theatre in Jamaica (see Walker 2002). The Jonkonnu masquerade still exists on the island today and remains an unchallenged symbol of the Jamaican identity, representing one of those core forms from which many of the popular music and dance forms emerged.

The Jonkonnu masquerade is a masked procession of dancers, actors, and musicians defined as

> a dance drama which is a living testimony of Jamaica's historical and social development. . . . It is a synthesis of the diverse cultural components that are the fabric of our heritage. . . . In common with masquerades the world over, it exhibits such features as dancing and music, singing and buffoonery, masks and costuming, street processions and feasting. (Barnett 1977, 1)

Mask dancing in Jamaica was recorded as early as 1687 by Sir Hans Sloane, a visitor to the island who wrote, "They would tie cow's tails to their rumps and add such other things to their bodies in several places as to give them a very extraordinary appearance" (Sloane 1707, 49). What Sloane saw and described was undoubtedly a description of early Jonkonnu. Long described one of these celebrations:

> In the towns during Christmas holidays they have several tall robust fellows dressed up in grotesque habits, and a pair of ox-horns on their heads, sprouting from the top of a horrid sort of visor, or mask, which about the mouth is rendered very terrific with large boar-tusks. The masquerader, carrying a wooden sword in his hand, is followed with a numerous crowd of drunken women, who refresh him frequently with a cup of aniseed-water, whilst he dances at every door, bellowing out "John Connu" with great vehemence. (Long 1774, 425).

The Jonkonnu masquerade evolved with the Jamaican culture. It adapted to the social and political structure of the island, refashioning itself into the present Jonkonnu celebrations, which are a fusion of mainly African and European masquerades with Asian influences. The embracing of other cultural icons resulted in a variety of creolized versions of other cultural masquerade icons being included the parade, complete with dance steps representative of each character.

Bettelheim, Nunley, and Bridges (1988, 46) state that "the Jonkonnu dance merged African/European steps." The European influence was represented by a character who wore on his head a houseboat filled with puppets of sailors, soldiers, and slaves at work on a plantation. Another European influence was the set girls, characters that came out of the red and blue balls that happened at Christmastime, which coincided with the Jonkonnu festival. Both sets, led by a queen, contended for elegance and beauty. In the end a play was enacted before the master at the great house. By the early 19th century, Jonkonnu was used to artistically reflect what was going on in the society. At Christmastime, the biggest news and events of the year were shown in a dramatic movement display in the Jonkonnu festival.

One of the steady maintaining Jonkonnu characters, along with cow head, is pitchy patchy. Both characters are part of what is called *Roots Jonkonnu*. *Roots* in Jamaican terminology refers to that which comes from the peasant or lower class; Roots Jonkonnu is more African in form, as opposed to the highly affected Fancy Dress Jonkonnu, which is more European in style (Bettelheim, Nunley, and Bridges 1988, 50). Bettelheim clarifies the difference: "The presence of Cowhead and other animal characters is one of the most important distinctions between Roots Jonkonnu and Fancy Dress . . ." (Bettelheim, Nunley, and Bridges 1988, 53).

Most of the newer Jonkonnu characters are manifestations of everyday life. (See table 3.1 for list of characters and origins.) Within the form there is much code switching and allegory, similar to the hidden motives behind Capoeira in Brazil, Bomba y Plena in Puerto Rico, and other African-based rituals in the Caribbean used as passive resistance to slavery and, later, to colonial rule. Behind the mask of Jonkonnu, performers protested against the state and ridiculed the ruling class without the fear of persecution, as these statements against oppression were hidden under what looked like light entertainment and revelry.

Table 3.1   Jonkonnu Characters

Character	Root	Costume or prop	Dance
Queen, daughter, and grandchild	European	Fineries befitting the characters	Regal steps of the court
Champion and warwick	European and African	Breastplate and two swords; head tie with cone-shaped head-dress with feathers at the crown, adorned with pieces of mirror and cutouts	Warlike, grounded defending and attack-ing movements

(continued)

Table 3.1   (continued)

Character	Root	Costume or prop	Dance
Satan	European and African	Black rags covering the entire body, blackened mesh mask with facial features painted on, red rim around the eyes, horns on top of the head, three-pronged fork in hand, cowbell attached to backside	Leaping back and forth from leg to leg in a rocking motion, performing stabbing movements with fork in hand simultaneously to the rocking
Whore girl or begga gyal	European and African	Usually short skirts or obscene fashions of trollops	Sexually suggestive movements, little jumps with wide-open legs and jabbing pelvis, with arms outstretched to the sides and fingers rhythmically performing a begging gesture
Messenger boy	European	Messenger uniform	Dances with queen and whore girl, also does a homosexual dance
Pitchy patchy	African	Scraps of fabric attached to overalls, hanging in a shaggy fashion; sometimes a whip in hand	Noted as the spirit of the dance, maintains order by using a cattle whip to keep audience away from the dancers; rapid jumps in circular patterns; shoulders and elbows move up and down and out and around, in counter tempo to the feet
Jack in the green	African	Shredded bark extending over the head to the shoulders, coconut leaves from the shoulders to the feet	Similar to pitchy patchy

Character	Root	Costume or prop	Dance
Belly woman	African	Fake pregnant belly and dress	Amusing antics, rolling and rotating the belly in time with the music, jumps like the whore girl
Madda lundy	African	Fake bottom and sometimes fake belly as well	Amusing antics, rolling and rotating bottom in time with the music, jumps like the whore girl
Policeman	European	Police uniform	Mimetic
Set girls	European	Elaborate gowns in the color of their set, sometimes provided by the lady of the house	Mimic the pageantry of ballroom dance with a competitive and creolized twist
Actor boy	European	Elaborate gown with lace and exaggerated fineries, a headdress that resembles a ship or sometimes a house	Mimetic; looking like a ballet master sometimes; clean, precise, and well-articulated leg movements with a rigid torso
Cow head	African	Calico head tie, halfcoconut shell with red cow horns attached, cow tail attached to the backside	Dances separately with jumping and bucking movements, successive leaps with circling arms and wobbling head
Wild Indian or Indian girl	Caribbean (of Arawak origin)	Tall cane and crossbow in hand; headdress with feathers, playing cards, and cutouts; pieces of mirror—silver heart worn on the chest	Grounded stomping with the torso generally in a forward curve
Babu	Indian	Dressed as an old Indian man	Frail movements

Jonkonnu celebrations were banned in Jamaica in 1841, but a 1952 Jonkonnu contest proved the value of this masquerade to the Jamaican people. The groups that performed displayed a tradition that obviously never died even though it was banned. Members of the Steer Town Jonkonnu Band attested to this. They stated that their fathers and grand-fathers "jumped Jonkonnu" (performed Jonkonnu) even though the government did not want them to perform it (personal communication, October 1998). Especially in the rural parishes of the island, Jonkonnu celebrations continued during Christmastime, when the "drums of Jamaica came out of hiding. Although prohibited, it is evident they are practiced all year, for some of the rhythms would challenge the excellence of a Haitian drummer" (Lekis 1960, 151). The two main instruments in a Jonkonnu band are the drums and the fife, and their sweet sounds, along with the banjo, grater, and pitchfork, were heard in rural areas during this time of prohibition.

As a child I was frightened of, and did not comprehend, the activities of Jonkonnu. But that soon changed as I began to understand and recognize images and dances, feeling a surge of pride whenever I heard the drumming of the Jonkonnu bands during the festival at Christmastime. I first watched through the living room window, then from the veranda, then from the gate, and then later as a part of the reveling crowd on the street. It was much more than mere entertainment, as stated by Nettleford in his contribution to *Caribbean Festival Arts:* "Festival remains a vehicle for communicating and affirming values and for strengthening the bonds in the new society . . ." (Bettelheim, Nunley, and Bridges 1988, 183). Even though Jonkonnu includes much buffoonery, it must not be confused with minstrelsy. Whereas the minstrel shows in North America perpetuated negative stereotypes of African Americans and sought to dehumanize the men, desexualize the women, and mentally weaken the race (Walker, Bailey, Bright-Holland 2003), the Jonkonnu masquerade was a satirical look at plantation life in Jamaica, an affirmation of a strong cultural past, and an opportunity for the creation and presentation of African-Jamaican art (through costume, movement, and music). It became a form of passive resistance to slavery, plantation life, and an oppressive colonial government.

Urban Folk

Urban folk is defined as dancehall movement as a direct derivative of Jamaican traditional and folk dance expressions. As people migrate from rural parishes to urban centers in Jamaica, there is a large transference of rural traditional and folk practices. In the metropolitan areas, many tradi-tional forms take on new shapes and purposes or are discarded altogether.

Certainly the physical projections of wake rituals in Jamaica's capital city of Kingston differ from those of the rituals found in the rural parishes. However, when examined closely, the Kingston rituals can be seen as an evolution, an abstraction, or a distillation of the traditional rituals. For example, sound systems replace the live and communal performances of traditional music, and urban folk movements replace traditional movement expressions.

The first wake ceremony I attended in Jamaica's metropolis was in 1987, two years after I moved there from the rural parish of St. Ann on Jamaica's North Coast. I had developed a fascination for wake rituals from attending many in rural Jamaica. They were essentially a celebration of life in the face of death, and they provided the bereaved with support for mourning and reflection. We younglings got to stay up late playing games, dancing, singing, and eating a variety of food, which is always in abundance at wake ceremonies. As I walked to this wake in Meadowvale, I could hear dancehall music and wondered if someone was having a party, which was very uncommon on a Tuesday night in our neighborhood. Meadowvale was a small sub-urban neighborhood, surrounded by other small sub-urban neighborhoods in Portmore, a place that many of my High School friends at Kingston College called the 'dormitories across the waters'. Portmore was a ten-minute car drive or a thirty-minute bus ride across the Causeway Bridge to downtown Kingston. It was dubbed a dormitory because many who lived in Portmore worked and played in Kingston. It was also a space where rural and urban cultures met on new soil—it was a safe space. I arrived at the address and soon found out that the dead yard was the source of the music. I thought I was in the wrong place, but I figured I would follow my nose and investigate further. There was a powerful smell of Escovitch Fish and Curried Goat permeating the air. I noticed that there were men playing dominoes in the outside lawn, children playing ring games under the mango tree in the front lawn, and young adults doing *scabbie, pedal an' wheel*, and other quick leg movements to the music in the empty lot bordering the house. Older folks were giving animated performances on the veranda to a laughing audience of their peers and teenagers seated on the lower and adjacent car porch. The children playing after eight p.m. on a school night, the smell of the food, and the intergenerational mixing told me this was not just some party—this was the nine night. I walked under a blue awning that stretched from the roof of the car porch to the high front gateposts, and upon hearing the oration coming from the veranda about the hilarious deeds of the deceased, I knew for sure I was in the right place. All the features of a wake were there, but I was experiencing something new with the music and movement.

The movements I witnessed at the wake were dancehall movements. For the first time and because of the context, I realized the similarity between the rural steps and what seemed like urban variations. The *scabbie* and *pedal an' wheel* were common social dances across the island, but there was a different message in how the movements were articulated in this space; there were a certain confidence, power, and assertion. I soon caught up with the flow and was in the thick of the dancing, though much more restrained in my expression. I felt most at home when a much older boy suggested that we "folk up the dancing." What followed was a fusion of Jonkonnu, dinki mini, kumina, gerreh, tambu, and other folk movements, all being done to dancehall music. We were on top of the world, soaring in our own creative atmosphere. I went home transformed, thinking that for the first time Kingston was beginning to make sense.

Kingston was about evolution, fusion, inclusion, change, and discovery. It was the center of Jamaica's arts and politics and was the amalgamation of the multifarious cultural expressions across the island. Fused here was a singular expression of hope and defiance against all odds—a singular expression of a Jamaican identity formed in movement and music and expressed through the lens of an urban Jamaican worldview. The energy in the streets of Kingston was a tangible, breathable power encased in the rich and collective cultural and artistic expressions of the people.

It is no surprise then that the musical icon of Jamaica, reggae, which was born out of an evolutionary fusion of ska, rocksteady, and rhythm and blues, came out of Kingston. There was constant adaptation within the traditional and folk and popular forms, with a solid projection of the Jamaican experience in rhythm, vocals, and movement. Dancehall music was a natural part of that evolution and also came out of Kingston in 1979-80. Like other Jamaican popular forms, it exemplifies the creolization, acculturation, and syncretism that are common in Caribbean culture. The interesting thing about these developments in popular Jamaican culture is that while there were influences from non-Jamaican sources, the root and projected dominance remained African Jamaican, especially in the physical response to these new music forms.

Dancehall Movers and Shakers

The rhythms and stories have always been the underlying motivation for movement development. Especially during the 1980s, different parts of Jamaica had different movement expressions for different songs, unlike today, where the majority of the island learns the same dances. I had the opportunity of consistently traveling back and forth between St. Ann on the North Coast and Kingston on the South Coast between 1986 and 2000. Being a party enthusiast—as my mother would say, "Every drum knock yuh deh deh" ("You are at every party")—I witnessed the migration of social dance practices from one region to the next by the many who traveled frequently between the coasts. Often people in the session (dancehall party) would look at the new movement with appreciation. Sometimes they would learn it, or sometimes they would just laugh because it looked strange to them. I could quickly distinguish Kingston dancers from St. Ann dancers just by the way they approached movement, but I never investigated how these dances were created or who was responsible for creating them until the phenomena of Bogle (Jamaica's most popular dancehall movement innovator) and Carlene (Jamaica's first dancehall queen) hit in the 1990s.

The Bogle dance takes its name from its creator and was made popular through the song of the same name by dancehall and reggae artist Buju Banton. The dance is characterized by a body wave with alternating arms reaching upward and over, slicing the space. The arms react to the melodic wave in the body that is initiated by a forward thrust of the pelvis. The leading arm sometimes mirrors this thrust in a percussive reach into a suspended slice as the movement travels up the spine, creating body waves in the torso. The stance is parallel feet flat on the ground, wide apart, with a slight bend in the knees. The difficulty increases with an incline of the torso—the dancer takes the torso back, all the time maintaining the wave in the body. Some dancers do this in a hinge position and others continue until their upper backs are on the floor. This dance relates directly to bruckins (a dance created in celebration of emancipation). In bruckins, dancers compete doing the silo, a movement that includes a bruck (break) and a small circle and wave in the torso. In both dances, very skilled dancers are able to go all the way backward in a hinge or to limbo until their upper backs touch the floor, all the while continuing the waves or brucks in the body, and then retrograde this back-breaking hinge movement to the starting position.

This partnering of music with lyrics relating to a specific dance is not new to the Jamaican social dance scene. Dances done to verbal cues and to specific songs and rhythms are a part of the Jamaican traditional dance aesthetic and have been a consistent feature in many of the popular music and dance forms. This partnership existed in mento, ska, and reggae, and it continues to exist in dancehall. Old hits parties in Jamaica testify to this. People go to these parties to drop legs (dance). Many of the old hits are dancing tunes, and songs such as Byron Lee and the Dragonaires' "Jamaican Ska" encourage dancing. These songs have danceable rhythms and descriptive lyrics that allow for a unified projection of movement ideas:

> Not any people can cha cha cha / Not everybody can do the twist / But everybody can do the ska / The new dance that goes like this / Ska ska ska, Jamaican ska / Now bow your heads / Swing your arms / Shake your hips / Now do a dip

The partnership between music and lyrics was also present in reggae artist Alton Ellis' "Rocksteady":

> You better get ready / Come do rocksteady / You got to do this new dance . . . / Shake your head / Rock your bodyline / Shake your shoulders / Everything in time

It was in dancehall artist Early Black's "Stuck": "Dance an go dung and dance and go dung and stuck." It was also in Flourgon's "One Foot Skank": "One foot skank, we do the one foot skank . . ." and "Jump spread out . . . and shake yuh body."

Though this partnership of rhythm and lyrics facilitating movement existed throughout the social dance forms, it was not a major feature. Diane Pottinger recalls sessions at Smurphy's Lawn in St. Ann's Bay during the 1980s; as a group, people would automatically start doing the scabbie on the first sound of "Buddi bi, buddi bi, buddi bi, buddi bi, buddi bi numba one." Other featured movements at sessions of the time included skank, one foot skank, Charlie horse, rent a tile, water pumpie, rub a dub, bubble, wine, and pedal an' wheel. "Though most people in the session would do the same movement, it did not have the same dancing feeling of oneness" that was apparent when "lover's rock and old hits" like the 1960s and 70s ska tunes were played in the session (Pottinger, personal interview, November 2006).

A New Era in Dancehall: Movement, Music, and Lyrics

Buju Banton's "Bogle" was not the first dancing tune, but it marked the beginning of a new era in dancehall. The dancing was once again becoming the focal point, and the recipe for that success was the combination of the visible dance creator Gerald "Bogle" Levy with insatiable dancing rhythms and lyrics. Buju Banton and Bogle reintroduced a unified music and movement expression: the dance in late 1991 and the accompanying song in 1992. There was something immediately galvanizing about the associated movement, music, and lyrics. The lyrics, like those of "Jamaican Ska," were encouraging and gave the impression that this was a dance that everyone was doing: "Uptown, downtown a rock to the beat." The dance was infectious, and all across the island people were doing it whether they were able to do it well or not. Dancing it poorly was OK and was jokingly encouraged in the song—"A mussi Nanny dat afta nuh so Bogle stay, dem cyan do it good but dem a rock same way" ("That must be Nanny, that's not how Bogle is, they cannot do it well but they are rocking nonetheless").

In the early 1990s, some friends and I drove from Ocho Rios to Kingston to see the Gladys Knight *Midnight Train* concert. We wrongly assumed that since the concert was a live performance, it would last all night like Jamaica popular music and dance events of the same nature. When the program ended and it was still not midnight, we were left energized by a wonderful concert that had ended too early for us to feel satiated. We decided to follow the restless crowd to a session that was just getting started in Lawrence Tavern in St. Andrew. As soon as we entered the lawn (an outdoor space where sessions are held), there was a rush of bodies running toward the entrance, which was also the only exit. It happened quickly. I was levitated by the mass and deposited in the streets. The crowd dispersed in record time and after a brief moment of uncertain silence, all could be heard with inquiring whispers—"You alright? You see Marge? A wha happen?" A few minutes later the crowd started to reemerge from behind trees, bushes, and parked cars, and those who had time to run were coming back into view from around the bend in the road. We soon found out that there was a fight and the turntables were damaged. Adrenalin was flowing, so when a vendor's boom box and mixed tapes provided the music, it became an all-night street dance. The first song on the tape was Buju Banton's "Bogle," and everyone within earshot gravitated toward that stall. A semicircle was formed, with the stall at the open end, and a friendly Bogle dance competition went into full swing. The dancing continued until the bus drivers demanded that we clear the streets for the morning commute. This story illustrates the nature of the dance in dancehall. Because everyone was familiar with the movement expression, it created an immediate feeling of belonging; a broken session was mended with movement. We danced freely without judgment to music that reinforced the solidarity.

Dancehall Moves

Carlene Smith is celebrated as Jamaica's first dancehall queen. She was a beautiful woman and a phenomenal dancer who moved with subtlety and grace as she waved and circled her body parts with boneless articulation. Carlene's image gave women a certain public power over their bodies—in essence, flipping the male gaze. I remember watching Carlene perform on the roof of the Parkway Restaurant in Ocho Rios. With a queen-like confidence, she seemingly floated across the stage. One of the guys standing next to me exclaimed, "She move like a cat," to which another responded, "Anuh regular house cat that though, a hunter that." As men, we stood there mesmerized and feeling like prey.

Carlene has been credited with the popularization of the butterfly. This dance movement is related to a similar pitchy patchy step. Usually the torso is bent slightly forward. The pitchy patchy inward and outward knee movements are fast and determined to give the shards of fabric hanging from the costume a life of their own. The action in the butterfly carves inward and outward, creating what seems like an abstraction of the graceful butterfly wings. The pelvis is an important part of this movement. The heels quickly lift from the ground as the buttocks are tossed backward and up at the start of the movement and then proceed fluidly in a contraction with the inward movement of the knees. A hyperextended release on the outward movement begins the backward toss again. Often women will circle the rib cage simultaneously. When men do this movement, they maintain similar accents with the quick raise of the heels creating a lift in the body, but unlike the women, who put a lot into the backward toss for the buttocks, they put more focus on the forward action of the pelvis. Dancers increase the difficulty by doing this movement very low, sometimes alternating legs. The arms often mirror the movements of the legs, but the arm movements tend to be a matter of moment and creativity when doing the butterfly.

Like the Bogle song associated with the Bogle dance, the song "Dance Butterfly" was largely responsible for the popularity of the butterfly dance. The movement was also a staple in Carlene's many public appearances. This association of movement to music, or the creating of music speaking to specific dances, became the norm for both the popularization and the validation of dancehall dances, most of which allowed for creative manipulation of the movement. According to Frederick "Tippa" Moncrieffe, dancehall and pop dancer and teacher at the Edna Manley College of the Visual and Performing Arts, the dancers who are aligned with the artists stand a better chance of getting their dances in the mainstream because the artists will write songs about the dances they create. Moncrieffe also stated that "people just get creative and mek up dance offa anything . . . cartoons, the way people walk or behave, things on television, politics . . ." (Moncrieffe, January 29, 2007). He says that the basis for movement creation lies in an individual's creativity and that the popularity of this vocabulary is based largely on who the dancer is associated with.

Of this creativity, Bogle has said repeatedly that he has been dancing since he was a child growing up in Kingston and that movement expression is something quite natural to him. In an interview with Montana of chicagoreggae.com (undated), Bogle stated that "dancing comes to me like sleeping and waking up . . . nuff time [often] when I dance I don't listen to music, I listen to my foot bottom. . . ." And his soles have contributed many dances to Jamaican dancehall. Dancehall artist Beenie Man celebrates Bogle's creativity in his song *row like a boat*, about the dance of the same title:

Mr. Bogle have di new brand style / Oonu row like a boat oonu row like a boat / Di whole dancehall a rock from coast to coast / Oonu

row like a boat oonu row like a boat / Rock to di wave then yuh
draw fi yuh rope / Oonu row like a boat oonu row like a boat /So
raggamuffin him muffin / Yuh raggamuffin from a child / Mr. Bogle
originate dat style / Bogle dance worl' dance / A dance gone dung
inna mi file / Cau him and Armstrong just come born for awhile /
Then urkel dance mek di place get wild / Then him remix, a find a
brand new style / Then him zip it [up] and log [on] it / And him fly
out for awhile / And return wid a new brand style

In these lyrics Beenie Man also mentions some of the dances that Bogle
has contributed in the past. Worl' dance is a rhythmically simple dance:
There is a foot action on every beat. On the right side the dancer proceeds
with step, step, step-drag-step. Between successive steps there is a deliberate
lifting of the leg and styling (personal interpretation) when it is placed
back on the floor. In the quicker part of the dance, where the steps are
almost connected by a drag, the movement looks like a little shuffle and
the hips relate to the movements consistent with the traditional wake
complex dances. The torso does a series of spirals with each step—the
left shoulder corresponds with the right heel, and so on. The movement
travels through space and is often done in a circular floor pattern.

Zip it up is characterized by the turn-in, turn-out foot and hip rotation,
a movement designed to bring two parts together. When done well, it looks
like the dancer is attempting to zip and unzip her body as the body halves
close in on each other before reopening. In a basic zip-it-up body pattern,
one leg turns inward and the ball of the foot taps the floor. The body
responds to this tap by breathing the heel of the other foot. The inward
rotation is to such a degree that the buttocks are visible from the front,
which then begins to unfold in an outward rotation initiated in the hip of
the turned-in leg. This outward rotation is in direct response to the tapping
of the foot and the raising of the heel. That rotation then travels down the
leg to a forward step on a now fully rotated leg. The movement continues
on alternating sides. The arm movements vary greatly for this dance. One
variation uses the hands to mime zipping up the fly. In the most common
variation, the elbows rest just above the hips, the forearms are stretched out
in front of the body, the palms face upward, and the fingers vibrate back
and forth in a calling gesture, as if to say, "Come."

Bogle was also responsible for creating the prang—a dance characterized by the lateral waves in the rib cage, the inclined position of the torso,
and the subtle bobbling head movements. The feet are wide apart and the
legs are bent slightly at the knees. There is a very small galloping action
in the feet, but the feet barely leave the ground and the wide stance is
maintained. The movement is initiated in the feet; the constant shifting
of weight from one leg to the other directs the energy up the body, caus-

ing the pelvis to shift from side to side, creating lateral waves in the torso and a subtle bobble of the head.

The Jerry Springer dance is an interpretation of the Jamaican reaction to the widely popular American talk show host Jerry Springer, whose guests are known for on-stage quarrels and physical fights. In a true Jamaican sense, the physical dialogue in the Jerry Springer dance states, "Mix-up an' cass cass mi nuh inna" ("I am not into or interested in gossips and brawls, or he said, she said"). The body is open. There are no secrets, and the dancers tend to show off as they navigate the space, moving through the crowd with a simple step-touch foot action. The dance is character-ized by both the attitude and the movement. It is non-confrontational, projecting a certain bravado and self-confidence—I am as I am, take it or leave it. The body is low, and the feet execute a simple step touch con-nected by a sideward glide with an ongoing bounce and body wave. The torso spirals toward the leading leg. The arms are generally held overhead, exposing the self even more.

The title *LOY* means Lord of Yard. Beenie Man's interpretation of the acronym in his song "L-O-Y" is more of an honor to Bogle: "Love, Origi-nality, Year after year." The only marked difference between the LOY and the Jerry Springer dances is the specificity of the arms, which in the LOY dance form the letters *L* (in front of the body), *O*, and *Y* (overhead). The footwork of both the Jerry Springer and the LOY dances can be found in the processional entrance movement of bruckins—a Jamaican tradi-tional form created in celebration of emancipation. The attitudinal and purely physical use of the upper body and waving pelvis (gestures and facial expressions, forward bending and spiraling of the torso, isolation of the rib cage, and so on) is consistent with many African movement retentions in Jamaica.

In several television, radio, and newspaper interviews, Bogle insists that he has always just done what comes naturally to him in creating these dances. In an interview with Merton "Scrapy D" McKenzie, Bogle said that he realized that there was a lull in the dancehall and that people were not dancing. He felt the people needed something to do because if there is music, people should be dancing to it: "Without the music there is no dance and without the dance the music *nah go* [will not] *come*" (Bogle, December 1997). He said he felt like he was in his lab and did what needed to be done, allowing a natural progression of movement expres-sion to happen. Though Bogle did not deliberately turn to the traditional rituals for inspiration, he was undoubtedly influenced by them. I contend that could have happened through the enculturation process as he was exposed to a Jamaican way of moving that is rooted in the traditional rituals and passed down in physical mannerisms/expressions. The major-ity of Bogle's movements are directly traceable to Jamaican traditional, neo-traditional, and folk forms. He has taken this knowledge himself, Jamaica's cultural inheritance of fusion and inclusion, and has remixed, updated, or refashioned a contemporary popular dance language to suit the needs of contemporary popular dancing culture. With that, he also returned permission to others to go ahead and create movements that express who they are and what they feel.

Tippa also grew up in Kingston and also did not study traditional dances. He started dancing seriously in 1982, focusing on the imported hip-hop dances but maintaining his Jamaican-ness with dancehall dances like the one foot skank and the old hits of the ska era. Tippa created such dances as the Chicago Bull, handi-cap dance, gangsta step, and reel rock. Tippa created the Chicago Bull dance around the success and eminent popularity of the team. The carriage for the dance came from the boldness and confidence of the team at the time, while the motivation for the base movement came from the foot action of the bull getting ready to attack, similar to the actions of the cow head character in Jonkonnu, which undoubtedly were a mime of bull movements. Further deconstruction of the dance forms revealed to Tippa the links between the traditional movements and the contemporary popular movements being created in the dancehall space. He stated, "Sometimes you think you create something and you see the same step . . . maybe a slight difference, in a folk dance form" (Moncrieffe, January 29, 2007). He went on to state that many of the dances that are being created in dancehall now are "remixes" of older dances. These remixes are fashioned by younger dancers and serve a new generation of dance goers who may or may not be aware of the influence of previous dances.

Though both Bogle and Carlene have paved the way since the early 1990s, it was Bogle who was the most prolific, and the Black Roses Crew was the most influential in creating dancehall dances. Since then there have been many male and female creators of dancehall dances. Even artists have contributed to the dancing scene, as Snagga Puss did with his song "Tattie" and dance tattie.

The objective of the tattie dance is to search yourself, and you twist your body into a series of tightly wound shapes as you do so. There is a change in the body on every beat. The arms work from the torso, and bent elbows respond to paroxysmal isolations that occur in the torso on every beat. The elbows move inward and outward, back and forth, side to side, and up and down as they respond to the changes in the body. The torso is bent forward, tilted sideways, and spiraled around the body at different points throughout the dance. Most dancers turn around themselves as they search; others move through space with simple steps accentuated by the pelvis shifting side to side rhythmically. Tattie is a fun and exciting dance that encourages partnering, as dancers often search others on the dance floor, encouraging different movements and shapes in each other. In this way Tattie leads to an almost familial relationship between strangers in the dancehall.

Another interesting dance is the screechie. The Jamaican word *screechie* means to move stealthily. It bears no relationship to the English word *screech* and has nothing to do with sound. It is an action and is used to refer to a mystical, contemporary, and cool way of moving through space. So when someone "screechie through the dance," he slips through the space unobtrusively. When dancing the screechie, the dancer crouches, and the hands create a visor, with the fingers meeting at the forehead and the palms facing down. The elbows remain in line with the shoulders throughout movement. Thus, with the torso forward, they are parallel to the floor. Like Pokumina, the screechie uses body halves. The weight is shifted to one side, which causes a change in the torso that by extension changes the relationship of the elbows to the floor. On the first weight shift, one elbow is low and the other is high, creating a diagonal line across the back. The feet also move out of a parallel, forward starting position, and both change to the opposite diagonal of the weight-bearing half. One foot lifts slightly to assist in locomotion, and the other shifts while maintaining contact with the ground. This is done while the dancer peers out from under the visor created by the hands. The body language changes on the retreat, and the foot movement often becomes a weighted turn-out action led by the heel.

More recent movement innovators who have gained exposure include Orville Hall for the dances matrix and chop out di grass, Colla Colla for the dances rhum ram and stookie, and Ding Dong for the dances bad man forward and summer bounce.

The New Wave

Bogle migrated to the United States in 2001 following the murder of his right-hand man, fellow Black Roses Crew member and community leader William "Willie Haggart" Moore, in April of that year. At that time there was a general lull within the dancing fraternity of the dancehall. People still went to sessions but resorted to the dancehall juggling stance of conversation and parading adorned masks in the form of dancehall couture. In Bogle's absence, Bogle's protégé and fellow member of the Black Roses Crew, John Hype, began to gain popularity through his appearances in music videos and his creation of the drive-by dance in late 2001. John Hype later created dances such as higher level, which made him hugely popular in the local dancehall scene. He then created pon di river, signal di plane, chaplin, head nuh good, rockaway, and blahzay, to name a few. He became a part of the force that brought back "niceness and dancing" to the dancehall.

In dancehall, the selector (dancehall disc jockey and vibes master) may or may not give credit to the creator of a particular dance during the ritualistic toasting of the session. Also, the artists who sing about these dances do not always give credit to the movement innovators. Sometimes there is conflict within the dancehall as to who created what dance. Bogle said he taught the log on to dancehall artist Elephant Man and dancehall queen Keeva (Bogle 2007), but in the song "Log On," Elephant Man mentions only Keeva ("Keeva tek dem to yu dancing school") and does not give credit to Bogle. There are many such cases where dancers feel that their creative work is not credited.

Elephant Man has contributed a new wave of dancing with his music and has generated a unified spirit in dancehall again. In his song "Signal di Plane," one of the first statements is, "Dancehall nice again / People smile again . . . / Dancing a Jamaica middle name," solidifying the expression as something truly Jamaican and as something that gives people enjoyment. His songs tend to group several dance steps, creating longer dances that are done in response to rhythm and lyrics. This is possible because of the codification of movement. In the following excerpts from "Signal di Plane" and "Pon di River," the codified movements are boldfaced:

> **Signal the plane,** mek we signal the plane / Nuh mek yu fren get buss, signal the plane / From yu know yu inna yu own suit / Labba labba, show dem di **parachute** / Parachute . . . parachute . . . / Everybody we a do di parachute / Yu drop pan di grung den yu do yu ting / Ey John, show dem di **chaplin** / Chaplin . . . chaplin . . . / Bogle gwine give dem . . .

> We tek dancing to a higher rank / We spen' pound, an' wi will spen franc / John have a new dance a lock Jamaica an' Bronx / **Pon di river pon di bank** / Kick out yuh shoes because yuh foot dem nuh cramp / Inna di river pon di bank / **Dung di flank,** wi a go dung di flank / Like a balla, wi go dung di flank / Yuh Jeep pretty, an' gas inna yuh tank / Bus di new dance, yuh nuh wear people pants (Cool) / **Gi dem a run** John, gi dem a run / We an' di girls a have fun (Bogle)

In "Willie Bounce," the lyrics of which follow, Elephant Man guides dancers through the entire dance. Every other line in the song is an instruction, written in similes and open to individual interpretation to allow for creativity. Between the images he asks the dancers to double the out and bad:

> All right bring yuh hand dem gwaan like yuh mad / Then yuh double, the double the out and bad / Look left, look right swing yuh hand like yuh bad / Then yuh double, the double the out and bad / Do the dip, do the dip like the dancing god / Then yuh double, the

double the out and bad / Walk with it mek up yuh face like yuh get rob / Then yuh double, the double the out and bad

Elephant Man directs the dancing in the session with his lyrics. This direction is successful because it is done in such a way that it (1) creates harmony (everyone returns to the base step at the same time in the music—in this case, the base step is the out and bad) and (2) allows for creativity ("Look left, look right, swing your hands as if you are bad"—these are instructions for structured improvisation during the song, which also asks dancers to "stop, make a pose, take a sip, shake your feet and then start do the dip, wacky dip . . . ").

This very song, which encourages creativity and the projection of the pure joy of movement, is a tribute to Bogle, who was murdered in January 2005. The chorus of the song states the following:

Dance will never die / Out and bad so badly bad / It a get intensify / I see the kids dem in the street / All the big man dem a practice fi dweet / Although Bogle pass and gone / We still a mek dem know him dancing live on

To affirm this statement, the song asks everyone to "Do the bounce / Willie bounce, everybody fi a do di Willie bounce."

Conclusion

The dance and the music in dancehall, as in the traditional forms, are inextricably linked. For every dance there are specific accompanying songs and rhythms. Even though everyone does the same movement, the dances are guidelines, and creativity is encouraged. Dancers are praised when they can do a movement well, especially when they bring some form of originality to the articulation of the dance.

According to Tippa, it is important that individuals learn the dance, and then they can add their own spice to the movement (Moncrieffe November 17, 2006). Personal interpretation is highly celebrated in the dancehall, be it through music, fashion, or movement. Right now, especially since 2000, there is a plethora of dances in the dancehall, and these dances are danced by both men and women. (See table 3.2 for a list of dancehall dances) Usually the songs will say if the dance is for a male or a female. For example, "Dutty wine my *girl* dutty wine" suggests that a woman should be doing the dutty wine, while "Bad *man* forward, bad man pull up" suggests that a man should be doing that movement. There are no hard rules about male and female movements; however, masculinity precedes movement in the dancehall culture, and so you will find more women doing the male movements than you will find men doing the more feminine steps.

Table 3.2   List of Dancehall Dances

<table>
<tr><td rowspan="7">1980s</td><td>1. Cool an' deadly</td><td>8. Booty shake</td><td>14. Scabbie</td></tr>
<tr><td>2. Rub a dub</td><td>9. Pedal an' wheel</td><td>15. Get flat</td></tr>
<tr><td>3. Leggings</td><td>10. Skank</td><td>16. Charlie horse</td></tr>
<tr><td>4. Wine and bubble</td><td>11. Stuck</td><td>17. General trees</td></tr>
<tr><td>5. Ticktock</td><td>12. One foot skank</td><td>18. Della move</td></tr>
<tr><td>6. Rent a tile</td><td>13. Water pumpie</td><td>19. Heel an' toe</td></tr>
<tr><td>7. Roun' di worl'</td><td></td><td></td></tr>

<tr><td rowspan="11">1990s</td><td>20. Butterfly</td><td>31. Peppa seed</td><td>42. Handi-cap</td></tr>
<tr><td>21. Bogle</td><td>32. Mock di dread</td><td>43. Heel and toe</td></tr>
<tr><td>22. Body basics</td><td>33. Prang (pram)</td><td>44. Nanny</td></tr>
<tr><td>23. Turtle</td><td>34. Pelpa</td><td>45. Bashment</td></tr>
<tr><td>24. Whip</td><td>35. Worl' dance</td><td>46. Chicago Bull</td></tr>
<tr><td>25. LOY</td><td>36. Limbo</td><td>47. Trinity</td></tr>
<tr><td>26. Boomshackalak</td><td>37. Position</td><td>48. Nutty Buddy</td></tr>
<tr><td>27. Jerry Springer</td><td>38. Batty rider</td><td>49. Head top</td></tr>
<tr><td>28. Angel</td><td>39. Skettel boom</td><td>50. Erkle</td></tr>
<tr><td>29. Santa Barbara</td><td>40. Wild out</td><td>51. Go-go wine</td></tr>
<tr><td>30. Hottie hottie</td><td>41. Armstrong</td><td>52. Bruk Up</td></tr>

<tr><td rowspan="15">2000s</td><td>53. Umbrella</td><td>68. Jiggy</td><td>82. Wash weh</td></tr>
<tr><td>54. Handcart</td><td>69. Weh di weh di</td><td>83. Back to basics</td></tr>
<tr><td>55. Mission Impossible</td><td>70. Iverson bounce</td><td>84. Formula</td></tr>
<tr><td>56. Shizzle ma nizzle</td><td>71. Exit</td><td>85. VIP</td></tr>
<tr><td>57. Chop out di grass</td><td>72. Defence</td><td>86. Online</td></tr>
<tr><td>58. Fan dem off</td><td>73. Tun yu roll and clear yu heart</td><td>87. Matrix</td></tr>
<tr><td>59. Drive by</td><td>74. Scooby Doo</td><td>88. Log on</td></tr>
<tr><td>60. Gangsta step</td><td>75. Sponge Bob</td><td>89. Hop di ferry</td></tr>
<tr><td>61. Reel rock</td><td>76. Sesame Street</td><td>90. Hotty hotty</td></tr>
<tr><td>62. Black peppa</td><td>77. Big Bird</td><td>91. In har heart</td></tr>
<tr><td>63. Tambourine</td><td>78. Air Force One</td><td>92. Matrix</td></tr>
<tr><td>64. Flowahs a bloom</td><td>79. Rain a fall</td><td>93. Zip it up</td></tr>
<tr><td>65. Sunshine</td><td>80. Dew rain</td><td>94. Pon di river</td></tr>
<tr><td>66. Thundaclap</td><td>81. Hard rain</td><td>95. Kick dem out</td></tr>
<tr><td>67. Thump di sky</td><td></td><td>(continued)</td></tr>
</table>

Table 3.2 *(continued)*

2000s	96. Di wave	116. Propella	135. In har heart
	97. Row the boat	117. Hot 97	136. Willie bounce
	98. Tattie	118. 3 pointer	137. Wacky dip
	99. Signal di plane	119. Chaplin	138. Tek buddy
	100. Anaconda	120. Head nuh good	139. Pray
	101. Screechie	121. Over di wall	140. Badda dance
	102. Pop di collar	122. Out a road	141. Out an' bad
	103. Diwali	123. Summer bounce/ Walk wid di bounce	142. Raging bull
	104. Tall up		143. Rhum ram
	105. Higher level	124. Crazy hype	144. Stookie
	106. Gi dem a run	125. Shankle dip	145. Hula hoop
	107. Parachute	126. Ova' di wall	146. Hot wuk
	108. Blahzay	127. Chakka chakka	147. Dutty wine
	109. Elbow dem	128. Chakka Belly	148. Tall up
	110. Shake dem off	129. Swing sang	149. Bounty walk
	111. Roc-a-way	130. Spread out	150. Killa swing
	112. Egyptian	131. March out	151. Tek weh yuself
	113. Shelly belly	132. Part di crowd	152. Roller coaster
	114. Swim by	133. Mad run	153. Helicopter
	115. Drive by/Bentley	134. Look outta road	

Compiled by Neila Ebanks and Chris Walker.

Approximately 90 percent of the dances being done in today's dancehall are unisex. The differences come out in individual projection and not so much in gender projection of movement. Also, the new wave of dancing has not introduced partner dances on any great scale. There are a few in which the men lift the women overhead, as in the helicopter, or suspend the women across the body, as in the roller coaster. Many of the other partnering movements seem to simulate sexual positions. Tippa contends that such expression is "not really dance . . . it's a vibes thing"—more about creating spectacle and excitement than about dancing (Moncrieffe, February 2007). This show of strength and virility has become increasingly popular and dangerous as dancers do these movements on top of fences, roofs, and even vehicles.

People learn the new dances by attending sessions, which are held every night in Kingston and on other parts of the island. These sessions

(Good Sunday, Hot Monday, Early Tuesday, Weddy Weddy, Blahzee, Passa Passa, Jiggy Friday) are laboratories for the development and subsequent dissemination of new movements. People from various parts of the island have access to these new dances through better transportation (people travel from afar to sessions of their choice), the Jamaica Cultural Development Commission's annual Festival of the Arts competition, the *Daily Gleaner* (which has recently started publishing descriptions and photographs of new dances), music videos that are broadcasted locally and internationally, dancehall videos and DVDs, and both global and local sites including the Internet, fitness centers, dance studios, schools, and dance companies.

The evolution of the dancehall movements continues into works of Jamaican dance theater companies, where dances are distilled for use in concert dance works. All the dance companies have dancehall or dancehall-informed pieces in their repertoire. The Jamaican contemporary dance language fused traditional and popular movements, while contemporary dance philosophies brought Jamaican and Caribbean realities into movement (see Walker 2007). The resulting synthesis is a physical alphabet to which dancehall has contributed in movement, rhythm, and attitude.

On the community level, the widely popular televised dancehall competition *Dancing Dynamites* is largely responsible for the national discourse at the grassroots level on dancehall movement as art. Neila Ebanks is a lecturer at the Edna Manley College of the Visual and Performing Arts and serves as a judge on the show. In speaking of the community's response to *Dancing Dynamites,* she states that there are some people who respect effort more than ability, while there are others who

> listen to the judge's commentary, which comes from a dance theatre perspective and recognizing that there are technical elements in movements and that there are elements of dance that some may or may not have. People are better able to articulate what they like about a particular dance group. The show is helping persons realize that there is much more to the craft of dance. There is a certain cry that comes when they see the groups persist, learn and improve. . . . We have always had a respect for people who can—now we are able to flesh it out in by expressing why, in critical dialogue about all the elements that make up the performance. (Ebanks, February 21, 2007)

Ebanks also stated that because the dances are codified, there is "galvanizing effect in terms of a community of people in the know." The dances have taken on a "kind of commentarial slant" that allows them to give persons outside of the dancehall community an idea of what is going on in that subculture (Ebanks, February 21, 2007). The traditional dance rituals and festival arts galvanize as well in that they consciously build community, much like what is happening on the artistic level in Jamaican dancehall. On a purely movement level, the dancehall allows for the refashioning of traditional and folk movement ideas and for the inclusion and development of new ones to express contemporary society. Coming out of a history of cultural collisions, forced migrations, enslavement, and years of colonial oppression and cultural denigration, the Jamaican dancing body paradoxically engages conflict and harmony in a singular expression. The dancehall articulates the basic physical characteristics of this rich ancestry of movement practices.

REFLECTIONS

Studying the way that dance and music capture a people's history provides us with a rich and complex narrative. Chris Walker, in his study of the Jamaican dancehall, reminds us that we cannot oversimplify the layers of meanings displayed and played out within particular cultural boundaries. In his discussion here, he provides us with a thick description of the cultural movements displayed in dancehall—movements that have been adopted and adapted from cultural rituals, traditional dance forms, and other cultures. In this particular history, which has been one of dominance and submission, master and slave, resistance took, at least in part, an embodied form. The body said that which was not allowed to be said. In the fusion of music and movement, a visual language was created that allowed the oppressed or disenfranchised to speak in a secret vernacular. The power of dance as a form of communication and resistance is hidden from those who do not know the language of the movement. Influenced by an aesthetic of community and connection, the dancehall provides a place where a common movement language can be danced, read, created, and recreated, all in an attempt to capture the experiences of a people and to remember the people's history. What Chris draws our attention to is the danger inherent in losing the meaning of the movement as we begin to fetishize the dance itself—a danger common in many cultures. Perhaps dancehall dances will go the way of ballet, in which we now teach the movement vocabulary disconnected from the narrative that the movements were intended to convey. Like African dance (in its many different forms), Jamaican dance might lose its way and become about competition rather than liberation, about winning or fame rather than community, and about those at the top rather than those not so fortunate. In a global society in which cultures become more fluid, commodification and fusion are inevitable, and the function of dance as a record of, and a modality for the hope, dreams, and struggles of, a culture can easily get lost. We must remain alert to what we are willing to give up, what we want to recreate, and what we do not wish to change.

PART 1 REFLECTIVE QUESTIONS

- Why might it be important for traditional dance or ethnic forms to remain unchanged and uninfluenced by other forms of expression?
- Is there such a thing as a pure ethnic dance form?
- How is our globalizing world affecting traditional dance, and is there a need to be critical of that process?
- What role could or should dance play in the formation of national identity?

part II

Politics of Belonging:
Disrupting the Norms

four

Writing in the Flesh: Body, Identity, Disability, and Difference

Lúcia Matos

Professor of dance and research methodology
Faculdade Social da Bahia
Brazil

Translation reviewed by Adriana C. Guedes de Almeida and David Iannitelli

This chapter discusses dance works involving dancers with disabilities as well as nondisabled dancers. These dancers were the subject of the doctoral research paper titled *Mapping Multiple Dancing Bodies: The Construction of New Corporal Territories and Aesthetics in Contemporary Dance in Brazil* (Matos 2006). Currently the dancing body, discussed as a network of relationships that go beyond instrumental and technical perspectives, encompasses biological, historical, and cultural aspects. With this purpose, dance is approached as an artistic product, and the body functions as the medium (Greiner 2005) and generator of (con)texts and senses in dance. In this chapter, I briefly reflect on inclusive education and accessibility in Brazil, using the research of disability studies as theoretical support. Within this context, the focus is directed toward the representations that are constructed and fixed in dance, both in teaching and in artistic production, and special attention is given to the concepts of dancing bodies, identity, and disability. Focusing on the body and the concept of difference, proposed by Deleuze (1988), I analyze the choreography performed in the *Festival Arte sem Barreiras* 2002 (Art Without Barriers Festival 2002). Though this festival proposes inclusion through the arts, some of its choreographic works utilized dancers with disabilities in ways that reinforce a paradigm of normality with respect to disability. Thus, this chapter discusses the implications of ability and disability in the teaching, choreography, and appreciation of dance.

Deconstructing the Dancer With Disability

During the past decades, different fields of knowledge that study the body have been searching for new ways of understanding this phenomenon, the body, and thus new horizons and theoretical conceptions have emerged. In the field of dance, some contemporary researchers of corporality (Albright 1997; Foster 1996; Greiner 2003; Iannitelli 2004; Shapiro 2002) contest the hegemonic, dichotomic, and mechanistic views that conceive of the body as an instrument with respect to its training and creative processes. Their discourses also favor the impossibility of making distinctions within the complex network of negotiations that interweave the physicality, subjectivity, culture, and identity of dancing bodies.

In this scope, this chapter presents part of my doctoral research, which maps four Brazilian contemporary dance groups[1] that mix dancers of different abilities, and focuses on issues related to dance, body, difference, and disability. These issues became part of my path as an artist and educator during different phases of my life when I worked with three students with distinct disabilities. My involvement with this process, as well as with other pedagogical and artistic experiences within different sociocultural and educational contexts, enabled me to think about the pedagogic praxis that I was developing, the introjections that were embedded in it, and the role of dance in society. In my quest to find other meanings to the practice of dance, I often had to confront the theoretical and practical methodologies for teaching dance that I had personally and theoretically experienced—even at the university.

When I began teaching in the state's public schools in 1992, I decided to improve my knowledge in special education. I longed to work with the deaf,[2] for I had often watched their conversations and was dazzled by their gestural sign language.[3] When observing them, I perceived their gestures as instigating elements for a research on dance movement, and I felt compelled to try to enter that universe.

This uneasy plunge into a world of people whom I knew of only by the stereotype of *disabled* was at times distressing and tiresome but was also pleasurable and full of discovery. During this journey I started noticing that in order for me to understand the relationship that people who are deaf have with their corporality, I would have to find new focuses that favored dialogue, so as to avoid getting stuck in our difference of references (universe of people who are deaf and universe of people who hear). These initial reflections led me back to the study that I carried out for my master's degree research (Matos 1998) in the corporality in dance of youths who are deaf.

As an unfolding of my master's degree research, my doctoral research analyzed the artistic product of four Brazilian contemporary dance groups with disabled and nondisabled dancers. This research was chosen due to the fact that while many contemporary choreographers have explored the singularity of the dancing body, some of them, including Meg Stuart (Damaged Goods), Les Ballets C. de la B, CandoCo, and Grupo Pulsar (Brazil), have researched movements based on different physicalities, exploring in practice concepts such as the aesthetics of pluralism, alterity, and difference. According to Schlicher (2001), the choreographers of the 1990s, namely Sasha Waltz, Jérôme Bel, and Meg Stuart, believed that there was nothing left to be invented and that everything could be reappropriated. Thus, "the image of the body in which they are interested is an *anti-virtuous* and *anti-heroic*[4] one" (31). Their starting point is often the examination of the imperfections and deficiencies of their own bodies and of their physical and individual limitations and possibilities. The differences present in other bodies may also stimulate creation, while the search to transform the body of the artist without disability opens up space for dialogue and displacements.

What was previously hidden, because it was considered an imperfection or a lack, may then be revealed and transformed into an element that generates other possibilities of movement and thus yields new approaches in both the creation and the perception of dance. The artists and the audience members are newly related to their own incompleteness by looking and contacting the other's body, forming a direct relationship among imperfection, perfection, and ambivalence.

Despite a current trend in contemporary dance toward deconstructing the idealized nondisabled dancer's body—a trend that often leads to constructing movements that resemble those of nondancers or of bodies outside the world of theatrical dance—paradoxically there remains a certain rejection of dance groups that include dancers with disabilities, along with a questioning of the artistic merit of their works. In addition, some choreographic works that utilize dancers with disabilities still sustain hegemonic visions of what it means to be such a dancer.

Bearing this scenario in mind and aiming to expand the reflection on body, identity, difference, and disability, I concentrate on issues related to inclusion and accessibility in Brazil. I also focus on the reflections of these policies that can be observed in artistic and cultural production, specifically in dance.

Exclusion Within Inclusion

Since the late 20th century, the term *inclusion* has gained ground in official speech and social policies of many countries thanks to the actions fostered by marginalized groups. In an attempt to give voice to the voiceless, the excluded have organized themselves as a social movement so they can not only acknowledge their diversity but also validate different ways of being part of the world.

Although people with disabilities have become more visible nowadays, there is still frequent discrimination from most members of the population, who, consciously or unconsciously, establish standards of social normality. These patterns are metanarratives[5] that point to closed and totalizing categories in favor of concepts of normality and static representations of gender, race, culture, class, sexuality, and physical ability. Thus, those who do not fit into the expected standards—in this case, people with disabilities—are excluded and stigmatized, while their actions are limited by the social environment.

In Brazil, one of the ways in which minority groups, such as people with disabilities, break this paradigm is to adopt affirmative action policies as temporary strategies to ensure that minorities receive their rights as citizens. Affirmative action involves questions of accessibility, equal rights, the labor market, and social and cultural inclusion. Even in societies where firm and inclusive policies have been implemented to protect the rights of people with disabilities, it is still possible to notice tensions among people with disabilities with respect to their social and cultural differences (*Animated* 2002).

The guidelines for inclusiveness outlined in official documents in Brazil face many obstacles. The first is their practical implementation, which is a problem due to the perverse social structure that institutes an uneven distribution of material and symbolic assets. Consequently, there is a dearth of effective public actions and representation of people with disabilities in positions of authority. Many of the cultural barriers that remain in our society result from a lack of education. In everyday life, for example, people with disabilities still find difficulty in moving from one place to another due to physical barriers in the cities or the lack of adapted public transportation to simplify free access.

Many educators are concerned with integrating those who are excluded in order to achieve educational equity, even though this has rarely been accomplished successfully. Many of these actions end up pointing toward the acknowledgment of diversity and not toward the subjects' emancipation in the Freirian[6] sense, for the latter would require considerable adaptations to the conditions of public teaching. Unfortunately, most of the efforts for inclusion apply to spatial occupation only, as if in the daily functioning of the schools all students were already included and free from ideologies and contradictions. Thus, the lack of qualification of public school teachers, the shortage of funding, the low expectancy regarding students with disabilities, and the scarcity of a reference of success among their peers all contribute to a new perspective of *exclusion* within this alleged inclusion.

Inclusive education policies, as described in official documents and in the media, make for an official discourse that in reality does not give priority to transformative educational goals. The policies have become a politics of inten-

Grupo Xis I.
Photo courtesy of Grupo Xis–Clarice Cajueiro.

tion, since the national economic plan gives priority to compliance with the requirements of the agreements made with international financing agencies (the International Monetary Fund and the World Bank).[7]

In relation to artistic formation, production, and access to cultural assets, there are practically no governmental policies that favor access for people with disabilities to the arts and to artistic production. Note that the perspective of art as therapy is not addressed here, since it has often been used in rehabilitation programs.[8]

By analyzing this brief panorama of the social, political, and cultural deficiencies in Brazil in relation to people with disabilities, and in light of the findings of disability studies,[9] we can affirm that the medical model that transforms disability into a pathology still prevails in Brazilian society. On the other hand, civil society is experiencing a movement on behalf of people with disabilities in an attempt to make their voices heard, to alter the hierarchy in relationships of power between people with and people without disabilities, and to transform the present reality.

For Shakespeare (1996), there are two ways of perceiving people with disabilities as a group. The first pertains to the medical perspective, or to the physical classification of the impairment,[10] and focuses on the medical dimension of the disability. The second conceives of disability as "an outcome of social processes or as a constructed or created category" (Shakespeare 1996, 3). Thus, in this model, disability is the result of a social, cultural, and political status that makes people with different physical conditions hostages of the social incapacity of dealing with difference. These two perspectives, which are broadly discussed in disability studies, lead us to question the way the disabled body is being approached in dance.

Difference Inscribed in the Flesh

The body as a cultural phenomenon is constructed not only through rational thought but also through the mediation and interaction of somatic experiences within a historical and social context. The construction of the body, in terms of both its physicality and its subjectivity, is susceptible to transformations (Matos 2000). Seen from this angle, the body is not only delimited by its biological configuration but also inscribed by culture. It is situated within its biological, historical, cultural, and social network. In its specificity, the body undergoes different production and reappropriation processes in which the subjects, by transcending the labels of *disability* and *normality*, can give new meaning to their own bodies. Thus, they engage in shaping an identity that is both symbolic and social.

The boundaries for the body that were established through dichotomies of natural and cultural, private and public, personal and collective, rational and emotional, and flesh and soul have been challenged in contemporary scholarly discourses. Thus materiality, subjectivity, culture, and environment have become part of the same network of experiences: the body itself. This resignification reminds us that the body is not only formed by corporeity, but by the game played with discourses and institutions that transcend and alienate it (Frank 1993). These discourses also interfere with the construction of identity because the way in which they define the body's limits, possibilities, and transmutations affects how we think about and experience them.

In *Difference and Repetition*, Deleuze (1988) states that the concept of difference cannot be bound to the guiding principles of representation (identity and similarity). Difference should be seen as rupture and discontinuity—as an element that disturbs a previously established order. In the Deleuzian sense, the being can express itself through difference:

He/she is not "the" difference in himself/herself, in the Platonic sense of the term. Rather, it is the difference by itself, in the sense adopted by the philosophy of difference: a univocal being expressed through the difference. Thus, he/she expresses himself/herself in the multiplicity and states the differences that form it, not as a whole that is closed, not even as something finite or infinite, but as something "finalized—unlimited." (Deleuze 1988, 355)

According to Deleuze, human beings are multiple and different and are "always produced by a disjunctive synthesis, while being disconnected and diverging" (Deleuze 1988). This game of difference is stressed by Pealbart (2004) when he states that Deleuze opens the way to an ethics of singularity that aims at producing new differentiations and unique modes of existence.

Deleuze's perspective contributes significantly to an understanding of difference and disability; his philosophy of immanence enables us to think about multiplicities and singularities. Seen from this bias, the disabled body in dance can change or break the concept of the ideal body and present itself in its singularity, with its physicality as a *possible* dancing body.

Greiner (2003) emphasizes that we should perceive the body as "its own subject and media of knowledge" (13). This view enables us to grasp the body as a complex structure that needs new epistemological bases for the reading of the significations and the multiplicities that are embodied in it.

For contemporary dance, the breaking of the univocal and the search for the multiple have opened space for investigating configurations for the dancing body that are outside of the universalizing systems of Western thought. Today the dancing body is not viewed only in terms of its kinesthetic relationship or expression. Some choreographers research the movement, the kinesthetic sensation or feeling, the physicality, the idiosyncrasy, the singularity, and the identity of that specific dancing body so that it is possible to identify and include differences, resignifying the representations and metaphors in dance that were built on and about the body.

Albright (1997) thinks that contemporary dance supported by current cultural theories can help us discover the various significations that are intertwined in the complexity of moving images, somatic experience (experienced, imagined, and perceived body), and identity. In this perspective, the dancing body and the representations that dancers bring to the dance are a result of social and cultural experiences. Thus it is not possible to conceive of the dancer as only a product of nature, void of social and cultural values and, consequently, of a fixed identity.

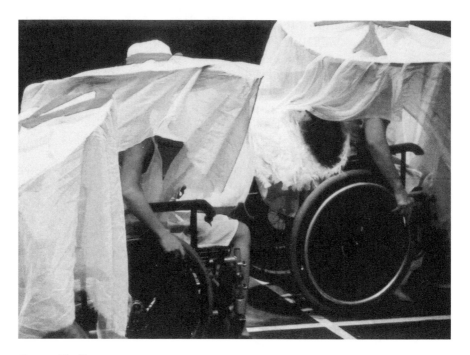

Grupo Xis II.
Photo courtesy of Grupo Xis—Clarice Cajueiro.

The subject's identity in contemporary thinking is neither separate nor autonomous. It is neither fixed through its biological characteristics nor bound to a single social position. It embraces the possibility of continuous formation and transformation in diverse sociocultural instances and interactions, and thus it is historically built. Hence, contemporary processes of identity take on an oscillating and multifaceted character that is no longer situated in a linearly unified continuity (Hall 1997).

In dealing with identity, Rubidge (1998) states that the postmodern subject has a multiplicity of identities (whether at the macrocollective or micropersonal level) that are in an ongoing flow, shifting according to the circumstances. In this perspective of a world where identity fluctuates, dance also potentially fluctuates since identity issues are directly related to its production.

For Cunha e Silva (1999), the dancing body has a moving identity that is based on the *polysemy* of the aesthetic material. In other words, "the body that dances, within this context, can work as an especially effective mediator in shaping an active plurality ['corplurality'] of the body . . . [in other words], in the perspective of assuming an identity based on variability" (23). The relationships established around the plural identity of the dancing body offer new possibilities to the field of dance, especially in terms of breaking the boundaries that up to now have confined the body to a normative technical and performative context. Within this new context, the concept of technique is transformed and relativized.

When talking about the new boundaries for the dancing body, Greiner (1999) highlights that one of the vital elements for this change in the dance of the 1990s involves new cultural dialogues. These dialogues are important because they establish "in a distinct way the thought of the dancing body" (Greiner 1999, 9). This way of thinking cannot be understood reductively as a translation of topics and concepts that belong to the cultural and social field of the dance language. As Greiner states, "This dialogue between things that are changing and the dancing body becomes real with the configuration of new organizations or, in other words, through the creation of new models of thought" (7).

These new models of dance thought are present in contemporary dance production. By the final decades of the 20th century, the dancer had broken the barriers of "thingification"—of being a mere performer and reproducer of movements created by a choreographer—to become a creator and interpreter, with the dancer's own body being considered an element essential to the creation process.

It is through the body, with its specific cultural, physical, and historical marks, that identity is exposed and recognized (or not), and it is through this recognition that we perceive the limits distinguishing the subject, the world, and the other, "the place from which alterity can be determined" (Tucherman 1999, 152). According to Tucherman, these social spaces demarcate the frontiers between what is identical (the same) and what is different (the other).

When we think about dance through this perspective, we are well aware that the expectation is to find dancers with "perfect" bodies, at least as far as their composition is concerned (the illuminist vision of the parts that make the whole), and that the idealized vision of the dancer's body is being thin and slender and having strong muscles. Thus, it is by appearance that difference first arises in dance: The body of the dancer with disability is not the one expected as a medium of this art.

Although contemporary dance favors diversity and polysemy, questioning the body that creates and dances, many restrictions can be noticed in the dance milieu when the dancing body itself does not fit within the expected standard of normality and goes against the canons of the aesthetically correct (Sodré and Paiva 2002). When a disabled body is inserted in dance, the feeling is that it is perceived in its incomplete state, or, in other words, in its abnormality. Therefore, in the state of being marginalized it becomes the "other"—the one that is not desired and that carries the stigma of negativity. This negative viewpoint can provoke reactions from audience members, from teachers, and from other dancers. These reactions range from laughter to disgust to excessive commotion. Undoubtedly this body, with its disquieting alterity, can evoke strange feelings, and most dance classes are not conceived for this kind of "other" physicality.

The participation of people with disabilities in dance, whether they are in search of educational, leisure, or artistic activity, has made visible bodies that are otherwise usually hidden. The dance scene in general has been affected by the presence (though limited) of these physicalities, and this presence has aroused reflection and has opened up spaces that were previously hermetically closed to people with disabilities. Thus the disabled body, in becoming a dancing body, can offer a new perception of identity to people with disabilities.

The inclusion of dancers with disabilities in Brazilian contemporary dance, however, raises other questions about the concepts of body and dance that have been disseminated throughout the artistic works of people with disabilities, about who is acting as dance teacher or choreographer within this scope, about the role that the disabled dancer takes on (or is allowed to take on) in dance, and about the interpretation or acceptance of this kind of dance as *disabled dance* or *inclusive dance,* according to the terminology currently being used in Brazil. These issues are addressed through a brief analysis of the *Festival Arte sem Barreiras* (Art Without Barriers Festival).

Art Without Barriers or Barriers in Art?

The use of the term *disabled dance* demonstrates the necessity of delimiting a cultural, political, and social territory that characterizes itself as art produced by artists whose disability imprints a singularity to their work. Quoting Pick (1992, 21), "Disabled art may have a different kind of greatness from non-disabled art, based on the uniqueness of the disabled situation and experience."

In the interviews I conducted in my research of four contemporary dance groups, what became clear were issues related to the use of the term *disabled.* The dancers with disabilities I spoke with did not identify themselves with the term *inclusive dance* since they thought that this term pertained only to integration. For them, their product is dance, regardless of the fact that they are dancers whose physicalities differ from those of the ideal body. Within the Brazilian dance context, this terminology may implicate other stigmas, raising questions of whether these dancers can be considered as artists and whether their product can be considered as art. All of the four groups analyzed included both nondisabled dancers and dancers with disabilities. This configuration can be decisive for not adopting a label such as *disabled dance* (a label that loses its full meaning when carried from English to Portuguese). In none of these groups did the dancers with disabilities act as director or choreographer, whereas in all of these groups they were presented as cocreators of the choreographies.

Utilizing Deleuze's (1988) concept of difference, we can perceive that the body of the dancer with disability can become a political body in the search to transform the hegemonic discourse and open up spaces for a body whose presentation was previously denied. Although I believe that is occurring, a change in what is understood as the normal dancer or artist, including dancers with disabilities in dance performances, does not necessarily free them from stereotypes. Stereotypes may subliminally or explicitly present a person with disability as a heroic figure who is in an endless quest to attain the paradigm of normality and who is thus subject to compassion.

The *Festival Arte sem Barreiras* (Art Without Barriers Festival) is one of the most important inclusive art events in Brazil, as it exclusively presents artistic and educational works aimed at people with disabilities.

Up to the year 2003, the Art Without Barriers Program was directly related to the *Associação Vida, Sensibilidade e Arte* (Life, Sensibility and Art Association) supported by Funarte (of the Ministry of Culture) and affiliated with VSA arts (United States).[11] As one of the few programs of its kind in Brazil, it has many important actions related to education aiming at the social insertion of people with disabilities, as well as to the development of artistic and educational activities for all people.

The goal of this program is to provide for "the incentive and the professional dissemination of works *that are apt*[12] and are to be presented in non-segmented cultural

Pulsar I.

Photo courtesy of Pulsar Cia de Dança—Mauro Kury.

spaces" (*Funarte* 2004). However, as far as cultural policies are concerned, neither this program nor the Ministry of Culture takes effective action to bring the person with disability into dance as a professional activity (this is also true for other artistic areas). Moreover, the program and the Ministry of Culture rarely promote the presentation of the disabled artists' products in nonsegmented circuits.[13] Funarte's Web page on the Art Without Barriers Program *(Funarte* 2004) describes its focus as the "discussion and elaboration of public policies for teaching through art" and states that it "carries out art procedures for people with special needs."[14]

Even though part of its mission is education, the Art Without Barriers Festival is mainly supported by Funarte of the Ministry of Culture, and this leads to questions about the relationship between artistic products and educational processes. Another issue relates to the structures and financial resources available to the Ministries of Education and Culture to subsidize their important but distinct concerns. At the same time, Funarte's role in outlining inclusive public policies for the arts is not clear. In Brazil the federal policies to foster the arts—more precisely, dance (maintenance, production, and circulation)—are almost nonexistent and are limited to public grants without focusing on an ongoing political plan for culture.[15]

While analyzing the guidelines of the Art Without Barriers Program, I perceived in its discourse and in the artistic performances it supports a vision of art as a process and a valorization of the amateur production of dance, although the program sometimes refers to art in a solely instrumental way. In order to have a better understanding of the program's profile, I focus on the analysis of dance productions presented at its first International Festival of Art Without Barriers, which took place in 2002 at the Sesiminas Theater during the activities of the first International Congress of Art Without Barriers at the Pontifical Catholic University of the State of Minas Gerais (PUC-MG).

First, it is interesting to note how the program was designed. Thirty national groups performed for five days. Fifteen groups participated in the afternoon performances of more amateur work, while the others performed in the evening. Many of the amateur groups were supported by rehabilitation institutions or special schools. Some were directed by therapists, educators, or physical education professionals, all of whom had limited knowledge of dance. This aspect favors the retention of ambiguous concepts of dance, the maintenance of the therapeutic vision, and the relationship of power between nondisabled and disabled populations.

In addition to the 15 groups identified by the organizing committee as semiprofessionals and professionals, two international groups were invited: Dançando com a Diferença (Dancing With the Difference) from Madeira Island, Portugal, and the professional English company CandoCo. The former was directed by Brazilian Henrique Amoedo and was sponsored by Madeira Island's Service of Art and Creativity of the Regional Department of Education. The latter was directed by Celeste Dandeker, whose coming to Brazil was partially subsided by the British Council.

The choreographies presented by the evening groups had the following stylistic profile: one ballet, three modern dances, two ballroom dances, one street dance, two folk dances, one dance without a defined style (a mixture of folk and ballroom dance), four contemporary dances, and one performance dance. Only three of the four groups classified[16] as contemporary dance performed differentiated works whose proposal for inclusion was clear. In them, the pursuit of dialogue between different bodies could be perceived in the choreographic work, and this helped to achieve a more meaningful result. These groups were dispersed in the general evening program. They were mixed with many other works that showed a more conventional and expected dance product: virtuosity and (e) (com)motion.[17]

In the view of Sodré and Paiva (2002), artistic works whose aesthetic category emphasizes affective reaction more than their compositional elements favor an emotional reaction from the audience. In this case, when people with disabilities were involved, the performance elicited compassion, horror (tragic), or amazement and laughter (grotesque).

The works presented in the afternoon evidenced strong amateur characteristics. They were the idea of what dance is to the general population, using the same conventions that are typical of end-of-the-year festivals at dance academies that lack, or do not count on, professionals who have a solid artistic and aesthetic background. The result was the use of recurrent clichés (namely, the use of standardized movements), a lack of spatial and temporal exploration, and the absence of research on thematic, artistic, or movement elements.

All of the works presented another element to be considered: the way the disabled body is addressed in the performance. I analyze this concern by studying the choreographies that were selected for the festival prime time and were identified as being semiprofessional or professional. Some of these choreographies displayed the same problematic characteristics discussed earlier in regard to the discourse of disability, while others displayed a therapeutic perspective, focusing on personal expression or even rehabilitation.

Therapy has at its core the promotion of heath and well-being. Dance therapy uses the creative processes of dancing and dance making to ameliorate the condition of the diseased body.[18] Within this context, dance is part of a process whose aim is not only an artistic product but also the reduction of human suffering. The danger occurs when there is confusion between artistic performance and rehabilitation. This problem was made clear in the presentation of the Crepúsculo Group, which was directed by two occupational therapists, one with a background in ballet and modern dance and one with a background in special education.

Near the end of the group's choreography, "Extension," a young man whose movements were clearly involuntary was brought to the center of the stage, sitting on an inflated beach float. While the other dancers were moving, he remained on stage in the same position, experiencing continuous spasms. The scene ended, the group thanked the audience, and the young man was left in the middle of the stage, stuck on the float. In the diagnosis presented by the therapists in the *Crepúsculo Manifest* this young man has quadriplegic spastic cerebral palsy with athetosis (*Crepúsculo Manifest* 2002). According to the group's directors, he presents a severe motor condition with major spasticity and involuntary movement, and he is without oral communication (he has only facial expression). The choreographer stated that he seemed to be "aware of his desires and longings," (ibid.) and for this reason he was integrated into the performance. I believe that the way he was inserted into the choreography raises some questions. For example, Which concept of dance—artistic or therapeutic—defines this work? Is it possible to present a therapeutic process (patient and therapist relationship) as an artistic product (involving dance, creator, interpreter, and choreography)? Did the young man make personal choices in terms of his movements or in regard to being on stage? What are the boundaries between the aesthetic and the ethical? In spite of these questions, most of the audience members were emotionally connected to and moved by the performance.

A hip-hop choreography presented by the group Bombelêla enabled a second reading that clearly revealed the relation of power between the nondisabled body and the disabled body. Many times in the musical background, the phrase "only a different body" was repeated as if the mere use of the sentence qualified the presence of the disabled dancer.

By analyzing the semantics and the relationships established in the choreography, it could be perceived that the different dancer was only a body who was passing by, whose trace was launched into the choreographic space and was soon erased or left to the outskirts of the work. The piece's movement was in many instances conducted by those who dominated the desired movement model. On other occasions, the disabled dancer was merely carried by the other dancers. This action changed the spatial arrangement while clearly suggesting the dependence of the disabled dancer. The choreographic climax showed the ability of the nondisabled body and the virtuosity of the soloist of the group, whose actions on stage set him off as the leader of one more urban tribe (in the Maffesolian sense [see Maffesoli 2000]).

This structure was repeated in several choreographies, mainly in those of ballroom dance, where the dancing relationship between woman and man was transferred to the relationship between nondisabled and disabled. This perspective reveals a clear hierarchy of power in which, in Foucault's sense, the disabled bodies became docile bodies trained to be subordinate.

A third alternative could be perceived in the presentation of the group Integrarte. Its classical ballet choreography was very well rehearsed, and the group showed high technical skill as well as a precise musical accuracy that the members of the cast who were deaf probably learned by heart with great diligence. This dance demonstrated one of the ways of impregnating the paradigm of overcome and normalization, which implies that the disabled body is the simulacrum of a nondisabled body and that by homogenization the disabled body may appear to be or have the body of the other.

This normalization pattern was actively demonstrated with the presentation of the dancers in wheelchairs. They emphasized their arm and head movements and the whirling of their chairs, aiming at nullifying the movement of their lower body, whose movement was beyond their control. In this approach, the importance of the nondisabled partner

Pulsar II.

Photo courtesy of Pulsar Cia de Dança—Mauro Kury

as a conductor in the performance comes into play and poses another question: If the dancers not in wheelchairs (the walking dancers) were not on stage, what kind of dance aesthetic might arise from the dancers in wheelchairs? What possibilities of movement and what time and space relationships might emerge?

The aspects that were implicit in the three models just described were either unnoticed or acceptable to most of the audience members. For most of the festival I observed a lively audience who cheered after each virtuous moment on the stage and was touched by the choreographies that were filled with appeals to emotion and the triumph of overcoming (after all, the performers were *dis*abled). In general, it did not matter how well the dance was performed or even what role the dancers with disabilities played in the artistic product. The only time when the audience's reception faded and remained cool was in response to the CandoCo performance. There was an unfamiliarity with the choreographic approach, and the company went on stage without adequate publicity. Thus the audience was expecting a presentation that was just like the other performances. The bodies that the audience expected (two dancers in wheelchairs, a dancer with an amputated leg, a dancer without a hand, and three dancers without disability) came on stage, but the dance embodied a different and complex approach.

CandoCo presented three choreographies that were part of its 2002-03 tour: "Phasing" by Jamie Watton, "Sour Milk" by Javier de Frutos, and "Shadow" by Fin Walker. Up until then these choreographies had not been shown in Brazil. The artistic direction of this company opted to work with renowned contemporary choreographers and intended to break taboos and the perceptions expected by the audience by inserting dancers with disabilities into the dance. In these choreographies, considering each creator's intentionality and specificity, the body differences and the dancers' singularities were interconnected, and thus the choreographies generated dances whose meaning was in the work, in the specific dancing body, and in its conjunctions and disjunctions, and not in the pathological concept of the disability. In CandoCo's work the dancers are not bound to a hierarchy. Their bodies trespass the rules of normality and abnormality, and "they do not try to conceal their physical limits, but work in the in-between space, namely in the space of conjunction, exploring the physicality of each body that interacts and acts with and on the other one" (Matos 2002, 182).

That is my way of understanding the reaction that the audience experienced while watching the CandoCo dances during the festival. At the end of the CandoCo performance, the audience's quiet applause was the response to a language that was still largely unknown as a possible medium of dance.

Conclusion

In this analysis of the *Festival Arte sem Barreiras* (Art Without Barriers Festival), we can see the importance of the questions of dance, identity, difference, and disability addressed throughout this discussion. The point that I want to make regarding the artistic product refers to the quest for new concepts of dance that are based on people with and without disabilities. After all, what are the specificities of a dancing body, whether disabled or nondisabled? How do we work different singularities and physicalities without reinforcing the same dualism of normal and abnormal, nondisabled and disabled? How do most people validate artists with disabilities in dance?

In general, the visibility of a disabled body can evoke questions concerning the image incarnated by these bodies, since they are beginning to occupy spaces that up to now have been dominated by ideal bodies. However, artists with disabilities can also support the privilege of the ideal body, trying to hide their differences and emphasizing a false overcoming of disability and thus invoking the image of a classic body and its ideological values.

There is an emergence of dancers with and without disabilities who have affirmed the artistic quality of their works through dance. Many contemporary works, namely the ones performed by CandoCo, DIN A13, and some Brazilian groups such as Grupo Pulsar (Pulsar Group) and Grupo X (X Group), present dancers whose bodies are often stigmatized in a different way. Through their choreographic works, these dance groups make the audience think about the reified conceptions of the body and dance.

Far from encouraging compassion, the presentation of the dancer with disability on stage can make the audience confront the story of this body with the stories, values, and preconceptions of their own bodies. These presentations can provoke disconcerting feelings as well as challenge the representations of the body that are established in the dance. In a Deleuzian sense, these bodies disturb the established order, and with their stories written in their own flesh, these dancers affirm themselves *in difference.*[19]

Just as the insertion of different bodies has implications for the relationship between process and product, it also requires and may guide changes in conceptions of the teaching of dance. Unfortunately, there is still a huge gap between research performed in the artistic field and its reflection in the area of education, since the spaces that can be accessed (both physically and artistically) by people with disabilities are still very limited. Most dance institutions, moreover, do not focus on transforming the philosophical and methodological proposals for teaching dance, which are based largely on measured aspects and performance skills of the body. Nonetheless, when the singularity of the dancing body is the focus of artistic exploration and aesthetic discourse, a greater plurality of poetics may arise in dance.

Persons with disabilities have claimed their rights as citizens with much difficulty through their struggle for emergence in society and culture. Dialogues concerning difference, and based on alterity, are being established and are no longer bound to binary pairs and to hegemonic patterns of culture and power. These dialogues make the frontiers formerly accepted as definitive fluid, and in so doing make the social and cultural ground more flexible and *moveable*.

In the groups including dancers with and without disabilities, the dialogues of these bodies as dance media have enabled an aesthetic construction that may take on a transgressing and critical character. It may take on this character by presenting the specificity of each dancing body in the network of relationships that can be created and researched and by creating zones of strangeness, convergence, and divergence. However, given the visibility of these works and the receptivity of the audience, it is clear that the presence of disabled bodies in the traditional dance circuits is still quite small. Beyond the talk of equality through difference, the (trans)formed bodies of the dancers with disabilities remain secluded to limited spaces. It is hoped that the small cracks in the idealized surface of the professional dance world will widen and become frontier spaces. In so doing, they may make possible a meaningful reconstruction of dance.

REFLECTIONS

In seeking to recognize the plurality of our societies, we have given much attention to issues of cultural and ethnic diversity. We have sought to become more culturally sensitive—that is, more educated about all those who participate in our society—and to respect our differences. To some extent, this is being done in our academies, corporations, religious institutions, and educational institutions as well as in our homes. Yet we still need to deconstruct our notions of difference as they apply to disability. In this chapter, Lúcia Matos asks that we examine more closely how dance defines disability. In raising this question, she suggests that we attend to what we consider to be the boundaries of normal. She reminds us that the body in dance mirrors our social and cultural ideals, falling prey to the same ideas of what is considered beautiful or physically perfect. We have recently begun to question our ideas of perfect bodies and the ideal dancer's body. Lúcia is now challenging us to expand that critical lens to examine how we define disability. Here we encounter questions of the rights and privileges of all as well as the notion of a democratic space. Lúcia states, "Beyond the talk of equality through difference, the (trans)formed bodies of the dancers with disabilities remain secluded to limited spaces." When bodies of different abilities appear before us on stage, in the studio, or in the classroom, they confront us with our own preconceived ideas of what dance and the dancer ought to be or can be. They challenge our curricula, our techniques, and our choreographies.

In dance, we try desperately to help students fit in and do as much as they can, but we do not question the underlying aesthetic assumptions we have about dance, the performer, and the performance. The ways we have tried to become more inclusive in dance by helping students to do their best in our existing structures need to be reconsidered. Many of us have interacted with individuals who do not fall within the boundaries of what is considered the normal dancer. Dance, however, can be a vehicle for self-transformation and social transformation, a process for understanding identity marked by history and culture, and a place where we might create new or alternative meanings. Who better than the people situated at the margins of society—the people whose difference marks them as less than those who are regarded as normal or able—can challenge our aesthetic assumptions and prejudices and bring us to recognize the world in which we exist in all of our multiple identities, abilities, diseases, and desires. How might dance change if we could release ourselves from old traditions and begin anew, recreating an image of what inclusive dance really is? What new aesthetic delights might we encounter?

Notes

1. Grupo Pulsar, Limites, Xis, and Ekilíbrio were chosen since their choreographies are not based on audience accommodation or on the overcoming or normalization of the body of the disabled dancer. These groups bring the audience to think about stagnant conceptions of the body, dance, and ability and disability. This chapter does not aim at analyzing these works.

2. I use the word *deaf* in order to place these subjects in a social group with its own culture. I also use it as the terminology adopted by the social actors themselves.

3. Since this language has a syntactic and semantic structure that characterizes it as a language, I use this expression only to highlight its spatial feature,

based on its visual perception, and the accompanying body language that is different from that which conventionally accompanies oral speech.

4. Author's emphasis.

5. Lyotard (1993) considers metanarratives to be the totalizing narratives that have marked modern times, such as emancipation and progress of reason.

6. This refers to the thoughts of Brazilian Paulo Freire, who defends an emancipatory, dialogic, and critical methodology as a means of promoting citizenry education and the access to symbolic goods (see Freire 1996)

7. Many of the agreements established between international banks and the Brazilian government include specific topics on education. Nonetheless, many of such aspects were restricted to the written agreement and do not occur in practice. An example of this is the increase of public resources for education and no teacher preparation for inclusive education.

8. Upon completion of the research in the second semester of 2006, Funarte and the *Programa Arte sem Fronteiras* published the first public grants specifically aimed at forming dance groups involving members with disabilities.

9. This area of research is beginning to gain ground in Brazil and is strongly influenced by British publications.

10. In Portuguese, there are no words to make a clear distinction between the term *impairment* and the term *disability*. In Brazil, both terms are related to combinations with the word *disability*. When in Brazil we refer only to *disability*, we are emphasizing the word *impairment*, which in Portuguese relates to abnormality or to a decrease in capacity. The term *disabled* is related to the person with a disability. In Portuguese, the literal translation of the word *disability* is *incapacity* or *deficiency*. There is no direct correspondence for these terms, and the Portuguese language cannot handle the specificity of terms such as *disability* and *disabled*.

11. Beginning in late 2003, this program started being directly incorporated into Funarte and the Ministry of Culture, and at this moment it is undergoing transformation, searching for new directions and guidelines.

12. Author's emphasis.

13. Nonsegmented circuits refer to artistic events that take place traditionally and are not directed toward only one social group. An example of a nonsegmented circuit is the dance festivals for persons with disability.

14. Term used in the official discourse.

15. For the first time in the history of Brazil, the government elaborated guidelines for public policies for dance, with the participation of artists and experts in the field of dance, by establishing the Sectorial Chamber of Dance in 2005.

16. This classification was made during the data analysis. In its event program, the organizing committee presented only the name of the group and the city of origin.

17. *(E) (com)motion* is a combination of *emotion* and *commotion*. This lexical play on these words ensures that their individual meanings are portrayed.

18. More questions on dance and therapy and the disabled body can be found in the author's dissertation (Matos 1998).

19. According to Deleuze (1998: 76) "Being is difference itself."

five

When Boys Dance: Cultural Resistance and Male Privilege in Dance Education

Doug Risner
Wayne State University
Detroit, Michigan

This chapter explores the dance education experience of boys and young men as a form of cultural resistance and as an important means for sharing a more common humanity through movement and expression. Although research indicates that 50 percent of male dancers in the United States are gay or bisexual (Bailey and Oberschneider 1997; Hamilton 1999), the dance community, until recently, has been silent on the subject of gay males in dance. Recent research on male youths in dance indicates that prevailing social stigma, heteronormative assumptions, narrow definitions of masculinity, heterosexist justifications for males in dance, and internalized homophobia exist in the field. For those boys and young males in dance education, however, choosing to dance may be an important vehicle for challenging dominant notions about gender, privilege, sexual orientation, and the body.

The ways in which male youths confront heterocentric bias, gender norms, and gendered bodies, as well as peer pressure and dominant cultural ideology, are explored throughout this chapter. The discussion focuses on key social questions of difference, pleasure, marginalization, and masculinity and on the larger, globalizing effects of the commodification of gay and bisexual culture. The author argues that a dance education that embraces all of its male students—straight, gay, and bisexual—can significantly influence homophobic prejudice and can disrupt the social stigma of difference in a global fashion.

When Boys Dance

Dance education and training have long been associated with gender and gender roles in world culture (Kraus, Hilsendager, and Dixon 1991; Posey 2002; Sanderson 1996; Stinson 2005). While many cultures have viewed and continue to view dance as an appropriate male activity, the Western European cultural paradigm situates dance as primarily a female art form, and it has done so since the 16th century (Hasbrook 1993). Moreover, research shows that the overwhelming majority of the student population engaged in dance education and training is female.[1] Researchers in dance education have gleaned considerable energy from the area of social foundations in education, especially in the realm of schooling and its effect on gender identity. With hybrid research agendas and methodologies from feminist thought, critical theory, gender studies, critical pedagogy, and, most recently, men's studies, the literature on dance education has begun to focus on the ways in which socially embedded assumptions about gender and dominant structural power relations produce unjust educational and sociocultural outcomes.[2]

Gender and its social construction play an important role in students' participation in and attitudes toward dance study.[3] Beginning dance training as early as three years of age, girls, unlike boys, often grow up with dance as a taken-for-granted activity of childhood, adopting values that "teach that it is good to be obedient and silent, good not to question authority or to have ideas which might conflict with what one is being asked to do" (Van Dyke 1992, 120). Traditional dance pedagogy teaches obedience and emphasizes silent conformity in which dancers reproduce what they receive rather than critique, question, or create it. Stinson (1998a, 118) cautions that "there is a kind of freedom in obedience, the freedom from responsibility." To deal with this sense of powerlessness, dance students often escape: "Some in dance escape into a world of beauty. Others escape into the world of self, allowing the image in the mirror, or achieving one more inch of elevation (in a jump), to become the focus of existence" (Stinson 1998a, 120). Although males begin dance training much later in their lives, this kind of escape or silent conformity affects both girls and boys.

A key consideration in studying gender and dance is to understand "the 'feminization' of theatrical dance in the west" (Thomas 1996). Because dance is viewed as a feminine activity, males who dance (whether gay or straight) are always in danger of being classified as effeminate, directly alongside the denigrated female. Approaches for confronting gender bias and inequity in dance teaching and curricula have been identified.[4] Central to most of these strategies are a concerted effort to make gender a conscious variable in all aspects of dance education (Ferdun 1994) and the affirmation of individual differences in gender and culture (Bond 1994; Kerr-Berry 1994).

At the same time, dance teachers often try to make boys and young men in dance feel more comfortable by inviting them to actively contribute ideas for movement, music, costuming, and choreographic theme (Risner, Godfrey, and Simmons 2004), by developing lesson plans and movements (sports movements, vigorous actions) that allow boys a feeling of ownership (Baumgarten 2003), and by emphasizing the challenge and satisfaction of jumping higher, shifting weight faster, moving bigger, and balancing longer (Gard 2001). In order to cultivate a larger male participation in dance, normalizing strategies over the past two decades have emphasized noteworthy heterosexual male dancers (Hanna 1988), made masculine comparisons between sport and dance (Crawford 1994), and minimized the significant number of male dancers who are gay (Risner 2002b; Spurgeon 1999). However, participation in Western European dance remains a culturally suspect endeavor for male adolescents, teenagers, and young adults (Gard 2003b; Leihikoinen 2005; Risner 2002a; Sanderson 2001; Stinson 2001).

Homogenizing Narratives

Because this book focuses on understanding dance education as a form of human empowerment as well as the struggle to survive a culturally homogenizing world, it is important to unpack some of the dehumanizing discourses on the male dancer and their continued implications for boys who dance. Much of the prevailing societal stigma associated with boys and male youths in dance can be traced to powerful discourses that, though sometimes meaning well, have produced a deleterious mythology about all males in dance, regardless of individual sexual orientation. At the same time, just like rampant globalization, these homogenizing narratives erase important cultural differences and struggles in the gay, lesbian, bisexual, and transgender (GLBT) population.

Hanna's (1988) *Dance, Sex, and Gender: Signs of Identity, Dominance, Defiance, and Desire* situated the study of male homosexuality and dance in a therapeutic, psychopathological setting in which gay male dancers ameliorated or eluded their "problematic" homosexuality in a comfortable and insular environment. Without regard for dominant sexual codes of heterosexuality or prevailing homophobic attitudes, Hanna's work focused on the anomalous number of gay men attracted to dance (ballet) and developed a lengthy rationale for such. Rather than exploring the social complexities of the experiences of gay and bisexual males in dance, Hanna repeatedly framed homosexuality as a problem for gays. In doing so, Hanna reinforced the narrow homosexual stereotypes:

Gay men identify with the effeminate yearnings, feelings, and romantic idealizations of the ballet. . . . Ballet presents an illusion experienced by some gay men as parallel to their relationships with women and the difficulties some gays have in establishing long-term relationships with each other. . . . Dancing (for gay men) may be an audition for lovers. . . . Ballet has had the attraction of colorful costume, glamour, and makeup. (Hanna 1988, 136-138)

In order to destigmatize dancing for boys and male youths and to "establish the respectability of a male dance career" (Hanna 1988, 146), Hanna championed projects like Jacques d'Amboise's National Dance Institute. While the efforts to bring dance to children, including young boys, and to a wider audience in general, continue to be admirable, these efforts and their rhetoric have often obfuscated larger social issues—most importantly, the significant gay male presence in dance and the considerable internalized homophobia found in the dance community in the late 1980s. Destigmatization and respectability, when read closely, meant minimizing the gay male population and its profound contribution to dance, cultivating the more respectable heterosexuals, "upgrading the status of male dancers" (Hanna 1988, 146), and silencing discussion of patriarchal and heterosexist practices in the profession. These discourses clearly illustrate the misguided effects of promoting heterosexual respectability, homosexual negation, and further homophobic attitudes in dance:

There are several approaches to the problem in addition to the d'Amboise strategy. . . . A male dancer (straight or gay) might handle the issue with nondancers by first acknowledging the stereotypical image (gay) and then establishing himself as an exception. He does this by revealing that he has a girlfriend, that he finds gays disgusting, or that his love of ballet makes him "put up" with gay men [attributed to O'Connor]. . . . A number of dancers said that there are very few gays in ballet today. (Hanna 1988, 146)

In previous works, I have criticized these kinds of hegemonic approaches (Risner 2002a, 2002b) and have advocated, with others (Crawford 1994; Gard 2001, 2003b), for more rigorous questioning that focuses on greater understanding of homophobic prejudice, dominant notions of masculinity, and societal stigma toward boys and male youths in dance. Most important, I have also advocated that researchers in dance education attempt to unearth cogent, relevant research about the experiences of all males currently in dance education. I believe what Crawford suggested more than a decade ago:

> Men have traditionally fulfilled roles as choreographers and managers, whereas women have been the prevalent performers and workers. Yet male dominance in dance has not led to an increase in male dancers, possibly because it conforms to, rather than challenges, the very structures that brought about the scarcity in the first place. (Crawford 1994, 40)

While I have acknowledged the appeal of cultivating a larger male population and audience in dance—a population and audience that more closely resemble those found in our communities, schools, and cultures—I continue to find it problematic to do so by denying the presence of gay and bisexual male dancers. Within our current political, economic, and social climate, attracting more males to the profession might conceivably bolster credibility and generate greater financial support for dance.

While efforts to bring dance to young boys and to a wider audience in general have been admirable, these efforts and their rhetoric have often obfuscated larger social issues of gender stereotypes and homophobia.

Photo by Steve Clarke.

However, attracting males by ignoring important cultural issues of sexual orientation, gender identity, and homophobic attitudes not only remains pragmatic and shortsighted but also forfeits vast opportunities for educating both the dance profession and our highly confused culture about sexuality and discrimination. Even with the best of intentions, the attempts to encourage young boys and men to pursue dance frequently reproduce narrow, derogatory stereotypes of gay dancers (Bond 1994; Crawford 1994). In doing so, these attempts demean rather than acknowledge and celebrate the gay male dance population and its contribution to the profession. I have asked dance educators to consider seriously the ethical implications of an empowering dance education for all boys in dance:

> It is one thing to promote dance, for example, as being an activity of self-expression and physical challenge for all children, both girls and boys. It is quite another to encourage involvement for boys by denigrating others, and thereby continually recasting the underlying assumptions and implicit sexism of the "sissy myth": *dance is for girls*. If we commit ourselves to cultivating larger male participation, thereby enriching the art form and its audience on the whole, then it would seem at least sensible to question the ways in which patriarchal Western society discourages young boys and men from participation. (Risner 2002b, 66)

Crisis in Masculinity

What is most worrisome concerning the current discourses on contemporary masculinity and gender, as well as concerning the leading researchers' findings on boys and males, is the direct correlation between postmodern masculine identity and homophobia (Kimmel and Messner 2001). More than a decade ago, the dance scholar Ramsay Burt gave a highly insightful and rigorous explanation of the cultural, social, and political history of masculine representation in dance, most notably the 20th-century construction of prejudice toward male dancers and the homophobia that today continues to surround gay—and for that matter, straight—men in dance. In his seminal book, *The Male Dancer: Bodies, Spectacle, Sexualities*, Burt (1995) charts the development of homophobia as a means for males to rationalize their close attraction to one another: Cultural norms necessitate a homophobic attitude in order for males to bond socially (which is a seemingly reasonable human endeavor). More simply, although men might certainly enjoy watching other men dance, in order to do so, they must profess an absolute repulsion toward homosexual desire or attraction. Straddling this important boundary between acceptable homosocial bonding and repressed homosexual attraction is the crux for the heterosexual male watching men dance. When extrapolated, this notion is a key element in understanding men's culturally prescribed anxiety toward gay men. It is instructive for dance educators to realize that similarly uncomfortable boundary crossings might apply to many fathers, siblings, and friends attempting to watch our male students dance. Without facing these foundational aspects of culturally defined masculinity (as narrow and destructive as they may be), there is little hope for any real progress. Recent research in men's studies finds much the same conclusion: Homophobia is a defining element in postmodern masculinity (Kimmel and Messner 2001).

Kimmel (2005, 220) notes the following in the current politicized debate about boys' achievement and behavior in schools:

> We hear about boys failing at school, where their behavior is increasingly seen as a problem. We read that boys are depressed, suicidal, emotionally shut down. Therapists caution parents about boys' fragility, warn of their hidden despondency and depression, and issue stern advice about the dire consequences if we don't watch our collective cultural step. Though we hear an awful lot about *males*, we hear very little about *masculinity*. Addressing the issue of masculinity will, I believe, enable us to resolve many of these debates, and move forward in a constructive way to create equity in our schools for boys as well as girls.

Although postmodern feminist theory has greatly expanded our understanding of multiple subject positions as well as the notion of diverse femininities or ways of being female, it appears that contemporary masculinity has become even narrower, like a "gender straightjacket" for boys and men (Pollack 1999, 6). In the pioneering *Real Boys: Rescuing Our Boys From the Myths of Boyhood*, Pollack (1999, 7) outlines the significance of a cultural reevaluation of the prevailing ideas about boys, men, and masculinity:

> The boys we care for . . . often seem to feel they must live semi-authentic lives, lives that conceal much of their true selves and feelings, and studies show they do so in order to fit in and be loved. The boys I see in schools and in private practice often are hiding not only a range of their feelings but also some of their creativity and originality. . . . The Boy Code is so strong, yet so subtle, in its influence that boys may not even know they are living in accordance with it. When they do (stray from the code), however, society tends to let them know—swiftly and forcefully—in the form of a taunt by a sibling, a rebuke by a parent or a teacher, or ostracism by classmates.

As many people have begun to acknowledge, the gender straightjacket and the Boy Code have profound effects on more than just the lives of boys and young males (Katz and Earp 1999; Kimmel 2005; Kimmel and Messner 2001; Pollack 1999). The unchecked traditional values of masculinity, such as emotional detachment, suppression of feelings, feigned bravado and self-confidence, dominance, aggression, and valorized individual achievement, diminish all human experience. Katz and Earp (1999, 3) describe this phenomenon as "the crisis in masculinity":

> It is vital that we understand that the real lives and identities of boys and men often, if not always, in some ways conflict with the dominant "real man" ideal. Behind the bravado and tough guy posturing, there is human complexity. In other words, behind the guise is the real boy and man, the results of a sensitive, nuanced experience of the world that rarely airs in public.

When we consider this mask of dominant masculinity that cultures across the globe perpetrate and place on boys and male youths, we see more clearly not only the disruptive cultural resistance to dance study for men but also the overwhelming courage (struggle) necessary for our male students to pursue dance study or to consider a career in dance. Moreover, as dance educators we should look more closely at the dominant social structures and cultural assumptions that guide our own practice and research, as well as examine the ways in which our actions wield the power to deplete or enrich an empowering common humanity. Whether in the United States or elsewhere, there are additional complexities for unpacking the gendered bodies of males in dance: marginalization as a male dancer in a culturally feminized field, combined with the privilege, benefit, and authority of being male in a patriarchal society.

Cultural Resistance: Challenging Dominant Gender Norms

Recent research in dance education and physical education in the United States, United Kingdom, and Australia has begun to explore the ways in which hegemonic masculinity (as an institution) can be challenged through the participation and experiences of boys and male youths in dance (Gard 2001, 2003a, 2003b; Keyworth 2001; Risner 2002a, 2002b). Central to this work is the notion that dance education may serve as an important means for disrupting dominant cultural assumptions about acceptable ways of moving for males and for challenging cultural stereotypes about male dancers and modes of sexuality other than heterosexual. Obviously, this is not to say that all boys and young men in dance consciously enter the dance studio with the intention of challenging dominant paradigms of masculinity. And it cannot be denied that some males in dance reaffirm narrow definitions of masculinity and heterosexism through their actions and discourses. Rather, this research suggests that the experiences of males in dance education can provide powerful insights into hegemonic assumptions about dance, gender, and sexuality and into the dominant codes that govern them all.

In his study, "Critical Autobiography: 'Straightening' Out Dance Education," Keyworth (2001) noted that the male participants expressed significant feelings of isolation as the "dancing queens" on campus. Although the participants enjoyed their dance experiences, many voiced unease with leaving the safety of athletics for the culturally pejorative dance studio. While optimistic that more males in dance will "question and ultimately subvert their own gendered conditioning," Keyworth (2001) concludes that the study's participants will "continue to carry their gendered legacy" (133).

Gard's recent work (2001, 2003a, 2003b) focuses on the possibilities that dance education offers for "disruptive and discomforting experiences," as well as pleasurable ones, for students in schools and universities. More specifically, these experiences involve exhuming the taken-for-granted aspect of gendered male bodies and heterosexual embodiment (Gard 2003a, 211). Gard notes the following:

> While I have heard male students use words like "weird," "stupid" and "dumb" to describe dance movement, my research suggests that the association of dance *per se* and particular forms of dance movement with both feminine and non-heterosexual ways of moving and being remains strong. And yet it is this knowledge, the knowledge that bodies carry and construct gendered meanings, which we might address through dance. (2003a, 220)

In a 2003 case study culled from a larger research project investigating male dancers, Gard explored the notion of gendered investments (committed ways of deploying the body) in dance education. In a life history narrative of Ralph, a professional male dancer, Gard (2003b) found an interesting correlation between the absence of enjoyment and the acute awareness that "boys don't dance" (109). This kind of love–hate relationship with dance stems from the idea that males are enculturated to manifest a particular kind of body and a specific way of moving that evidence a strict heterosexual regime (or set of governed practices). Although Ralph was a highly proficient professional dancer, his narrative account of dancing is one of repeated ambivalence, "bereft of any talk of bodily pleasure" (113).

Gard argues that this kind of uncertainty hinges on a struggle to reconcile enjoyment of dancing with other bodily investments more consistent with dominant male heterosexuality, such as Ralph's skills in rugby and surfing. Challenging dominant gender norms, whether done intentionally or not, requires an intense internal struggle with external forces and expectations.

In previous research on sexual orientation and dance participation by male undergraduates that I conducted in the southern United States with six introductory-level male dance students, I found five important themes that reveal a deeper understanding of social stigmatization: homophobic stereotypes, narrow definitions of masculinity, heterosexist justifications for male participation, the absence of positive male role models (straight and gay), and internalized homophobia among male dance students (Risner 2002a). Three of the participants in this study self-identified as heterosexual, while two self-identified as gay and one self-identified as bisexual.

For these young men (average age of 19 years), resisting cultural norms began with confronting the homophobic stereotypes held by their families and peers. Their own negative preconceptions of male dancers figured prominently as they contemplated and began dance study. At the same time, these participants later spoke eloquently about the personal satisfaction they felt while studying dance. Similarly to Gard (2003b), Keyworth (2001), and Lehikoinen (2005), I am interested in understanding the ways in which young men in dance balance these powerful competing narratives:

> On the one hand, their dance education is an important source of joy, satisfaction, and affirmation. While on the other, their masculinity and sexual orientation is repeatedly questioned and surveilled. Complicated meta-narratives require equally complicated coping mechanisms for young men in dance. (Risner 2002a, 87)

For young men who dance, justifying participation in dance emerges as an important arbiter of masculinity. Justifications, or *excuses* as Gard refers to them, frequently result in heteronormative half-truths—that is to say, a real male would never actively choose dance study on his own volition. AJ (pseudonym), whose degree program in theater requires course work in dance, acknowledges the following in his narrative:

> If you *have* to take dance, rather than if you just chose to take it, it frees you up. By it being a requirement, you don't have to show that you're interested, but of course I am. I did use it (the requirement) as an excuse with my friends back home, my family. (Risner 2002a, 87)

In a follow-up interview, AJ also made clear not only that dance was required for his degree but also that he felt a deep and profound attraction to both women and sports. Still other male dancers reiterate the similarities between dance and sport in their rationale to others. For example, "Most people have misconceptions of dance, that only weak people take it so they won't have to play sports, that dancers couldn't play football. I let them know it's just as difficult as sports" (Risner 2002a, 87).

Many of the male students described their frustration with the lack of positive male role models in dance, citing the need for more affirming examples of men as dance teachers and professional dancers as well as the need for popular media images of men dancing. Without strong role models to challenge narrow views of masculinity, homosexual stereotypes become so imbedded in the culture's associations with dance that young male dancers often become complacent (as some of the case study participants suggested), taking for granted the homophobic responses their dancing frequently elicits.

While I have little doubt that the physical demands of dance are commensurate with those of football or soccer, like Gard (2001), I am

For boys and young males in dance education, choosing to dance may be an important vehicle for challenging dominant notions about gender, privilege, sexual orientation, and the male body.
Photo by Steve Clarke.

concerned about discourses that colonialize dance with the intention of making it more accessible and palatable. I do not doubt, for those participants who are straight, the ontological significance of their hetero-sexual orientation and the ways in which dancing may challenge their deepest feelings about what it means to be male. However, I do find it problematic that justifying male participation in dance requires testimo-nials that not only buttress homophobic stereotypes but also erase the otherwise positive experiences of these young men in dance. First, why do these young men, gay and straight, reaffirm the very stereotypes that they repeatedly confront themselves? Second, why do these men feel it necessary to deny the presence of gay and bisexual men and youths in dance education in order to legitimatize their own participation? While we can certainly acknowledge the enormous courage that these young men require to confront social stigmatization, we must also recognize the myriad of ways in which denigrating some people serves to privilege others—in this case, heterosexual males.

Marginalized in a Marginal Field

For young males who are gay, the protection offered by the dance studio often carries the high cost of extreme isolation for a number of reasons (Risner 2002b, 68). First, young girls significantly outnumber their male counterparts in dance. Second, boys (gay and straight) experiencing the negative stigma associated with males in dance often go to great lengths to display traditional heterosexual markers. Social support networks and positive role models for gay youths in dance are rare. Leaving the dance studio often means returning to the embarrassment, humiliation, and contempt of being labeled as the pansy, fag, or queer. In addition, research shows that males in dance who are not heterosexual receive far less paren-tal and family encouragement for dancing than their heterosexual peers receive (Bailey and Oberschneider 1997, Risner 2002a). I have noted the following in previous research:

> The lack of parental support and approval experienced by gay male dancers may be attributed to parents' more general disapproval of dancing, or to dance as a career choice for their sons. It may well be that the larger fears of homosexuality inhibit parents from encour-aging their male children to pursue dance study, especially if one or both of the parents harbor homosexual suspicions about their male child. (Risner 2002a, 90)

Young boys' avoidance of their homosexual orientation is facilitated by countless devices perpetrated by a pervasively heterocentric culture, especially when considering the overwhelmingly ridiculed status of sissy boys in American society. Rofes (1995) notes that the widely accepted sissy and jock paradigm operates as a key element in male youth culture; through it, traditional masculinity is narrowly described in highly misogynist ways. Boys in dance, unlike boys in athletics and team sports, are participating in an activity that already sheds social suspicion on their masculinity and heterosexuality. For gay male youths in dance, coping with this double bind (marginal in a marginalized field) is a complicated dilemma.

Young gay males tend to begin homosexual activity during early or midadolescence; lesbians begin similar activity around 20 years of age (Anderson 1995, 18). Dance educators must realize that because adolescents are only beginning to possess the capacity for abstract thought and the formal reasoning needed to cognitively integrate their sexual experiences, boys and young gay males in dance are extremely vulnerable to gendered criticism, homophobic attitudes, antigay slurs, and the absence of positive gay male role models. Moreover, young self-identified gay males in dance experience far more alienation in dance class than their straight male peers experience (Risner 2002a, 89).

Young gay males may develop internalized homophobia, in which self-hate, low self-esteem, destructive behavior, and further confusion characterize their underlying attitudes and conduct. Many gays who are incapable of resisting persistent heterocentrism and homophobic prejudice internalize negative attitudes about homosexuality, themselves, and other gay people (Lehne 1976; Margolies, Becker, and Jackson-Brewer 1987). As Luke (self-identified as gay) told me in 2002,

> I never talk to men in class. I prefer straight women because they're not as difficult to talk to as gay men . . . we don't identify with other gay guys. This sounds stupid, but I really don't like gay people that often. And the ones I do like really get on my nerves . . . I mean, who wants to talk to a bitchy male dancer? (Risner 2002a, 89)

Or as Brett (self-identified as gay) told me in the same study,

> I know many openly gay people in theatre, but in dance, many are closeted. I don't understand why. I get so frustrated with them. I mean, I know it's difficult and I don't judge them, but please, we're in dance . . . and these closeted guys try so hard. It's all about their girlfriends . . . I'm not gonna (sic) waste my time. (Risner 2002a, 89)

Because I found the internalized homophobia surprising, I asked the gay and bisexual participants if they felt that dance was a supportive environment for gay men. Although the participants uniformly believed that dance provides an open and supportive atmosphere for gays, they struggled to articulate how they experienced the support to which they attested, telling me, "There's some sense of support in that nobody's calling you names. It's not hostile." They also said, "It's a big escape in the studio . . . when I come out of dance class I feel it all back on me." And finally, "There's no harassment from the other dancers and that feels extremely supportive" (Risner 2002a, 90). The interesting picture that these young gay and bisexual men paint depicts a contradictory landscape characterized by a strong sense of gay and bisexual support and affirmation on the one hand and a deeply internalized homophobia on the other. This landscape, when combined with the homophobic attitudes characteristic of homosocial bonding, tends to isolate gay males from their straight male classmates and from each other. What this small picture may be showing us is that young males in dance—gay and straight—tend to distance themselves from gay males and homosexuality.

This kind of environment is stressful and often threatening for gay male students, particularly since they are vulnerable young people who are struggling to claim and affirm their sexual orientation in an often hostile atmosphere of homosexual denigration. For closeted gay youths, keeping this aspect of their identity hidden over time causes many other psychological and emotional hardships, though at the time these dilemmas go unacknowledged (Besner and Spungin 1995, 95). Deceiving others ultimately leads to deceiving the self, a deception that goes well beyond sexual orientation.

Moreover, gay adolescents often have far fewer resources available to them for understanding homosexuality and same-sex sexual harassment and abuse in a balanced and unbiased manner. Because the field of dance education often suppresses candid and forthright discussions of gay issues, it rarely, if ever, addresses the sexual harassment and abuse that sometimes occur (Risner 2002b). Hamilton (1998, 92) reports that though there are far fewer males than females in dance, male students are three times as likely to experience sexual harassment than female students are, and perpetrators of sexual harassment are more than seven times as likely to be male than female. In addition, teenage male dancers are propositioned for sex by their dance teachers, directors, choreographers, and fellow dance students at a rate of three to one when compared with female dancers, and the gender of the solicitor is male nearly 70 percent of the time (Hamilton 1998, 92).

The silence surrounding sexual abuse in the dance profession is deeply troubling, but it also speaks to the unwritten pact the profession maintains for the *unspoken*. Instead of keeping quiet, we should rigorously question the motivation and perpetuation of the secrecy that allows this kind of abuse to be perpetrated on youths in dance education. For dance educators, three grave dangers emerge:

1. Male students rarely, if ever, come forward about sexual harassment and abuse.
2. Sexual abuse performed by male dance faculty is often trivialized or ignored.
3. Within the muted discourse of the dance profession, sexual abuse and homosexual orientation are wrongly equated with one another.

These disconcerting, if not incriminating, facts certainly exacerbate the continued absence of serious discussion surrounding gay issues in dance education. When faced honestly, these issues should compel dance educators to speak more openly about the truth of the matter in its entirety. Gay men have been and continue to be an important part of the dance landscape. The dance profession must counter society's negative message about gays by answering it directly, not by avoiding it. Taking a critical stance on sexual harassment and abuse should not require that we deny the significant presence and contribution of gay men to dance education. However, all too frequently, this denial has been the case. What I find even more troubling is the way in which the lack of response by the dance profession serves to equate homosexual orientation *with* sexual harassment and abuse and thereby reproduces negative attitudes and stereotypes about gays.

Male Privilege in Dance Education: Negotiating the Margin and Center

Dance, already marginalized in its status, funding, and curricular equity (Garber et al. 2006), remains widely misunderstood by the general public. Due in large part to dualistic thinking that separates mind from body and intellectual activity from physical labor, and due to dance's close association with girls and women, dance is often perceived as part of the women's domain, whereby its denigration for its dense female population is possible. Historical notions about the body often linked the feminine with intuition, nature, the body, and evil; conversely, intellect, culture, the mind, and good have been perceived as masculine (Risner 2001).

Being critical of that which already functions from a place of social and cultural weakness is a difficult task and is doubly confounding when we acknowledge our own unwitting participation in systems of domination and oppression. From the outside, the most stigmatized of the marginalized in dance is the gay male. When we also consider race, as DeFrantz rightfully reminds us to do, the Black gay male dancer is likely the most marginalized (DeFrantz 1996). However, from inside the dance profession, the oppression that women experience in general society is reproduced. Dance does not necessarily offer more opportunities to women than it does to men despite the women's majority of the dance population. Because of the seeming legitimacy that men bring to dance, they often receive more attention and cultivation in their classes and training even though they make up a definitive minority.

If the field commits to cultivating larger male participation in dance, thereby enriching the art form and its audience on the whole, then it would seem at least sensible to question the ways in which patriarchal Western society strongly discourages young boys and men from participation.
Photo by Steve Clarke.

Despite the fact that women constitute the vast majority of the dance field, males hold a disproportionate number of directorial and administrative authority positions in the United States (Clark 1994; Hanna 1988; Lodge 2001; Risner 2006; Samuels 2001; Stinson, Blumenfeld-Jones, and Van Dyke 1990; Van Dyke 1996). For example, data from the National Endowment for the Arts, the American Dance Festival, and the National Corporate Fund for Dance report that men in dance have benefited disproportionately from scholarships, grant funding, education, income, and employment (McGuire 1999; Samuels 2001; Van Dyke 1996). Recent reports in the United States indicate that as increasing numbers of male dancers have returned to graduate school to obtain advanced degrees in order to parlay successful performing careers into positions of authority in higher education, the last decade has seen a 40 percent increase in male leadership in dance education (Higher Education Arts Data Survey 2003, *Dance Magazine* College Guide 2004-2005).

Research also indicates a larger, more troubling outcome of gender inequity in dance in higher education (Warburton and Stanek 2004), in which the typical faculty profile is a 49-year-old female working part time in a nontenure track, teaching up to six classes per semester and reporting no creative activity over the past two years (Risner and Prioleau 2004). In U.S. public institutions, the salaries of male professors, associate professors, and lecturers in higher education dance exceed those of females in the same positions by a yearly average of more than $3,000 U.S. (Higher Education Arts Data Survey 2003).

For gay males acting as faculty members, choreographers, managers, and administrators, the paradox of having one foot in the center and one foot in the margin emerges. The nature of this double bind (Sedgwick 1990)—privileged through sex, race, and position of power but marginalized by sexual orientation and art form—presents interesting possibilities for disrupting dominant asymmetrical power relationships and for developing imaginative pedagogical approaches. Exposing mechanisms of stigmatization and dehumanization means interrogating one's own participation in their production. At the same time, mining the potential for resistance from this double bind is also demanded.

However, in hopes of establishing legitimacy (raising funds, attracting corporate and private sponsorships, developing audiences, recruiting men) through male participation and direction and in hopes of garnering wider social acceptance (rather than further homosexual stigmatization), the gay male presence in dance is often suppressed by the dance community itself—often at the hands of those males in authority whose sympathetic response seems at least logical, if not obligatory. As a gay, White male department chair in dance, I am equally implicated. Some of my recent work has sought to more clearly align my position of privilege and authority with my ethical responsibilities for fostering a more humanizing dance education (Risner 2003a, 2003b, 2004a, 2004b, 2005; Risner, Godfrey, and Simmons 2004; Risner and Thompson 2005).

Rise of Global Masculinity (Commodifying Gay Male Culture)

It is now necessary to draw some of the complicated issues articulated throughout the chapter into greater coherence; therefore, I want to extend these arguments to a national and global realm. It is critical to examine the ways in which the commodification (or repackaging and selling) of gay male culture and the globalizing effects of hegemonic masculinity dehumanize all of our lives in general and liberatory dance education in particular.

Globalization aims at the transcendental intensification of political and socioeconomic homogenization across the globe (Akindele, Gibado, and Olaopo 2002). Its primary target is to achieve the universal homogenization of ideas, cultures, values, and lifestyles (Ohiorhenuan 1998, 6). While globalization is certainly rooted in the unbridled spread of capitalism, for our purposes here I concentrate on the aims of political and social homogenization inherent in the U.S. globalization agenda[5]—specifically, the global swathe of hegemonic masculinity, including the commodification and commercialization of gay male culture.

Shapiro and Purpel (2005, 367) remind us that globalization, "the process by which human beings and societies become ever more interconnected with one another[,] has been developing for hundreds of years. . . . [Globalization has] occurred in ways that are asymmetrical in terms of power and cultural influence." As we have seen throughout this chapter, the current definitions of masculinity in the United States are rife with narrow and highly limited views of what constitutes "real men," male bodies, and appropriate gender investments for boys and male youths. In discussing global terms of what it means to be male, Kimmel (2005, 223) suggests the need for understanding and affirming the diversity of American (U.S.) male experiences and masculinities:

> Despite biology and the traditional cliché "boys will be boys," there's plenty of evidence that boys will not necessarily be boys everywhere in the same way. Few other Western nations would boast of violent, homophobic, and misogynist adolescent males and excuse them by virtue of this expression. If it's all so biological, why are European boys so different?

The notion of a globalizing masculinity rooted in this kind of a singular definition is easily conceivable, especially when we consider the asymmetrical power and cultural influence of capitalistic approaches, advanced technologies, and the homogenizing narratives discussed earlier in this chapter. Dance educators have much to lose in this dehumanizing process, and in many respects, we may have unintentionally paved the way through our past efforts to cultivate male participation in dance through masculinist and homophobic approaches (e.g., promoting dance as sport or competition and emphasizing straight male dancers and demeaning sissy and jock narratives).

Couched in these approaches is the misguided assumption and narrow view that all boys are the same and "the non-athletic qualities of dancing are unlikely to be of any interest to them" (Gard 2001, 219). Moreover, the crux of the matter (when boys dance) goes unacknowledged and thus reproduces the same homophobic stereotypes that dance educators seek to redress. While we do not know all the reasons why boys and male youths dance, it should be obvious that these strategies ignore and potentially negate some of their motivations, such as creative expression, interest and aptitude, curricular requirement, recreation, dance as a complementary skill to theater, and so on. Because these approaches valorize dominant heterosexual masculinity to such an extent, they may also render invisible gay and bisexual males who are questioning their sexual orientation. In a sense, these males are bleached or homogenized through an acceptable heterosexist lens of masculinity. This kind of gay male commodification, and its subsequent commercialization in the United States, is a key component of a globalizing masculinity.[6]

A cogent example of gay male assimilation and reappropriation comes from popular media that, although gay male culture appears to have unprecedented visibility, are clearly situated from a dominant male heterocentric perspective. *Will and Grace*, one of the most successful U.S. television programs produced by the National Broadcasting Company (NBC), focuses openly on the lives of two 30-something gay men. In its eight-season run (1998-2006), the weekly comedy series traced the hip yet traditional *I Love Lucy* antics of Will Truman, a successful New York attorney, and of his flamboyantly gay friend from college, Jack McFarland. Will, though gay, literally and figuratively plays the straight man to Jack's over-sexed gay stereotype. Week after week, Will and his high school girlfriend, now interior designer, Grace Adler, continue the long and tortured relationship they began in high school—struggling episode to episode to reconcile themselves to the fact that they will never be together because *Will is gay*. This heterocentric yet immensely popular situation comedy has little to do with meaningful gay male experiences or the lives of gay men, and it does not pretend to do so. Rather, acting as a gay recapitulation of the misogynist saint and whore archetype, it typifies the commodification and commercialization that are characteristic of the account of gay men that is relayed by global masculinity, an account that reaffirms gay stereotypes while homogenizing gays from a straight perspective. As Battles and Hilton-Morrow (2002) note, the show's immense mainstream popularity, now seen widely in syndication throughout the United States and in 27 countries on six continents, arises from "straightened out" representations of homosexuality, in which the characters of Will and Jack are heterosexist constructions that satisfy heteronormative expectations of gay men.

This example of *Will and Grace* sheds greater light on the dehumanization fueled by the rampant cultural homogenization in the United States and also demonstrates the cost of gay male repackaging for mainstream acceptance:

> This tragedy is familiar, but even more pronounced for the gay community. Gay men actively courted corporate America in the hope of being taken seriously. The cost is the commodification, and thus the loss of, a discrete ethnic identity—the postmodern tale of ethnicity meeting global capitalism. (Bryson 1999, 422)

The remaking of the world is presumed in the globalization process (Diagne and Ossebi 1996) by changing the way in which major actors think and operate across the globe (Biersterker 1998). While some dance educators will likely disagree with me, I believe that much of our discourse about males in dance has buttressed the current narrow, masculinist view. We are remaking the idea of who the boys and men who dance are to satisfy external pressures and expectations. Not always intentionally, but sometimes through silence or consent, the dance field itself may have facilitated the marginalization of both dance students and dance education.

Conclusion

> The more you are like me, the more I know the true value of my power, which you wish to share, and the more I am aware that you are but a shoddy counterfeit. (Gilman 1986, 2)

This passage from Gilman summarizes some of the ideas in this chapter. Gilman (as the privileged center) warns of the stranger's (the marginalized individual's) temptation to erase his difference in exchange for access to validation and emancipation by the inner circle. This passage illuminates many of the complicated intersections articulated in this chapter, such as gender and gendered investments, human empowerment and homogenizing narratives, masculinity and homophobia, cultural resistance and dominant gender norms, marginalization and privilege, humanization and globalization. These intersections frequently overlap and inform one another, especially when we consider this passage in terms of ethnicity, gender, social class, dance form, and academic discipline. What remain the primary issues, however, are those of difference and affirmation.

In the context of dance education, Gard may have skillfully, though not intentionally, articulated these primary concerns in terms of the sacrifice that dance education will undergo in order to gain affirmation by garnering increased male participation and legitimization from patriarchal systems:

> The reasoning seems to be that "if only dance were more like football, then more boys would want to dance." If there really is a special reason for boys participating in dance as opposed to, say, football, then making dance more like football would likely seem to compromise whatever this mysterious quality of dance is . . . by starting from a position that most boys like football, the category of "boys" becomes frozen. Not surprisingly, then, this approach has nowhere else to go other than to position dance, and not the category of "boys," as the problem. (Gard 2001, 220)

Remaining in the margin, addressing the inadequacies of the dominant center's game of affirmation and emancipation, reveals that this game is yet another one of domination, one that erases the margin's difference (experiences, needs, achievements, and struggles). Keeping a sense of isolation, of not completely fitting in, provides the deeper sensitivity and wider awareness necessary for resistance that is both critical and affirming. What is essential is the notion that marginalized peoples and art forms can live and learn, as Welch (1999) describes, from and within difference. This kind of cultural resistance arises not purely from the inside, nor wholly from the outside, but rather it emerges from the two and with the dialectic that runs between. The marginalized learn from and with their differences—unbleached, present, and worthy. The language of the margin is one of resistance that transcends by literally connecting the world we live "in here" with the world "out there."

It is of tremendous importance that we see the larger geography of our current world while simultaneously recognizing its trajectory into our own dance education locales. It is also critical that we understand the ways in which our actions can deplete or enrich human experience through dance education in our schools, studios, classrooms, performances, and programs.

REFLECTIONS

Across the globe young boys and men struggle with the gender norms of male culture. This struggle is heightened in the world of dance. The questioning of masculinity can be inherent in the act of dancing, particularly if the dance role differs from the accepted male role of the culture. As Doug Risner reminds us, gender norms, prevalent in all cultures, are heightened in dance, where homophobia continues to strongly discourage male participation. Dance offers the possibility to disrupt or challenge the dominant cultural assumptions about masculinity. With the participation of gay boys and men, it becomes critical for us in dance and dance education to take a stance in response to homophobic culture. There is a need to recognize the stressful, threatening, and often hostile environment that our young men face both in the larger world and in the dance world. The complexity of social positioning means that males in dance may hold positions of power and authority and simultaneously be marginalized because of their sexual orientation. With this knowledge it becomes more pressing both to challenge male dominance in dance and to foster, as Risner calls for, "a more humanizing dance education." Our current and dominant definitions of real men and masculinity can be deconstructed. Increasing male participation in dance and exorcising homophobia can help break the oppressive masculinity and can open avenues for new modes of global being.

Notes

1. Though seemingly obvious, see, for example, Adair 1992; Higher Education Arts Data Survey 2003; Sanderson 2001; and Van Dyke 1992, 1996.

2. The last decade's work chronologically includes Arkin 1994; Clark 1994; Horwitz 1995; Marques 1998; Shapiro 1998, 2004; Smith 1998; Green 2000, 2002-03, 2004; Doi 2002; Schaffman 2001; Keyworth 2001; Risner 2002a, 2002b, 2004a, 2005; Blume 2003; Letts and Nobles 2003; Gard 2003a, 2003b.

3. Social construction of gender in dance education is explored chronologically in the following works: Stinson, Blumenfeld-Jones, and Van Dyke 1990; Flintoff 1991; Van Dyke 1992; Cushway 1996; Sanderson 1996, 2001; Stinson 1998a, 1998b, 2001; Gard 2001, 2003a; Green 2001, 2002-03, 2004.

4. Approaches for confronting gender bias and inequity in dance teaching and curriculum are articulated by Arkin 1994; Bond 1994; Clark 2004;

Crawford 1994; Daly 1994; Dils 2004; Ferdun 1994; Kerr-Berry 1994; Risner 2003b; Stinson 2005.

5. In previous work (Risner 2001), I have discussed the limitations of a capitalistic democratic society in terms of liberatory social policies for gays and lesbians.

6. See Harris (1997) for a well-argued treatise on ethnic and cultural assimilation of gay culture.

six

Acts of Love Under a Southern Moon

Lynn Maree

Chair, KZN DanceLink
Durban, KwaZulu-Natal, South Africa

Acts of Love Under a Southern Moon was a dance work performed in the South African city of Durban in May 2005. It is a fitting title for an essay describing the dance scene in that city. In a country in conscious transition, a country with a fractured past, a great many strands of change and conservation occur at once, crisscrossing, reinforcing, and contradicting each other. Dance in Durban, in the eThekwini Metropolitan Municipality of KwaZulu-Natal, is a potent example of this exciting, challenging, and even explosive change. The dance scene cannot be called a *melting pot*, for a pot in which disparate things are, through heat, melting together is assumed to be producing one appetizing dish. In Durban the dance community doesn't really know what it is producing. But there is one thing the dance community does know: It is not homogeneous. These words by David Gouldie, a local choreographer, offer insight into the state of dance in the city:

> We all come from many different places but there is a real sense of caring and of journey among ourselves as choreographers and companies in Durban, which I really think is fantastic and I don't often see in other places. I just know that it's also about combining energies. (Gouldie, August 2005, 83)

Cultural Conflict

Culture, that overused and catchall term, needs some South African expli-
cation. In South Africa there is a Ministry of Arts and Culture, and for
a time after the arrival of democracy in 1994, it seemed that the phrase
arts and culture was being used as a rolled-together phrase: artsandculture.
Included in arts and culture were such things as the circumcision of adolescent boys in the Xhosa culture, hut painting and face painting, and a
cappella singing (like that of Ladysmith Black Mambazo).

One of the main aims of our Arts and Culture Ministry is to restore the
esteem of those cultures and art forms that were discounted and devalued
by the South African apartheid government, which began its grand scheme
of apartheid in 1948. Indigenous dance, together with the community
values and ceremonies it enriches, deserves celebration and acknowledgment. But we must also recognize that some of our existing culture is
being contested, and should be contested. For example, the Ministry of
Arts and Culture finds a clash between the cultural practice of small girls
dancing with nothing on beneath their skirts and the constitutional right
of those young girls to dignity and respect. Also, the national government
is trying to regulate and make safe traditional circumcision ceremonies
in which young boys sometimes die because of a lack of skill in some of
the ritual practitioners.

Cultures are not static. They have an internal dynamic and they interact
with other cultures. Certain aspects of them are always being contested.
And when we consider the arts end of arts and culture, we know how
mongrelized the arts already are. Creative people have always stolen,
borrowed, remade, and made new. Hollywood, American soap operas,
and American rap are all are seen as Americanizing the world, and yet the
counterflow of influence on American culture from, for example, African
music, dance, and art remains unacknowledged.

In KwaZulu-Natal there are Zulu dance groups in rural areas, in town-
ships, and in hostels inside cities that are dedicated to preserving and
advancing their traditional dance form. There are also Indian communities whose families take their daughters to Bharatanatyam, which is
the Indian equivalent of ballet and is seen by mothers as helping their
daughters develop the poise and grace of middle-class Indian girls. And
then there are suburban communities in which White parents take their
daughters to ballet. So the cultures' use of dance goes on, though perhaps the reasons for using dance change. But there are Black, Muslim,
and Coloured children in those ballet studios as well. And the township
children who perform their traditional dances also learn dances such as
pantsula, kwaito, hip hop, and contemporary. Indian traditionalists are
experimenting with the Bollywood trait of slipping in and out of roles,

changing from submissive and sweet feminine milkmaids to sultry hip-swinging sirens, and they can do it all tongue in cheek.

What there is less of is the learning of African dance by White, Indian, and Coloured South Africans. This is because the racial hierarchy that was apartheid bit deep into society, and middle-classness is equated with White. Now, in the striving after the middle-class lifestyle, children of all races attend schools previously reserved for Whites. This trend has led, in some cases, to Black parents removing their children from these schools because of a perception that the school population is getting "too Black." But *less* does not mean nothing at all: There are dance students in drama departments at universities, including the University of KwaZulu-Natal, learning to move in a variety of ways and not treating dance genres as belonging exclusively to particular racial groups. There is also a new Learning Area (what used to be called a *school subject)* in the National Curriculum, that of Arts and Culture. In theory at least, all children are meant to know something of all of South Africa's art forms, and the curriculum pays particular attention to previously disadvantaged forms such as traditional African dance in all of its manifestations. As of now, South Africa has neither the teachers nor the resources to do this, but it is a start, and in-service courses do exist.

So there is some reclamation of what seemed to have been shattered and devalued by the White rulers. In some places dance is vibrant, imbued with new thinking, new technology, and new influences. And it is very confident. Two examples of this constructive reclamation follow; one is the music department of the University of KwaZulu-Natal, and the other, which is located about 60 kilometers west of Durban, is a children's home in Cato Ridge where a performing arts academy is being set up. A theater has been built and a production has already toured England. In both of these examples traditional work is being restaged, refined, and put into new contexts.

Music From Africa

The African Music and Dance Programme is part of the music program at the University of KwaZulu-Natal. Its director is Dr. Patricia Opondo, a Kenyan academic of great determination and imagination. The students study music and dance from all over Africa, and the department's African Music and Dance Ensemble travels to many parts of South Africa and the continent. Each year the program hosts an artist in residence; this artist usually brings a group of dancers and musicians from his or her country. This group works with the South African students to produce and perform a new work. The staging is accompanied by a music and food event, with food from many parts of Africa being offered in stalls set up around the hall. The food is all supplied and cooked by representatives of the different countries of Africa who live in Durban. The significance of the cultural interchange—the spirit of the people involved and the richness of the cuisine—carries an important political message in a society where Black Africans from other parts of Africa are feared, disliked, and often dismissed pejoratively as makwerekwere (the English equivalent of the word *makwerekwere* would probably be *bloody foreigners*).

In 2004, Jackson Mamengi Kumesu from the Democratic Republic of the Congo (DRC) was the artist in residence. His production, *Epoppée Likelembe*, included dances from many provinces and ethnic groups in the DRC. These dances were woven into a story of conflict and reconciliation in a rural community untouched by city or Western life. The values espoused in the story were those of forgiveness, of the need for communities to support their members, and of gratitude for the harvest. What was of note was the combining of different traditions into one production that put together Congolese dancers from Kumesu's company, Ballet Salongo Bonganga, with South African student dancers on an indoor stage with sophisticated lighting. The celebration ended with two newly choreographed works, one thanking the administrator of the course for her hard work and constant support, and the other thanking Dr. Opondo for her inspiration, for her belief in Kumesu, and for her continuous dedication to the promotion of African music and dance throughout the continent (of Africa). The technology and personnel and the place—the newly democratic South Africa—gave a fresh context in which to make sense of and appreciate the interethnic performance. The evening underlined the fact that tradition is not frozen even though some members of a society may try to freeze it. Tradition changes with time, and everywhere people are wrestling with the desire to preserve, critique, and hold on to that which is known while at the same time acknowledging that slippage is inevitable.

Self-Help Begins at Home

God's Golden Acre is a rural outreach development project that, while situated in a very poor part of the province, runs an arts program. It was started by an extraordinary woman, Heather Reynolds, as a home for young children who had been orphaned or abandoned through the pandemic of HIV and AIDS. It has expanded into a project that offers support to all the rural communities by feeding those who cannot sustain themselves; helping to plant trees and provide chickens so that self-help programs can begin; providing school fees, books, and uniforms for many children from the valleys; and running a soccer league and a dance and music program.

The history of the dance and music program needs to be told. In Durban there is an umbrella organization for dance, KZN DanceLink, which is a membership organization that links the companies, choreographers, and dance schools of the province. In early 2000, DanceLink began holding weekly dance classes in a wide range of dance genres at God's Golden Acre. In July of that year, the International Conference on AIDS was held in Durban and the class participants from God's Golden Acre performed a cross-cultural piece titled "Asimbonanga." The performance piece used music of the same name by the South African artist Johnny Clegg and was taught to the participants by Surialanga, an Indian dance company that is part of KZN DanceLink. The weekly workshops continued, but the appearance at the AIDS conference began a performing career that led to a 2002 production, the *Young Zulu Warriors*, that toured England for six weeks. This tour raised enough money for Heather Reynolds to build a theater at the children's home. In October 2004, the theater opened with a new production, *Thulasizwe.*

In June 2004, God's Golden Acre acquired the services of Thulabona Mzizi, a dancer and choreographer who had worked with the project some years earlier as a KZN DanceLink teacher. He had been a member of two

The theater at God's Golden Acre.
Photo by H. Reynolds

of Durban's professional dance companies, but his personal life had fallen afoul of the violent crime in cities and the corruption within elements of the police force. The opportunity to work with children, away from the mess and muddle of his life in the city, resurrected Mzizi's working life, while his availability as an experienced dance teacher came as a timely boon to the artistic development at God's Golden Acre. Mzizi brought to his work a confidence born out of his knowledge of his own traditions, his training in contemporary and creative dance, and the experience of professional stages and music technology. He borrows and incorporates with a sure touch. In 2001, when the children from God's Golden Acre took part in KZN DanceLink's annual showcase, Imbumba, they were the weakest dancers but survived by a sympathy vote. At the 2005 Imbumba they were better rehearsed, and they had a stronger sense of performance than any of the other groups had.

At the time of this writing, more than 70 young people from the valleys are studying dance and music (mostly singing) every day at God's Golden Acre. The training incorporates teaching in the local schools and working on performances. The dance training is based mainly in traditional Zulu indlamu (warrior line dance), but KZN DanceLink is able to provide teachers of African contemporary dance, and this technical training underpins the professionalism of the work the children are learning to perform.

Dance to Empower, to Challenge, to Express Injustice

During the struggle in South Africa, many people were introduced to modern ideas, ideas about democracy, freedom, creativity, and women's rights. Imperialism, colonialism, and apartheid had entered traditional societies and destroyed the elements that allowed those societies to function. However, those traditional societies were not perfect (there is no such thing as a perfect society). They were authoritarian, patriarchal, and hard on their children. Placing the ancestors at the heart of a values system keeps a society stable, but it also maintains the status quo. And those who are in power, as Gramsci's concept of hegemony[1] shows, have a way of using that values system to maintain and extend their power.

Musa Hlatshwayo, a young contemporary choreographer, speaks about growing up in this kind of hegemony, where those in power demand that the oppressed minority keep silent. Musa draws on his background and culture in creating his works. He has won awards and is invited to dance festivals throughout Africa and across the seas. He experienced his move into the city, into university culture, into a global culture, as bringing tension. When he visits home he is seen as a role model, and he goes home when he wants to be refreshed and to soak up home. But he is not uncritical of the culture in which he grew up:

> I also mentioned that I grew up in a culture of silence where, if you are a youngster, you remain a youngster. But the fact that, at this point in time, I'm . . . noted as a young choreographer, . . . somebody whose voice is emerging and talking about issues, shows that I have taken a step forward to discovering a voice. What I am trying to do is break through from the tradition of KwaMaphumulo . . . I am aiming at breaking through the culture of silence so that obviously means breaking away from the tradition . . . What I do is question what happens. Just like tradition says "you have to follow", I say, "Do I have to follow without questioning?" (Hlatshwayo, August 2004, 57)

Musa can question in safety because the South African Constitution, which came into force in 1996, granted individual rights that challenged the traditional structures and granted rights to women to give them controls (or potential controls) that they did not have before.

In Durban it is individuals with strong political and moral convictions who see the power of dance to challenge. In this context, I focus on two case studies: first, a girls' project in a township in the eThekwini Metropolitan Municipality designed to help them to understand their rights and to grow strong, and second, the products of two dance companies and their choreographers, who are currently making work that challenges the new received wisdoms. Can a White person belong here? Can a newly enriched Black person lose his humanity? Can a society recover its heart or, indeed, grow a new one?

Beauty and the Butterfly

Dudlu Ntombi: Arise iMvemvane[2] is the girls' project run by the Flatfoot Dance Company in KwaMashu, a sprawling township located some distance out of the city that was built for Black South Africans under the now abolished Group Areas Act. In KwaMashu poverty is great and crime levels are high, unemployment is widespread, dysfunctional families are many, rape and domestic violence are commonplace, much of the community support that exists in rural parts of South Africa has broken down, and local support services are minimal.

Dudlu Ntombi is a group of girls who were chosen not for their dance talent but for their potential for growth. In the audition they had to explain why they are special, present a scene focusing on what they considered to be women's role in society, and dance a taught sequence while adding their own dance language as they saw fit. The group members work harmoniously, and each participant has a clear sense of why she is there and what she wants to gain from the process—that is, the girls have ownership of their work. They perform with growing confidence alongside other young people.

Time is spent in discussion each week. Not every discussion topic finds its way into the group's performances, but these discussions clearly strengthen the girls' physical confidence and readiness to take criticism and make demands of themselves and to work as a team with their tutors and with each other. As women they are becoming more fulfilled and they are learning that the rights they have heard about are accompanied by responsibilities.

We (Flatfoot Dance Company) have facilitated sessions on speaking out and reporting child abuses to the police and local authorities. We encourage the girls to take an active role in ensuring that their rights as children are defended; in doing so, we encourage them to develop self-awareness and pride (Flatfoot Dance Company 2005).

Crossing Altogether to Another Place

Jay Pather, the artistic director of the Siwela Sonke Dance Theatre, has taken work to the World Social Forum in Mumbai, to the steps of the Cathedral of St. John the Divine in Manhattan (of New York City) for Season South Africa, and to Constitution Hill, a part of Johannesburg's cultural arc. Siwela Sonke, the name of which means crossing over to another place, runs extensive outreach programs and training projects, as do most professional dance companies in this country. Pather is an exceptional writer and speaker and is often in demand for interviews. His personality and his work would make a worthy subject for another chapter or book. But here I want to focus on my understanding of his politics—the political place that he wishes to occupy, in 2005, in a South Africa that, while a miracle state compared with the authoritarian, undemocratic, and exploitative police state it once was, has disappointed many who worked for its overthrow. The new South Africa has a model constitution but is mired in corruption, crime, and defensiveness toward criticism, all of which bring fresh problems, while poverty, unemployment, and fatal disease are a continuation of old problems.

Pather began his dance career as a young Indian intellectual who supported his father's struggle to overthrow apartheid but saw his own struggle as being on a different terrain—that of commenting as an artist. Growing in confidence as a gay man, as an Indian South African with

The Siwela Sonke Dance Theatre in Season South Africa, New York City.
Photo by Storm Janse van Rensburg

two degrees and a Fulbright Scholarship behind him living in a changing South Africa, and as an artist and choreographer, he returned to Durban from Cape Town in 1996 to direct the Siwela Sonke Dance Theatre and to be the midwife in its emergence as a professional company. The immediate challenge was to make a dance performance to take to India. He titled it "Ahimsa-Ubuntu," and it was a work that used Black, White, and Indian dancers to depict the history of South Africa from the arrival of both White settlers and Indian indentured laborers to the overthrow of the White regime. This was followed by an overtly angry and polemical piece, "Unclenching the Fist," that dealt with domestic violence and the abuse of women.

Since those early days his work has become increasingly oblique. Using a multimedia approach that is often site specific, his formal comment is harder to fully grasp in a single viewing, but it is strongly there in the complex layers of sound, film, text, and movement. As he states, "The political framework is skeletal, threadbare, a structure of very fine, almost invisible, thread. It is there, and then it slips" (Pather 2003, 83). His personal connection to the issue or, rather, to how the issue affects him, is not apparently significant in the narrative. He has become an omniscient commentator: His maleness, his gayness, his Indianness, and his identity are not the issues that concern him when he creates a performance. What is conveyed to the audience is a larger morality, from a detached perspective, where the artist is working with the material—the idea, the content, the site, the specific skills of the performers, the film that can be found—to build a postmodern creation. Pather argues, "I don't think I've got to make a political point in the actual work" (Pather 2003, 83). The aesthetics generate that.

The piece created for Constitution Hill in March 2005 exemplifies where Pather stands in relation to dance, power, and difference. Ayi Kwei Armah's novel about corruption, neglect, and decay in postindependent Ghana, *The Beautyful Ones Are Not Yet Born*, provoked the title and underpinning of the work, which Pather entitled *The Beautiful Ones Must Be Born*. As Pather explains, "South Africa needs them. We cannot go down that road (to neglect and decay)" (Pather 2004). These are the messages implicit in his title.

Johannesburg is the site of the Constitutional Court in South Africa. The court is built on the side of a hill next to the Old Fort, a prison constructed in 1892 by the first colonial rulers of the Transvaal Republic. In its time, the prison housed both British and Boer prisoners. Later, when it became a prison for Blacks, other people, including pass offenders, people on trial for treason, Nelson Mandela, and even Mahatma Gandhi, were incarcerated there. The Old Fort Prison and the women's prison next door were both incorporated within the area now known as *Constitution Hill*.[3] The complex is open to visitors; only the chambers of the court's judges are not open to the public. Much has changed from the Old Fort's days as a prison; it has been transformed into an inspiring place, filled with the works of artists and craftsmen. The doors, the name displayed on the front wall, the carpets—all were tendered by artists. And Durban can lay claim to many of those tenders.

In his Constitutional Court piece, Pather used first the broad, shallow steps alongside the court, then the courtyard outside the court entrance, then the exterior of the Awaiting Trial Block, and finally a lit cell as spaces for his performers. He projected slides and film onto the blockhouses used to guard the prisoners. At one point the audience was stationed on the artificial hill that forms one wall of the prison, from which the whole Constitution Hill complex is visible, and was looking down on a circular stage, on which a Mbeki-like ringmaster strutted (South Africa's president is Thabo Mbeki). Pather's performers ranged from White ballet dancers wearing white tutus and white face paint to Black Shembe (a Zulu form of Christianity) dancers in white robes and white face paint to a Kathak dancer dressed all in white, with a full satin skirt, bare feet, bells on her ankles, and white face paint, to a Black beggar in ragged jackets to a Black male in a smart suit representing a 1950s political activist. In Mandela's courtyard, while a Black man in a pinstriped suit walked on an exercise machine, a film of a poverty-stricken informal settlement so speeded up that its image was blurred was thrown onto a blockhouse. Meanwhile, two ballet dancers in romantic tutus and green gloves tended the grass growing around the running machine. The Kathak dancer occasionally, and laconically, sped up the exercise machine, and Mr. Sleazy Entrepreneur began to trot, and then to run, and then to hurtle. Then the film slowed little by little until every detail of the poverty—the dirt, the ragged children, and the clogged stream—could be seen.

During the section of the piece taking place in the cell, film blown up on a blockhouse was accompanied by text from an account of the numerous bail hearings of Thulebona Mzizi, the artistic director of God's Golden Acre Performing Arts Academy who was arrested on suspicion of two murders, crimes for which there is proof that he is innocent and for which he is currently out on bail. The text unemotionally records the chaos that sometimes enters our legal system and the loss of human rights and dignity of those whom the police decide to persecute. Layers of irony permeate the reading—a reading that is taking place in a jail alongside the spanking new concrete realization of all the ideals of the new democracy and new constitution: the Constitutional Court.

Pather's next piece created later the same year, another site-specific work, was created for the centenary of the Natal Society of Arts and held in the society's gallery. It had as its threadbare structure the relationship between a rural Black woman and an urban White boy. It's an unlikely scenario but the audience must use its own experience to make sense of it. One member of the audience interpreted it as "this thing with the maid." For many White men, the Black women they see the most often are the servants in their homes, and "this thing" occurs, in their minds at least. There is power in it, and there is difference, and now, in the 21st century, there are ghosts. The ghosts hang heavily around everything we say and do; everything is loaded. In South Africa the people are aware of this, but it is true of everywhere. It means that a person can create something that is intensely political but can seem simply off the wall; the creation can sound familiar but prod unfamiliar thoughts.

As a sophisticated postmodern man in a postmodern world, the world of Africa, Pather knows that art cannot be used to tell someone something, that all messages are received differently, that what we "get is not what we see." He now hopes that "a healthy uncertainty . . . may be our salvation" (Pather 2004).

Politics of Belonging

As I write this in 2005, Durban has four professional dance companies. The university dance company known as Flatfoot is the second example that I am including in my case study of dance companies who produce political works. In addition to producing performances, Flatfoot runs outreach projects such as Dudlu Ntombi. The artistic director of Flatfoot is Lliane Loots, a senior lecturer in the Drama and Performance Studies Department of the University of KwaZulu-Natal and the director of the Jomba! Contemporary Dance Festival that is run by the university's Centre for Creative Arts. The eighth Jomba! festival loomed as this chapter was being written and was seeking to build on the success of the 2004 event, which celebrated 10 years of South African democracy and included a conference on African contemporary dance, questioning issues of a performance aesthetic for a developing and independent continent.

Loots works with a more personal political agenda than Pather does, describing her politics as the politics of belonging. She was involved in the overthrow of the illegitimate White regime that introduced apartheid and that put legalized racism on the statute books. During the struggle to overthrow the regime she spent some time in jail. She is a White woman who loves the country, loves its landscape and its people, and she deals with her feminism, her environmental radicalism, and her Whiteness in her performances. She believes that the more personal you get, the more universal you get. She also deals with the stories and hurts of her dancers. One of her dancers, Musa Hlatshwayo, is a choreographer in his own right and choreographed "Abakhwetha" for Jomba! 2002. This work dealt with the issue of circumcision for adolescent boys in the Xhosa tradition and depicted the death of one of the initiates.[4] For Jomba! 2004, Hlatshwayo choreographed "Umthombi," in which he dealt with the pathways and rites of the passage to manhood of a young rural Black man.

I want to focus in particular on Loots' May 2005 season, *Acts of Love Under a Southern Moon*, a work that is described as being choreographed and devised by Loots, though her method is effectively one of collaboration. During the crafting of the work, the dancers often create the movements. Loots is clear as to the shapes and spaces she wants, and as the choreographer she weaves the movements the dancers have created into the sections she requires. She often uses poetry, sometimes her own poetry, in her works. In her collaboration with poets, they talk first, and then she sifts and edits their material.

Six dancers and three poets work with no set, just striking lighting, slides or film on the back of the stage, music, and slides about love projected onto the floor at the front of the stage. The audience watches in quiet bemusement as a series of narratives—a series of small moments—unfolds

"Umthombi," choreographed by Musa Hlatshwayo.
Photo by Val Adamson.

before their eyes and ears. It is left to them to work out how it all fits together; there is no directing narrative. It is a work that benefits from many viewings—its layers cannot be taken in on one viewing. The first section has the poets in the middle, in a circle of light, with the dancers in different configurations moving in and around a square of light that is also moving. The poetry is about personal love, that of a man for a woman, a man who is softened and made whole and full of awe by his love. In one section a man keeps falling, and the woman with him keeps picking him up, righting him, and leaving him to manage on his own, again and again.

The stage darkens, and a new narrative starts. A jigged-up "Somewhere Over the Rainbow" signals a change of pace, and bounce and freedom appear in the movement. Slides show Nelson Mandela and the others accused in the Rivonia Trial, which led to sentences of life imprisonment on Robben Island. On the floor appear the words LEARNING TO LOVE BY BEING STILL AND WAITING. As the dancers flow happily about the stage, the audience realizes that there is always one, though not always the same one, standing still.

The next section starts with the voice of a man who cannot be seen and with three women in glamorous dresses standing in three separate pools of light. The women fall over, and the man's voice apologizes to his woman for beating her. He promises to never do it again. The women stand up. They fall to the ground again, and the man's voice repeats his repentance. Then the three male dancers put on girls' dresses, and a young man's voice tells the story of how, when he was little, his granny would notice that men had come to the village, and she would make him put on his sister's dress for the duration of these men's visit. On the floor we see the words LEARNING TO WEAR A DRESS, and we hear the child's voice explaining that these men had come to take the boy children away to fight in the battles over "who will lead us when we get our freedom." Each section ends in an atmosphere of quiet dignity.

LEARNING TO LOVE MY INNER VOICE, says the slogan on the floor, and the poets get angrier and more perplexed. "How did our minds accommodate freedom so suddenly? How come the Bush becomes so powerful? How come honesty's become a rarity?" We are told the story of a dream in which a young couple goes to the beach to enjoy quiet time alone. She is abducted, and he is "too full of holes" to be able to save her. But, the poets say, "We're living, we're loving, we're surviving."

In LEARNING TO LOVE THE THERMAL UPDRAFT, the voice is that of Loots speaking about her difficulty in looking up and out at the world and about how she puts her trust instead in the ground in front of her. Meanwhile the dancers lift and fly and lilt and roll, using each other's support as they do so. Loots speaks the following:

> The wandering albatross mates for life. They find each other and remain committed to a journey back every second year to the same breeding ground. They are solitary birds, spending up to nine months at a time at sea, drifting, fishing, and using the thermal updraft to hold them in the air. But come mating season, instinct, cosmology, and weather lead them home.

> I am mated for life to this country. It is as if my internal meteorology and magnetic cues kick in and, no matter what, I am always coming home. It is like an internal love song that the wandering albatross has begun to teach me.

> I have been made to feel like the displaced White woman that walks like an exile in her own land. But displacement, like the wandering albatross whose instinct brings it back to remembered geography, has little or nothing to do with earth justice. The earth holds a place for all of us; ashes to ashes and dust to dust. Regeneration and a cycle that goes on beyond even our imagined life spans. I am learning to trust the thermal updraft to hold me.

And in LEARNING THAT LOVE IS A PILGRIMAGE, the poets speak about Mecca, a "place" to which one must journey to "find the Mecca in me," to find a comfortable identity in the new South Africa. This journey is about "a rebirth of faith, hope, and trust."

Both Flatfoot and Siwela Sonke work across genres. Very seldom do they make pure dance works. They use text, film, and actors. Doing this enables them to be political, to be nuanced, and to find wider audiences. They are making the work that they feel personally inspired to make. Dance is their starting point. They invariably have something to say, and their visual and aural senses and their relationships with other artists allow them to think widely.

Pather and Loots are not the only choreographers in Durban in 2005 making work that challenges and criticizes. Sbonakaliso Ndaba of the Phenduka Dance Theatre, the 2003 winner of the DaimlerChrysler Choreography Award (a national dance competition), makes work that provides her young dancers with a means of finding their anger at the way apartheid provided the context for them to be treated like and to feel like lesser beings and of coalescing that anger so that it is turned into a work of art. This is a form of empowerment that helps to make both the choreographer and the dancer whole. It helps them to find the "rebirth of faith, hope, and trust" that Loots speaks of.

David Gouldie of the Fantastic Flying Fish Dance Company, a winner of multiple awards and a finalist in the DaimlerChrysler choreography competition of 2003, created a piece for that competition that allowed White dancers to express their confusion, their ghosts, and their desire to make new, real, and honest connections. None of these choreographers allows their anger to get in the way of their art and their morality, as we all struggle to free ourselves of the ghosts and to deal honestly with our confusions and hurts. What could be more powerful? What society can do without artists offering their pain and their analyses?

Dance as a Unifying Force With the Potential for Nation Building

There are idealists who know that nation building is an awesomely difficult task and that patriotism can be dangerous and divisive. Groups come together at the expense of other groups. These activists want to bring people together and to encourage them to work together, so that they learn both to respect other ways of doing things and to make new ways of doing things together.

KwaZulu-Natal has an umbrella dance organization, KZN DanceLink that includes professional companies of all genres and races as well as community groups and dance schools. Its members work together and

Dance for Youth, held October 2004 at God's Golden Acre.
Photo by P. Taylor

share teachers, and once a year the organization puts on a large-scale open-air production that brings together all its young members in a celebration of Dance for Youth. The year 2006 saw its fifth production, and the dynamics of that production, as well as its outcomes, form the next case study.

KZN DanceLink has been in existence for 10 years, and it now enjoys funding from lotteries so that it is able to run an office, respond to invitations to perform, and implement its own projects. One of its first initiatives was to run the weekly workshops at God's Golden Acre. It now runs workshops in three children's homes, and it also funds Dudlu Ntombi. It offers an annual showcase, called *Imbumba*, featuring the work of member groups. It has workshops for dance educators in the Arts and Culture Curriculum in schools, and it gives annual awards in Durban for choreography, dance, and technical support, such as lighting, design, and publicity. The organization gives these awards in the belief that its dancers, choreographers, and support industries are of a very high standard and deserve recognition. The fact that membership cuts across all dance genres and all dance levels means that developing the ground rules for each of these initiatives leads to debate. Through this process the members learn about each other, and they learn how to negotiate, compromise, show respect for each other, and welcome each other. As such, this process is a strengthening of the dance community. Given South Africa's history and the walls that existed between all communities, the need for spaces in which we can learn about each other and be honest with each another is urgent as we build our nation. KZN DanceLink offers a small but powerful reason to hope.

Conclusion

This chapter has focused on dance as an example of political activism, pressure groups, single-issue groups, the influence of history, the influence of struggle, and being part of a larger social and political change. It has not focused on dance as dance, an art occasionally affected by outside influences. There are people in Durban with a mission, and their chosen vehicle, because it is what they most love, is dance and the making of dance. The province as a whole has a striking number of such people, and they feed off each other. That reinforcement is itself a sociological phenomenon worth investigating. Most of all, in a world where much is in flux and confusion, where there is a danger of losing what is most valuable in our relationships with each other, as individuals, as groups, as nations, and as Bush-like axes, it is a cause for celebration.

The choreographer Gregory Maqoma, a keynote speaker at the 2004 Jomba! Conference, was speaking for all South Africa and Africa but especially for Durban when he said the following:

African Contemporary Dance marks a new wave of choreographers who are breaking barriers and who have adopted a "tell it as it is" slogan. These dance makers are thriving and carrying contemporary dance into another level that transcends cultural barriers and creates a new dynamic culture that is constantly reproducing history by virtue of how they actually live and respond to your circumstances. Our contemporary moment is particularly exciting despite the political quagmire in which this continent is mired. More in the area of finding an appropriation—the work we are putting on our stages signals change, signals artistic freedom that fuses mud, hearts, intellect, Armani suits, ball gowns and naked bodies. This is innovation and a true reflection of our continent today. (Maqoma 2005, 29)

REFLECTIONS

Reverend Gardner C. Taylor, one of America's preeminent preachers, speaks of the difficulty of African Americans who, in the United States, must find their freedom within the culture that has long oppressed them. So too must the South Africans who were oppressed by an apartheid government; who suffered physical, spiritual, and psychological violence; and who heroically sought to regain their human freedom and dignity find their freedom within the oppressing culture. They tell their powerful and moving stories through the arts. Anyone who has seen the paintings of Nelson Mandela, as he gave color to the gray surroundings of his prison on Robben Island, has witnessed the healing and transformative action of art as it captures the hope of possibility or the vision of that which does not yet exist. In the works of the artists that Lynn Maree speaks of in this chapter, we find the embodied meaning of the lives lived within the context of oppression. Social reality is placed before us as a narrative of political and aesthetic struggle. These works lead us to examine the relationship that we ourselves have with the story being told. In this artistic space, where none are guilty but all are responsible, we come face to face with our own humanity. Allowing others to share their stories with us connects us in ways that supersede art for art's sake—it pushes us beyond our own artistic boundaries, demanding a human response that is grounded in our ethical beliefs and commitments and not simply in artistic appreciation. We move beyond the realm of rational knowing into the world of passion and social justice. It is surely the latter that grounds the desire for a different kind of world—one of compassion, love, and justice. Remembering in this sense is the act of identifying the self in all of its creative, critical, spiritual, and ethical dimensions and its responsibility to the other. It is the process of finding a home in a torn and afflicted world.

Notes

1. Gramsci's concept of hegemony referred to the way a social group could maintain its dominance over others in society less through overt coercion or force and more through the achievement of shared beliefs, assumptions, and values that persuade the subordinate groups that they have common interests with those who rule over them.

2. *Dudlu Ntombi* is a traditional Zulu compliment paid to young girls who possess inner beauty and strength and who are seen as deserving of respect by members of their community. *IMvemvane* is isiZulu for butterfly. The

essence of the project is to embark on a sustainable process of gender awareness for young girls between 10 and 20 years of age and to help them realize their self-worth and power as individuals within a community.

3. See www.constitutionhill.co.za.

4. "Abakhwetha" was later invited to the Fifth Choreographic Encounters of Africa and the Indian Ocean held in Madagascar.

PART II REFLECTIVE QUESTIONS

- How has dance historically reinforced prejudices and stereotypes about the "normal" body?
- Is it possible to modify our assumptions about what constitutes excellence in dance performance? (Do moral considerations require that we do that?)
- Does modern dance disrupt or reinforce dominant conceptions of masculine identity?
- How do the arts and dance provide a sense of possibility and hope toward changing the conditions of human suffering and oppression? Can you give specific examples of the ways that dance contributes to liberation and social transformation?

part III

Conversations on Dance for a Multicultural World

seven

Common Experience Creates Magnitudes of Meaning

Ann Kipling Brown

Professor in dance education
Arts education programs
University of Regina
Regina, Saskatchewan

In this chapter I explore, through personal story and description of experiences with schoolchildren and preservice teachers, the role of dance in helping us to consciously connect with our bodies and to creatively express ourselves. On the one hand the learning from these experiences is personal and multifaceted, but on the other hand it coincides and connects, creating a community of learners. In my teaching I plan for a safe and caring environment in which we can explore our uniqueness as well as our place in the group. I want students to understand the importance of context and the role of those students on the margins. I believe that through the dance experiences that I design, students are able to resist and reframe social contexts and to learn to become critical and visionary thinkers so that they can imagine their world differently. Together we can examine globalization through economic and political shifts and question how it detraditionalizes some dance forms, taking away the essence of and respect for the form. We can also look at the exciting and challenging opportunities afforded by taking a global perspective and viewing the world as a unity of all individuals and interacting cultures.

Dancing Together

The students move one by one to join each other in a shape sculpture, clasping hands, grasping shoulders, leaning on torsos, touching feet and legs. Their bodies make various shapes—big, small, and twisted—at different levels and with shades of gentleness and firmness in their connections. And then there is stillness. I ask the group to slowly melt to the floor. Each student accommodates the other, melting more slowly; the students adjust bodies, rolling over another, sliding from beneath someone, so that they do not take another's space. Finally there is a collapsed shape on the floor—some bodies are intertwined, some are curled tightly, and some are spread out to provide space for others. I ask the students to form the group shape once again. They carefully remold, adjusting and accommodating each other. We repeat the melting, and this time it happens more quickly but still carefully and thoughtfully. I ask them to move away from each other, and they roll, wriggle, slide, pull, and push themselves as far away as possible. I ask them to move back to the group and remold. They do this with mindfulness of each other and the space around them. The dance ends in stillness.

The students like the challenge, and when the group is reshaped and has held for a few moments, they collapse in a heap of laughter and chatter as they realize they have succeeded in the task without anyone being hurt or left behind. They recognize their commitment and are proud of themselves. I read this in their laughter and hear it in their comments: "That was fun!" "Did you see me as I rolled over you?" "I didn't know where I was when we went back to the group."

The group is made up of 36 young people, both male and female, and of mixed race and ability. Half of the group is a class of 13-year-olds from a local school, and the other half is a class of undergraduate preservice teachers from the Arts Education Program in which I teach. I have brought these young people together for two reasons: first, to create a positive dance experience for young students who do not have a dance program in their school, and second, to provide an opportunity for the preservice teachers to work closely with students in a school environment. When the group has finished its task, the classroom teacher and I applaud the group members on their work and acknowledge that they were responsive and responsible. The teacher draws her students' attention to the role of communication, an area that she has been working on with this class for the year, and says that this dance demonstrates the students' understanding and ability to work together and exchange ideas. I talk about the idea for my group dance and how our earlier activities have led to this final dance. I describe the clear shaping of their bodies as they moved and came to stillness. I mention the care and attention they exhibited as they melted together, moved away from the group, and then returned to remake the shape. I talk about the expression of their movements as they changed their direction or speed to accommodate someone else and about how the joining together was done with gentleness and attention for others.

This dance was the final piece of a series of lessons with this group of 13-year-old boys and girls who do not have regular dance classes. In the previous lessons we had explored various ways of moving in place, in the room, and with another person, always attaching a theme or mood to the moving. We had practiced skills, such as traveling across the room in various rhythmic locomotor patterns. Each student had paired with a preservice teacher, and there were conversations about dance and the movements that we were exploring. At times there was laughter as the group struggled with a new concept or found a movement awkward or strange. There were interesting and caring comments about the work we

A shape sculpture.
Photo courtesy of Ann Kipling Brown.

observed, whether we were observing the video footage I had selected or their own dance phrases. And verbal comments and written observations demonstrated that there was obviously some deep learning about the self and the possibilities for expressing oneself through movement. The group members saw connections to their everyday world and to the popular culture surrounding them.

I am always disappointed when I learn how little dance takes place in the classrooms of a province where arts education is part of the core curriculum, in which dance together with drama, music, and visual art has 50 minutes allotted each week. I am pleased to work with teachers who are keen to weave dance into their busy schedules, and I hope that when I leave they continue with the dancing. I know that the dance experience I facilitate will influence the students, particularly those who enter the space with reluctance and ask me in skeptical and challenging voices about what we are going to do. They tell me that they don't want to dance and describe it as "sissy" and "silly." How many times have I heard those comments and risen to the challenge to prove that dance is a worthwhile endeavor that can be part of their lives!

Talking About the Experience

The group dance experience is also an opportunity to provide learning experiences for the preservice teachers, to confirm the role of dance in young people's lives, and to show that it is possible to introduce dance into a school program. In my university dance education courses I try to provide dance experiences with children of varying ages, from the preschooler to the senior grade levels. I pose three questions to the preservice teachers: What did these experiences mean to you? What did you learn? How could you use these experiences to plan your own dance lessons? The preservice teachers comment positively about the group dance experience. Several stated that "they are much more confident going into the classroom and teaching dance" (Anne). One felt that he had "been able to grow not only as a professional, but as an individual. For example, I never realized how much I enjoy working with young children. Watching them grow and get excited about learning, to me, is a beautiful experience" (Ryan). Personal and professional growth were mentioned by many of the preservice teachers, and the experience confirmed for them that they have made the right choice and that "taking these opportunities make you better able to teach" (Bobbi). Several said they had learned much about themselves, about how they "react to different situations." They learned that their "enthusiasm really rubs off on young people" (Diane), that they were able to talk and motivate young children, and that listening to the young students was most important. They felt that they had learned at first hand "that children learn differently and that children at the same age may be at a different stage of development" (Cherry). One preservice teacher who had never taken dance lessons until university said that she had "learned the magic of dance and imagination working with the students" (Lynette). Several of the teachers felt that "it was important to make learning fun for students and see students enjoy their learning experience through the arts" (Mary). Several agreed that "creative dance is beneficial to students" and that it "helps with their creativity" (Susan). The students learned not only about dance but also about other life skills, such as "trusting others" (Mary), "fairness and respect for others" (Sarah), and "skills in relating and supporting others" (Anne). The majority of the preservice teachers agreed that "a well-planned lesson is worth the time" (Paul) and that the experiences provided "valuable resources" (Bobbi). One person explained that she would "take these experiences into consideration, as they will help me to determine appropriate activities" (Cherry). One student stated, "I could use these experiences to plan my own dance lessons because they are already set out for me and I know that they will work" (Tara).

The classroom teacher and I proudly related this experience to the other teachers in the school and then I retold the story to my colleagues in the Arts Education Program. We wanted them to understand what we had witnessed. The students had worked together and through the medium of dance had demonstrated their understanding and their ability to work collaboratively and collectively. The classroom teacher was overjoyed that her work on communication skills had paid off, and I was ecstatic to have another experience that confirmed my beliefs in the power of dance and its role in the education of young people. More important, the experience strengthened my involvement in dance and my exploration into what occurs when we learn and teach dance.

Our Dance Journeys

This group dance experience has become a part of a journey that I have been taking for many years. I believe that in telling stories of experiences like this one, we unearth what is truly important in the education of young people. One of the first things that I ask preservice teachers to do when they begin their work in dance education is to relate their previous experiences in dance and to reflect on how those experiences had affected them. We investigate the stories of those who have made dance their life, including local dance teachers and artists as well as dancers who are celebrated nationally and internationally. We consider the significance of dance in the lives of people in our community as well as in the lives of people from other parts of the world. My preservice teachers and I live in a community where we encounter families that have immigrated to Canada for varying and often tragic reasons. It is exciting and rewarding to learn about each other through our language, dance, and other cultural practices. It is often a challenge for teachers, particularly for young preservice teachers, to deal with the social, political, and personal pressures of each individual in their classroom and to juggle dealing with these pressures with the academic and administrative requirements of the school environment. On the one hand we can tell stores of incidents in which we missed a valuable insight into a situation or stories of teachable moments that flew out of our grasp, and on the other hand we can talk of the influences that shaped our lives and made teaching a rewarding experience.

Each year I examine my own story, and in it I find interesting parallels to and ideas and values that intersect with the stories of the preservice teachers. The following stories relate some of the values and processes that have guided me in selecting dance experiences for others and myself. Collectively they are my story of finding those values, working collaboratively with colleagues in arts education, and establishing my role as a dance educator. Good stories are usually filled with details and complexities; their plots and subplots take the reader in several new directions while maintaining a central theme or flow. Story is an appropriate metaphor for my journey in dance education. Weaving through all my stories is dance. The following selected stories particularize and highlight the effect that dancing has had on me and on others I have danced with.

The Beginning Story

I have always wanted to be a teacher. At an early age I was interested in teaching geography. Maybe I was interested in teaching because I did well at school and interested in geography because my family traveled so much. At age 10 I moved to India with my family and was able to study Manipuri, an Indian classical dance form, as well as pursue ballet, tap, and acrobatics. I loved my dance classes. I adored my teachers. I was happy to spend private time practicing the steps and patterns. I believed that I had found a place where I was truly at home. My experience in Manipuri and the friendships I formed with several Indian girls revealed to me some of the culture of those friends and of my teacher. My teacher unraveled the stories we were dancing and explained the deeper meaning of the particular movements and dances as they related to the customs and religion of the people. While these dance experiences added to my interest in dance, they also made me question what I was doing in the ballet class. Though I retained my passion and love for dance, the ballet class had started to bore me. The exercises became tedious, and we never seemed to dance. It also became apparent to me that the ballet teachers did not enjoy teaching the mixed dance class of young English, American, and Indian girls. Then a new teacher arrived. She was much older that our previous teachers were. She was tall and elegant, had an exotic name, and smelled of expensive perfume and cigarette smoke. She shared her love of ballet and the history and background of the genre. The most important experience she gave me was the opportunity at the end of ballet class to improvise and create my own version of the classical ballet stories as well as create my own dances. I was in heaven. Even though at the time I could not articulate what she had given to me, I now know that a seed had been sown.

The Study Story

The seeds sown by these gifted teachers were nurtured during high school and college. I was still passionate about dance, and it was very clear that I wanted to pursue the teaching profession. However, I wanted to teach dance, not geography. At that time it was not possible to study dance as a discrete area of study, so I entered into a physical education program in a college of education. The program embraced the philosophy of Rudolf Laban and prepared teachers to focus on the child's needs in modern educational dance, gymnastics, and games. It was important to provide the analysis and vocabulary for these movement areas and for the children to experiment and discover their own ways of moving, both functionally and expressively. The focus in dance was to find a personal way of moving to express an idea, thought, or feeling and to introduce the prescribed and distilled vocabularies of the adult dance world, such as ballet, jazz, and modern dance, at a later stage. This open and unrestricted way of moving was a delight to me, providing me with opportunities to create choreography on themes such as oppression, struggle, and freedom. I remember creating a duo with a very good friend that reflected the tensions of power and how the class was moved by our dance and applauded our choreography. I knew that the class had understood our message and that what we had said could have been said only through movement.

The Teaching Story

Even though I was excited by the personal and imaginative approach to dance, I also wanted to understand the vocabulary and choreography of others. And I was lucky! One of my first teaching jobs took me to London, where I could attend a great variety of dance classes and performances. I would find myself participating in a contemporary jazz class during the day and attending an Indian classical dance performance in the evening! This immersion in the London dance scene was an exciting and stimulating professional development for me. It certainly influenced my teaching, at times sending me into a tizzy of possibilities for my students. I wanted them to experience what I was experiencing and to find the joy and passion in dance that I had found. And I think I succeeded in the public school setting—not with everyone, of course, but with many who realized that they could dance and had something to say through movement. I was not as successful in the private studio setting, where most directors expected that the students would follow the traditional dance syllabus and examinations.

I decided to focus on the public school setting and to create opportunities for young people who had never danced before or for young people who wanted to extend their dance experience. It was at this time that I realized that my dances often had a political message. I created three dance groups for the different age groups that attended the free extracurricular dance classes provided by the education authority. As the groups became more defined in their membership and eager to share their dances with others, I asked them to choose their names. One student from the teenage group said very clearly that the group should be called *Vision and Sound*, since "the dances were about what was happening to people in the world and we made sure that people heard the stories" (Personal Journal 1979). I realized that the themes and music I was selecting resonated with these young people. It was the time of the popular television production *Roots*, which told the story of Black slavery and its devastating effects on the people and their cultures. One dance group, which was predominantly made up of British and Jamaican girls, embraced the theme and music. The girls created their own story and performance, and the choreography was emotionally received by their parents, their friends, and the school administration.

All of these experiences, many of which are retained in dog-eared teaching files and journals, made teaching a joy for me. However, I was not blind to what Hart (2001, 165) was talking about when he said, "Contemporary schools often embody a 'culture of fear,' from fear-based reform to the fear engendered in students who must produce one right answer, to the teachers who must deal with extraordinary demands from others and their own limitations, to the fearful separation inherent in the dominant objectivist ways of knowing." I was cognizant at that time and am still aware today that school is not always a happy or safe place for some of my students and that what they experience in the dance class is not viewed as significant.

I know full well that at that time the arts were not accepted and that today they are still not fully accepted as mainstream curriculum. The first areas to be cut from the school program are the arts. I am also aware of the disempowerment of teachers who are faced with oppressive curricular demands, expected to focus on competition and standardized testing, and provided with little or no support for personal or professional development. I know that at times I protected myself by being silent and avoiding conflict with school administration and that it would have been easier to be compliant or to drop out. However, I know that I did empower some of those students and gave them a reason to attend school and find their own voice. It was this knowledge, which was often reinforced when I heard news of their careers and endeavors—not always in dance, but that does not matter—that shaped my career in education.

The Teacher Education Story

While working with students in the public school setting, I had opportunities to present my work to college students, to lead dance education courses with preservice teachers, and to supervise undergraduate and graduate students in teaching contexts. It seemed possible that I could help future teachers to notice the inner significance of their lives and to understand and care about others through dance. I felt that there was a possibility to implement change at this level and to encourage future teachers to be courageous and use their imagination. I am still convinced that educational change is possible and that the arts will be viewed as contributing to the education of our young people. As Horan (2000, x) stated, "Substantive educational change cannot occur without conversation. Not the kind of conversation that currently is ubiquitous in our schools, but a post-formal conversation that facilitates new educational designs, creative problem-solving, and personal and collective critical reflection on theory and practice." We delude ourselves into thinking that change is optional. However, change is inevitable, and our responsibility is both personal and communal. Change does not often occur in substantial measures; rather, through small and incremental actions people can be agents in their own transformation as well as in the transformation of others. According to Hart (2001, 153), "Transformation is a dialectic of expression and reception, contraction and expansion, self-separateness and union, autonomy and interconnection, intention and surrender, initiating and allowing, control and flow, structure and freedom, and so forth." This dynamic interplay reverberates with my understanding of teaching as providing times when the control of the experience involves letting go of the leadership and entering a place of collaboration. The interplay also exists during the times of creativity that demand hard work and intention as well as inspiration and vision. Hart explains that these attributes can appear to be bipolar and far apart. However, when viewed from a different perspective, "they emerge as different aspects of the same wave, an undivided unity" (Hart 2001, 153).

Dance Meanings

Dance makes way for possibility, allowing for multiple meanings, personal invention, and reconfiguration of ideas. This feature of dance furthers the students' ability to engage in critical and visionary thinking. It is imperative that we encourage students, particularly those who will be working with future generations, to fully engage life and to enter into and debate the viewpoints of others. The dance educator can be viewed as a person who opens the doors to the potential of living life to the fullest, using the arts to question, to explore, and to dream. I have no doubt of the power of the arts and of the particular role that dance plays in comprehending events and finding a fruitful and an energetic way of living in the world. Whether you are attending your first full-length ballet or creating a dance to show your response to a disaster in another place or dancing freely with your friends, dance has the potency to exemplify life. I know personally of the effect that dance has had on my life; at times it has provided solace, excitement, and renewal in both my personal and my professional lives. Nancy Beardall (2005) revealed the effects of dance on a diverse group of students in her chapter, "Dance the Dream: Reflections on an Eighth Grade Dance Class." In the dance experience she describes, she "wanted to give everyone the opportunity to look at our differences in order to come to a better understanding of each other" (7). The results of this project were powerful:

> The gift of Dance the Dream was the chance for individual students to move from not knowing each other and even being intimidated and afraid of each other to dancing together in a community. By doing so, each student came to recognize her authentic voice and her movement voice, which allowed her to trust herself enough to be true to who she was and open to the possibility of connection and partnering in a creative dance that expressed a relational model of community and support. (Beardall 2005, 15)

A four-year-old group and I dance our interpretation of "Jack and the Beanstalk." The varied shapes of the beans, the growth of the beanstalk, the strides of the giant, and the alertness of Jack transpose the story into an embodied knowing of the tale of good and evil. The four-year-olds tell me how they thought the giant strides were fun to do and how they liked hiding from the giant when they played the role of Jack. They draw their curly and twisted beanstalks and explain how important it was for Jack to take home the treasure to his mother. A third-grade class skips and gallops across the room, the students excited about achieving the technical skills of the locomotor patterns as well as successfully following the changing floor plans I present. Sixth-grade students articulate what they have learned while attending a powwow. Preservice dance educators describe a dance from Korea and share the background information they have found. Another group of preservice dance educators creates and performs a dance that focuses on an issue of discrimination that has affected them personally. In all instances I ask the students to reflect on what the dance experience and knowledge provide for them in their particular context.

I am inspired by the knowledge that these young people bring to their dance classes. I observe them communicating through dance, developing a discipline and a way of living in the world, exploring and coming to understand an issue in a different way, transferring this knowledge into other parts of their lives, and, most of all, developing their cultural knowledge. Dance ethnographer Deidre Sklar (1991, 6) explains that "dance is a kind of cultural knowledge" and that "dancing is not just somatic, but mental and emotional as well, encompassing history, beliefs, values and feelings." She explains that "cultural knowledge is embodied in movement, especially in the highly stylized and codified movement we call dance" (6). This view is reflected in many of the dance curricula found in schools and higher education today. The role of the reflective audience member or dancer is as important as the dance event, the description, or the performance of the movement and its organization or the appreciation of the historical background. Sklar articulates this idea when she says, "In attempting to understand the 'other,' I was forced to reflect on myself" (8). The development of a dance vocabulary, both physical and verbal; the understanding of our own cultural traditions; the knowledge of how dances come into being and are reshaped by time and cultural changes and exchanges; and the ability to observe and describe the dance event are skills that dance educators require of their students.

Our knowledge of dance and our expression in dance today have emerged from the local and global transitions of the past. We have come to understand contemporary forms of world dance by examining the past and the changes that have occurred throughout time. Our recognition that who we are is embedded in our cultural forms of expression, such as dance, enables us to explore and create today. The importance of dance has been substantiated through recent developments in cognitive science and neuroscience. These recent developments have shown that the brain and the body make up a single, fully integrated cognitive system. Likewise, as thoughts occur, often well below our conscious thought, we are continually responding to sensory information. We consistently represent the abstract through metaphors that we associate with physical experiences and emotions. As we know, dance represents such metaphors in a special and an individual way. I believe it is safe to say that through varied activity with dance, students develop a sensitive and global perspective not only on dance but also on the world around them.

Preservice Teacher Program

Today I find myself in a program whose task is the creation of the future. This task is not high minded or arrogant but is realistic when considering that the focus is on individual students, inclusiveness, and participation. Content is important but is seen as "the means of dialogue, the means of communication, and the means of participation" (Ritenburg 2001, 262). Since its inception in 1982, the Arts Education Program in the Faculty of Education at the University of Regina has established a five-year bachelor of education (BEd) and a BEd after degree in Arts Education. The students in the program take courses in aesthetics, education, dance, drama, literature, music, and visual arts and are provided with experiences in kindergarten through grade 12 schools and in various community settings. These studies and experiences lead to a comprehensive education in the teaching of the arts, full teacher certification, and a combined bachelor of arts in some art areas. Many of the courses, particularly those at the senior level, include projects in which the students experience as well as develop community programs. The Faculty in the Arts Education Program continually debate what kind of person we wish teachers to be and what kind of program should support that end. We want our students to be able to respond positively to the reality and the challenge of a changing society and to consider what is possible in the education of our children. Hinchey (2006, 5) states that "teacher education courses focus most often not on the *whys* but on the *hows* of schooling." In the Arts Education Program we strive to foster critical and reflective thought, aesthetic sensibilities, an understanding of how knowledge is socially constructed, an appreciation of the diversity of human experience and expression, and an understanding of the importance of creativity and lifelong learning.

There is a close relationship between the Arts Education Program at the University of Regina and the Arts Education curriculum in schools. The aim of the school curriculum is to enable students to understand and value arts expressions throughout life. This aim describes the main outcome for students and the primary reason for including Arts Education in the core curriculum for all students. This is an exciting relationship, as both the Arts Education Program and the Arts Education curriculum emphasize the importance of personal expression *and* the arts as ways of knowing. Both also echo Eisner (1996, 11) when he writes, "There are multiple ways in which the world can be known. Artists, dancers, and writers as well as scientists have important things to tell us about the world." I would not be telling the truth if I said that the acceptance of the arts as part of the core curriculum in schools and as a major program in the Faculty of Education has been an easy passage. It is to the credit of our faculty, our partners in education, and our graduates that arts education exists in the public schools and the university. I attribute this success to the strong belief of my colleagues and students that we do not have to conform to economic and political powers.

In "Globalizing Education: Policies, Pedagogies and Politics," Michael W. Apple argues that schools are more concerned with reflecting the marketplace and focusing on "high status knowledge" or technical knowledge (2005, 1). This is a response to economic expansion and the trends associated with globalization. These globalizing tendencies are often seen as internationalization, marketization, universalization, Westernization, and deterritorialization (Scholte 2000). Singh, Kenway, and Apple (2005, 1) believe that globalization has "many and varied implications for the educational policies, pedagogies, and politics of nation-states" and imply the devastating effect that this can play on cultural identification. Perhaps on a more positive note Tomlinson refers to globalization as "the rapidly developing and ever-denser network of interconnections and interdependencies that characterize modern social life" (Singh, Kenway, and Apple 2005, 4).

Educational institutions and processes reflect globalizing tendencies. Thus we must pay attention to the complex and diverse responses to globalization in educational settings and be alert to how globalization affects our life and the lives of others. Such concerns reflect the argument of Beyer (2000), who quoted Bowles and Gintis (1976, 53) in saying that schools continue to reproduce the vertical lines of power and authority that become part of the everyday classroom experience, in which students are at the low end of the power continuum, with teachers overseeing their work and administrators providing direction and incentives. Little has changed, and there is no doubt that institutions such as schools and universities maintain our social identity and reinforce important political consciousness, economic realities, and cultural practices.

Conclusion

So how can I—or how do I—address such issues in dance? I plan for a safe and fun environment in which the participants can express themselves freely through dance. I attempt to work with the dialectic of transformation, leading and following, control and freedom, and so on. I focus on dance as a tool the students can use to consciously connect with their bodies, to accept their bodies, and to creatively express their thoughts and feelings. I provide occasions to perform for peers or public, which in turn provide opportunities for students to share their ideas and to develop pride and confidence in their ideas and selected movement vocabulary. I use the dance language to teach about membership, the importance of context, the dynamics of identity, and the role of those on the margins.

Throughout this chapter, I have tried to emphasize the importance of not only the content and knowledge of dance itself but also the dialogue and communication that dance provides to both the participants in the dance and the audience members. In creating dance experiences for the beginner as well as the experienced dancer, the focus should be on the student and what the experience provides in terms of personal growth as well as knowledge of the dance form. Watching a well-known choreographer such as Eduard Lock explore and express risk or a personal choreography exploring the same theme may encourage students to deeply examine their own understanding of risk taking. The experience and knowledge of creating a new work and the specific roles of the choreographer and dancer provide a dialogue about the creative process and the examination of one's own creative process. Investigating the dance of a selected people opens up knowledge about others as well as the self and allows us to examine cultural practice and change.

Preservice teachers have great concerns about the management of classroom behaviors, and in many instances they are encouraged to examine their classroom management style. Often the overt or silent behaviors demonstrated by young students occur because the students are disinterested and do not understand the point of the experience. They become disengaged. "Why do we have to do dance?" Rather than resorting to "the vertical line of power and authority" (Beyer) by making threats or allowing the administration to deal with the situation, it is more strategic to take a different approach. Finding ways in which the content of dance connects with the students' lives and enables the students to make sense of what is happening in their world has powerful results. Acknowledging who the young students are in your classroom and how dance plays a part in their lives is an excellent starting point for the dance experience. This does not mean that you have to focus solely on what interests the young student and provide dance that reflects popular culture. Close examination reveals that there is someone in the class who understands clearly why his parents wanted him to take Ukrainian dance lessons, how the experience connected him to his heritage, and what he learned through those lessons. There is the girl in the class who knows why she begged for ballet lessons even though no one else in her family had ever studied the dance form. There is the new child who has recently moved from another country and is feeling isolated and lonely. Respectful conversation and questions about his past home and how dance figures in his life begin to open him up to his new home. The recounting of these experiences opens up possibilities for the dance educator to connect with students on many levels, to explore with students the deeper levels of our existence, and to learn how our experiences have shaped and continue to shape us.

Through dance it is possible to resist and reframe cultural contexts and to become critical and visionary thinkers so that we can imagine our world differently. We can examine globalization through economic and political shifts and question how such practice detraditionalizes some dance forms, taking away the essence of and respect for the form. We can also look at the opportunities afforded when taking a global perspective and viewing the world as a unity of all individuals and interacting cultures. I remain optimistic that through the arts we can provoke more dialogue about what is happening in the world, encourage individuals to explore their identity and context, educate the uninformed, empower the invisible and disenfranchised, raise questions about our situation, and provide a vision for the future.

REFLECTIONS

As teachers, dancers, choreographers, researchers, historians, citizens, or players of whatever role we undertake that has a part in the enterprise of education, we must ask ourselves what we are teaching and why. Ann Kipling Brown shares her stories about how her experiences and passions shaped her work in dance education. Through her stories she reminds us that dance education, like any education, can and does have underlying outcomes that may or may not be something we consciously articulate as teachers. Our role as educators, if taken seriously, must address not only the basic discipline-specific content but also and more importantly the students' lives and the larger world in which the students live. Much about the incorporation of the arts into education, and the value it offers, has been argued for many years.

Some countries, such as South Africa, have learned through their history that all of education, including the arts, must address the larger social issues. For them this is stated clearly in national curricular terms focusing on democratic citizenship and issues of social justice. In the following statement, copied from the South African National Curriculum Standards, we see both the why and the how of dance:

> Dance Studies focuses on building values and attitudes of respect and inclusivity, providing access for learners facing physical and social barriers. It promotes the value of diverse South African cultural and artistic practices. Through exploring dance, learners reflect on ways of promoting cultural fairness and learn to respect cultural and other diversities, in keeping with constitutional principles and the Bill of Rights. Through the inclusion of indigenous dance, learners realise the important contribution that indigenous knowledge systems make to the understanding of dance and its practices. (Wiki Books 2007)

And, in seeking to address both local and global cultures, the South African National Curriculum Standards adds a section on the scope of dance under the heading *Recommended Dance Forms:*

> Acknowledging the cultural diversity in this country, schools can offer various dance forms on the condition that they subscribe to the range of Learning Outcomes and Assessment Standards set out in this document. (Wiki Books 2007)

These dance forms must contribute to the development of dance in a transformational South Africa for the following reasons:

- It is in keeping with local and global concerns to develop contemporary South African culture.
- It serves the purposes of redress and restoring balance.
- It reflects an evolving, contemporary South African identity.
- It encourages the development of South African performances that are meaningful and attractive both locally and internationally.

The Revised National Curriculum Statement of South Africa speaks to the way a culture understands and values education for its ability to help us understand our identity, our history, and our values and to challenge us to reflect on who we are as a people and who we are in the broader context of a global society. We may then stop asking what value the arts have in education and instead ask how the arts can help us understand who we are and help us to become better at making meanings and developing our imagination. Perhaps, most importantly, we may begin to ask how we may contribute to the transformation of our world so that it becomes a place of greater justice and dignity for all.

eight

Dialogical Pedagogy, Embodied Knowledge, and Meaningful Learning

Eeva Anttila

Theatre Academy
Department of dance and theatre pedagogy
Helsinki, Finland

In this chapter I describe an approach to dance education in public schools that has evolved during my last eight years of research and practical work within the school context. A dance teacher since the early 1980s, I reached a turning point in my professional career in the late 1990s when I asked myself a simple question: So what? This question embraces a deep concern of the purpose and direction of my work with young dance students and schoolchildren. Having established a method of dance teaching that I was confident and comfortable with, I felt that there had to be a deeper meaning in dance education. The modernist assumptions on dance pedagogy that I had accumulated during two decades of studying, teaching, and researching dance began crumbling. I started searching for deeper meaning and noticed that I was not alone. My colleagues and mentors in dance education, such as Karen Bond, Isabel Marques, Sherry Shapiro, and Susan W. Stinson, had started their quest for meaning long before I had. Reading their work (Bond 2000; Marques 1998; Shapiro 1998, 1999; Stinson 1995, 1998, 2001, 2004) and discussing ideas with them became immensely significant for me. With their help, I became familiar with ideas such as critical and feminist pedagogy, and I became very curious about the concept of dialogue. Through my doctoral work (Anttila 2003a), I became immersed in the origins of these ideas and began to incorporate them into my own pedagogical practice. My search for deeper meaning thus generated a pedagogical approach that I like to identify as *dialogical dance education*. Following are a brief description of key ideas related to dialogue and an account of a practical pedagogical project based on these ideas.

Dialogue in Dance Education

The concept of dialogue is complex but fascinating, and there are many variations on the meaning of dialogue. I developed my conception of dialogue largely with the support of work by Martin Buber (1937/1970, 1947) and Paulo Freire (1972, 1996, 1998a, 1998b). Although their backgrounds and views on dialogue differ considerably, I have been able to glean several key ideas from their works. These ideas are foundational for my thinking about dialogue in the context of dance education. First, both Buber and Freire see dialogue as more than a method or a tool. Freire claims that "dialogism is a requirement of human nature and also a sign of the educator's democratic stand" (Freire 1998a, 92). As a sign of humanity and an essential quality of human life, dialogue is also the indispensable aim of education. According to Buber, the longing for relation is fundamental to human beings. His basic premise is that humans become persons through their relationships with others and with the world: "Man becomes an I through a You" (1937/1970, 80). Becoming a person happens through relating and associating with others; in contrast, becoming an ego happens through separating from others (1937/1970, 112).

Second, Buber and Freire share the view that education denotes a purpose and a direction. However, they claim that the content and direction of education are to be determined through dialogue instead of being predetermined (Buber 1947, 101-102; Freire 1996, 112). Thus dialogue is a significant ingredient in *purposeful education*. Buber and Freire challenge educators to see the possibility of genuine dialogue in an educational relationship. Freire points out that "a dialogical relation does not, as is sometimes thought, rule out the possibility of the act of teaching" (1996, 117). According to Freire (1972, 65-66), the content of education should be neither a gift nor an imposition but should be based on the things about which the students want to know more. The starting point for critical pedagogy is the students' present, existential, and concrete life situation and their awareness of it that reflects their aspirations. Freire says, "It is not our role to speak to the people about our own view of the world, not to attempt to impose that view on them, but rather to dialogue with the people about their view and ours" (1972, 68).

For Buber, education as a purpose means that the teacher presents a selection of the world to the student. However, the world itself influences and educates the child. The educator is just one element of influence, and this influence must proceed from the educator's integrity in order to be an integrating force (Buber 1947, 90). Buber is as concerned as Freire is about the need to base education on students' interests and life situation. His concern is apparent as he admonishes that "the educator may carry out his selection and his influence from himself and his idea of the pupil, not from the pupil's own reality" (Buber 1947, 100). This concern reflects quite accurately the premise of critical pedagogy.

The concept of inclusion is central to understanding Buber's thinking on dialogue. Inclusion means experiencing from the other side (Buber 1947, 96). It can be mutual, as it is in friendship. In mutual inclusion both persons experience from both sides. It can also be one sided, as it is in education. This means that when educators practice inclusion, they take part in the students' experiences on being educated, but they cannot expect that the students can or should "experience the educating of the educator" (Buber 1947, 100). Thus, not all dialogical relationships consist of mutual inclusion, and relationships that are characterized by one-sided inclusion have not lost anything of their dialogical character (Buber 1937/1970, 178). According to Buber, inclusion constitutes the relation in education, and "the relation in education is one of pure dialogue" (1947, 98).

Dialogue in education does not mean that the teacher and the student have similar roles, tasks, and responsibilities. What is needed, however, is a resolution of the traditional teacher–student contradiction. In critical or dialogical education, the teacher and the students are jointly responsible for a process in which all grow: "Men teach each other, mediated by the world" (Freire 1972, 53). In Buber's words, dialogue in education means that "now he [the educator] no longer interferes, nor does he merely allow things to happen. He listens to that which grows, to the way of Being in the world . . . he encounters" (Buber 1937/1970, 109).

The last idea on dialogue that I discuss here is its nonverbal nature. Although bodily dialogue is discussed more fully in Buber's writings, Freire also sees dialogue as more than words. His idea of praxis—uniting reflection and action—may help us to grasp how important it is to embody ideas through action (Freire 1972, 60). Buber (1947, 21-22), on the other hand, speaks of a basic movement of turning toward the other person. The attitude and the basic movements include both inner movements and bodily actions, such as the "very tension of the eyes' muscles and the very action of the foot as it walks" (Buber 1947, 21). We communicate by our way of being and relating to others—how we focus on others, how we lean toward others, how we are present in our bodies to others, and how communication streams from our bodies to others without reserve. Buber also says that "for a conversation no sound is necessary, not even a gesture" (1947, 3), and that "a shared silence can also be dialogue" (1947, 97). In its essence, dialogue is a prelinguistic, bodily, and concrete happening that streams from one body to another body.

These ideas closely resemble those of a recent discourse that endorses concepts such as embodied knowledge and tacit knowledge. Exploring dialogue and its nonverbal nature led me to study conceptions of knowledge and the significance of bodily processes in constructing consciousness and in learning. It is exciting how barriers separating natural science, human science, and philosophy are fading and how the quest for understanding human consciousness, and the role of the body in consciousness, has created a space for dialogue among people from different areas. As a result of this increased understanding, a growing number of scholars are conceiving of the mind and the body as one. According to Shapiro, paying a renewed attention to the body is central to critiquing the Western epistemology that dominates education. She asks, "How can we understand through our *embodied knowledge* what it might mean to live freer and more empowered lives?" (Shapiro 1998, 9), and she insists that education must start from lived experiences. Viewing the body as a subject, or as a vehicle for understanding, shifts us from disembodied knowing to embodied knowing. Thus, "The intent of the learning experience moves from one of learning movement vocabulary for the sake of creating dance to gaining an understanding of the self, others, and the larger world for the possibility of change" (Shapiro 1998, 15).

I return to this idea of embodied knowledge and holistic learning after describing a dance education project that took place in 2004-05 in an elementary school in eastern Helsinki, Finland. In this project, my aim as a dance teacher was to apply these ideas of dialogue and embodied knowledge in a spirit of collaborative searching.

Background of the Project

The project was initiated in spring 2004. At that time I was playing the role of parent and spectator, witnessing a school play performed by a fifth-grade class. As a dance teacher and a trainer of prospective dance and theater teachers, I saw that the approach used in creating this play was quite traditional and teacher directed. The play was based on a children's story and was adapted for the stage by the teacher, and the roles were assigned largely by the teacher and a visiting drama teacher, who also directed the play with a traditional theater director's approach. The children seemed to be somewhat lost onstage, performing memorized lines, tasks, and movements. In a discussion following the performance, the classroom teacher disclosed to me that she had hoped to create another kind of experience

Students' art works were used as background projections for creating a sense of time and place in the performance.
Photo courtesy of Helka Nurmi-Niemi.

for the children, an experience in which the children, acting as performers, would have a sense of meaning and personal agency. Recognizing that her aims were akin to my aspirations as a dance teacher, I agreed to work with her in the performance project she was planning for the coming year. Soon I found myself fully immersed in this endeavor.

The school itself appeared to be interesting and different from schools I had worked in before. I was especially impressed with its architecture. This school was built recently and around the idea that the school building itself is a learning tool, almost like a three-dimensional book. The school has a big central area, the heart, which consists of a large, fully equipped stage and a cafeteria that can be converted into the seating area for the audience. Also, this area is a very tall space, with staircases and open hallways circling around, and it is very light, with many walls made of glass. The school curriculum is interesting, incorporating craft, design, and technology and emphasizing students' active inquiry and integration between different subjects. The classroom teacher, who now taught a combined class of fifth and sixth graders, wanted to strengthen the arts education program in the school and utilize the great possibilities that the school had for performance projects. Thus she and I planned to unite our areas of expertise and create a project in which art and technology would support each other.

Facilitating Meaningful Learning Through Generative Themes

Initially, the classroom teacher and I discussed a theme related to history. However, to remain faithful to my ideas on critical pedagogy and dialogue, I wanted to suspend this decision and include the students in the process. According to Freire (1972), the starting point of critical pedagogy is the students' present and concrete life situation, and thus the content of education should be based on the things about which the students want to know more; educational content should be based on themes that are significant to them. Significant, or generative, themes are meaningful ideas, concepts, hopes, doubts, values, and challenges; they are found in the students' perception of reality (Freire 1972, 73-75, 81). Generative themes are embedded in human beings' relationship with the world, and we create these themes in collaboration with other people. Thematic investigation, thus, aims at awareness of reality and self (Freire 1972, 78-80).

In dance education, Shapiro (1998) and Marques (1997, 1998) have developed artistic and pedagogical approaches based on generative themes and collaborative investigation. Marques writes the following:

> The student's context—the intersection of lived, perceived, and imagined realities—should be both the starting point and the continuation of what is to be understood, constructed, unveiled, transformed, problematized, and deconstructed in a transformative educational action. . . . The chosen context should not only be interesting and motivating, but it also should be meaningful and open to ongoing development of the dance contents themselves. (Marques 1998, 181)

For Marques, choosing a theme for a dance class or a starting point for a choreographic process "requires attention, sensitivity, respect for the other, critical understanding, competence, some degree of structure, and specific contents and movements to convey our ideas" (Marques 1998, 182). She also claims that both teaching and creating dance call for flexibility, openness, and nonpreconceived programs in which unpredictable outcomes are generated. Thus, the process of creation and transformation is enhanced.

For Shapiro, students' lives are the core of the curriculum that is based on the belief that human beings are capable of understanding their own experiences and able to act upon the reality they live in. She views education as praxis, as an emancipatory act. By using generative themes in educational and choreographic processes, she has become convinced that dance can be a process of liberation (Shapiro 1998, 19).

In theater education, many forms of community theater and so-called *devising methods* have been used to empower students or performers and to include them as creative agents (Boal 1992, 2000; Oddey 1994). Many choreographers and dance educators include their dancers when creating movement material. In many cases the students or dancers are also engaged in reflective work. Including them in a critical investigation of the thematic content of the performance is, however, a demanding and complicated process, and to my understanding, it is not very widely practiced among dance educators and choreographers.

I now return to the early phase of my project with the classroom teacher and our initial discussions, in which I explained my desire that the students create the material and ideas for the performance. This meant that we, acting as the persons responsible for leading the performance project,

Boys making headpieces for their characters.
Photo courtesy of Helka Nurmi–Niemi.

had to put off our ideas and visions about the content and form of the evolving piece. Suspending your own ideas is sometimes very difficult, but on the other hand, listening to others' ideas and letting them resonate in your mind—and body—is an exciting experience, and it generates unforeseen ideas that may never have come up without the suspending phase. In this way, I think it is possible to base educational projects on Buber's idea of listening to that which grows (1937/1970, 109). By listening to and encountering the students and their worlds and ideas and by practicing inclusion, the teacher can take part in students' lives without forgetting her or his own life, experiences, ideas, and needs.

At this stage, it was still a little unclear to me who was to participate in this project. Our meetings were scheduled during physical education classes, in which girls and boys were in separate groups and the combined class of fifth and sixth graders was further combined with girls or boys from another sixth grade class. My first meeting was with about 20 girls and took place while the boys participated in another activity. The girls, ranging from 11 to 13 years of age, seemed to be at different places in their lives—some were still childlike, and some were more like young adults—and had different interests and attitudes toward this project. However, I found that most of the girls present were interested in history and were willing to choose a topic related to history.

The fifth graders had just begun their studies in ancient history, and the sixth graders still remembered details—names, places, and events—about their previous studies in ancient history. Some students had recently visited Egypt and wanted to share their experiences. I had also been to Egypt and so had the classroom teacher. Egypt was also familiar to the students through one student whose father was from Egypt and through another student whose cousin lived in Egypt. The discussion around the theme soon became vivid and engaged most of the girls.

Before making a final decision on this topic, however, we did an activity that I hoped would give the students some perspective about the history of human culture. We drew a timeline on the floor, and then the students chose significant landmarks in the history of humankind, converted the years into meters and centimeters, and located the events on the timeline. This activity seemed to surprise the students as they exclaimed how short the time of history is that we know more accurately. We also discussed the concept of culture and identified key events in the history of human culture. The process of actually walking through the history seemed to make the concepts of time and history more tangible for the students. Regular steps represented a long passage of time, and the tiniest steps possible represented a lifetime of one person, or a generation, at the most. Approaching history via physical activity made studying more playful and engaging, and at this point everyone agreed that ancient Egypt would be a good topic for this performance project. Our choosing of the performance topic is a simple example of what embodied knowledge and embodied learning might mean. I return to these ideas in the closing of this chapter.

Feminist Underpinnings

During the first phase of the project, I worked only with girls. This created a space for us to investigate ancient history from a feminist perspective. Feminist educators (e.g., Ellsworth 1992), aiming at justice and equality, as do critical educators, have questioned critical pedagogy. They claim that critical pedagogy has failed to provide justice for women in educational settings. Most critical educators are male, and a female perspective has been almost completely absent from the discussion. Feminist critique has targeted Freire's pedagogy for not problematizing gender or even noting it in their work (Kenway and Modra 1992, 157). Also, many dance educators have expressed concern about dance education as a gendered practice and discussed the need to become aware of the gender aspect in dance pedagogy. Most notably, Sherry Shapiro and Susan W. Stinson have developed approaches to teaching based on feminist pedagogy. According to Shapiro, imagination, creativity, and body memories can lead women to a more critical understanding of their lives in dance and in their culture, taken that imagination and creativity are underlying powers to envision and recreate the world in which we live (Shapiro 1998, 7, 11). Stinson has developed feminist pedagogy for children's dance. She encourages even young children to be their own teachers and to listen to their bodies instead of focusing on a mirror or on the dance teacher. She works to help her students to find internal awareness and opportunities to speak, to find their own voice and own movement. She also looks for ways to help students to perceive relationships between and among students and to share their ideas with each other and with her. Other relationships that need attention are the students' relationship to their own body and the relationship between what goes on in the studio and what happens outside of it. Recognizing relationships is important in learning to take responsibility for the other, for the world, and for ourselves (Stinson 1998, 39-42).

Dance education for young girls in contemporary society can hardly follow the traditional thinking that views girls as the silent gender who easily obeys authority. Today, fewer girls are willing to fit into a traditional girl's role; assertiveness, strong views and opinions challenging adult authority, and even aggression have surfaced among girls. Empowering girls in our contemporary world is a complicated matter, when some girls seem to be already so empowered that their concern for others, so typical of the traditional female role, all but disappears. For me it has been a great challenge to include contemporary girls in constructive, meaningful, and collaborative work.

In this particular project, I gave the girls the challenge of portraying a strong female character through body movement, hoping that allowing them to associate themselves as bold, strong, and even somewhat deviant characters would be meaningful for them and support their struggle for both identity construction and adult acceptance.

We proceeded into this phase by exploring with a more detailed timeline. I brought along pieces of paper inscribed with the names of the historical people (and the years that they lived) that the students had remembered in the last meeting. I also introduced them to influential female characters they had not heard about previously. The students' task was now to place these names on the timeline. We found out that most of the names had to be placed very close to each other, while the rest of the timeline remained almost empty. We concluded together that this was

Working toward a performance strengthens mutual bonds.
Photo courtesy of Helka Nurmi-Niemi.

an interesting stage in history and decided to focus on it. For me it was inspiring to learn how women living in ancient Egypt during that time had considerable influence in their society. I shared these stories with the students and hoped that they would also become inspired by these stories. I wanted to establish a connection between these stories and the contemporary world, and I approached this task by discussing women's rights in different cultures today.

An Anticasting Philosophy

At this point, many of the girls became eager to decide on their roles and tasks in the performance. Others were still hesitant about the whole project, saying that they couldn't dance or that they didn't want to be onstage. I think that this is one of the most challenging and crucial moments in a performance project: to support each student in finding a meaningful role or task and to let the students take part in this casting process. I think that the content and structure of the performance should be derived from this initial, collaborative process. If teachers want to support the students' process of making meaning, they must allow space for the students' own views and interests in the different roles and tasks, even when doing so seems to lead to a mess in terms of teachers' aesthetic and artistic views. Moreover, taking the initial reactions literally and viewing them as fixed may crush covert dreams and desires. Some girls—and boys—do not dare to express their interest in performing because they are concerned about their peers' opinions.

Another objection I have to traditional casting is that the philosophy embedded in it implies that those who have a lot (skills, self-confidence, looks) will gain even more. My anticasting philosophy implies that those who seem to have less potential as performers should be given as much responsibility in a performance as they are willing to take, and even a little bit more. This philosophy, however, comes with its own problems and conflicts. I return to these challenges shortly.

I told the students that we were not going to make any decisions about roles yet and that I wanted them to have time to think about what they would like to do. The students, apparently used to being assigned roles by the teacher, were surprised but agreed to wait. We did movement improvisations based on the idea of status. We divided the room into four areas, each denoting a status. The first status was called *divine*, the second was called *royal*, the third was named *ordinary people*, and the fourth was called *subordinated* (as in slaves or prisoners). As the students moved within each area, I asked them to imagine how the status affected their movement. They could move freely from one area to another, but

I asked them to explore all four areas. After this, I asked them how they felt and which of the areas was their favorite status. We also discussed how in many countries these different kinds of status still exist today and how in our country these kinds of differences between groups of people are more subtle but continue to exist. I also asked the sixth graders to compare these thoughts to the Finnish history that they were currently studying. I asked them to what extent these categories could be detected in the recent history of our country.

The next step in our project was somewhat more elaborate in terms of movement. I had copied pictures of a book called *Ancient Egyptian Dances* by Irina Lexova. I had discovered this book by accident—unplanned events often give a project like this a new direction. Thus, being open to the world is important in creative work. Using pictures as a basis for composition was an approach that I had rarely used, but for this project, it immediately felt right, because the visual material from ancient Egypt is very rich, detailed, and fascinating.

I had grouped these pictures according to the type of movement or purpose of dance they represented. Some pictures depicted pharaohs and their spouses performing elegant upper-body moves, some portrayed servant dancers performing acrobatic, full-body moves, and some depicted men and women moving with objects such as musical instruments, swords, and sticks. I had the students choose a picture from the group that matched their interest—for example, they chose the group that moved elegantly or the one that moved acrobatically. Then, in small groups, they connected their pictures and created a small choreography based on the pictures. This way, I got an idea about their movement preferences and about their group dynamics and friendships, which always influence students' choices.

After this activity, which generated interesting movement sequences, we proceeded into an initial discussion of each student's preferences in terms of movement quality and character. Most girls said that they wanted to be dancers (dancers were identified as ordinary people or servants whose profession was to entertain the pharaohs). A group of four sixth graders who were friends wanted to be royal characters. A few girls indicated that they also wanted to be divine characters.

The students continued to work in small groups, choosing more pictures and making the movement sequences longer and more refined. I also brought in some readings about royal women in ancient Egypt and asked the four girls who wanted to be royal characters to study the readings and to think about which character they would like to be. At this point, they realized that these characters were related to each other.

Having met with the fifth- and sixth-grade girls three times, I found out that some boys were already anxious about their involvement in this project and had already started to make some dances with their class-room teacher by using the same pictures and procedures the girls used. One group of boys had choreographed a stick dance, while others had created a small royal sequence of elegant movements. Our next meeting involved the whole combined fifth and sixth grade class. The classroom teacher had asked everyone to bring Egyptian artifacts and photographs to class, and they had arranged all these items to be a display. We watched a video that I brought with me called *Secret Egypt*. I was glad to get the boys involved, and they eagerly demonstrated their movement sequences. The boy whose father was from Egypt brought in Arabic music that the boys used to accompany their movements. The project was in full swing.

Dialogue at Test: Negotiating Groups and Tasks

As the work continued, some groups proceeded very well, while others did not proceed much at all. Some girls started arguing. In groups that had chosen more challenging movements, some students were not able to keep up with others who wanted to do cartwheels and other gymnastic moves. I also became concerned about their safety.

I faced a difficult dilemma. Clearly there were some girls who were very apt physically and wanted to make use of their skills in their sequences. Some girls had chosen their groups based on friendships and not because of their interest in acrobatic movement. It was simply not safe for them to participate in those activities. However, it would not be fair to deny those girls who were able to move skillfully a chance to make use of their skills. I believe that students perform best when their movement suits their skill level and interest. My task was now to make everyone understand that simple movements and sequences, if performed gracefully and with presence and intent, are as valuable as the more difficult sequences in the whole of the production. I discussed these thoughts with some girls privately and in small groups and suggested forming another group of dancers. Some girls protested at first but agreed to give it a try.

The groups gradually became more specialized in their styles. One group, for example, created a sequence that was joyful and light in its quality. I suggested that this group, consisting of four girls, be named *the children*, and they agreed. The new group consisted of six girls who were a little bit more reserved, so I suggested that they be called the *women*. They agreed as well. They still had some difficulties in figuring out their dance, and I suggested that they dance with objects (fabrics, pottery) and start with everyday movements (lifting and carrying water, doing laundry). The concreteness of the tasks seemed to help them. At this point, we also had a group of four boys who danced with sticks. They became the *men*.

I then suggested that the two remaining girl groups be combined to form a group of six *dancers* who would create a more acrobatic dance. They agreed. In addition, we had the group of royal women that had formed earlier. These girls gradually developed a simple but elegant sequence.

When I asked the rest of the boys about their interests, some of the boys, as I had anticipated, were extremely eager to get a "big role." I asked them if they wanted to be pharaohs or gods, and they wanted to be both. As some boys were reluctant to be involved, I let them have double roles. Four boys with double roles as gods and pharaohs were to study the legend of Osiris together with two girls who also wanted double roles as goddesses and dancers. As these students studied the myths and the relationships of the characters related to the legend of Osiris, they learned that they were related to each other. Everything seemed to circle around Pharaoh Akhenaton, and everyone agreed that the best student for this central figure was the boy whose origins were in Egypt. He seemed proud and pleased about this decision.

There were a few more boys who were not involved. One boy played the violin but said that he did not want to dance onstage. We agreed that he would be the musician. I had hoped for a group of musicians, but since no one else was eager to play music onstage, and this boy was happy to

Men, women, and children lift a grape vine in preparing a feast for the pharaohs.
Photo courtesy of Helka Nurmi-Niemi.

play by himself, I thought a solo performance was a good solution. I had found an abundance of taped Arabic music, another fascinating exploration into the richness of this culture. We listened to a traditional Arabic theme and notated this theme for him to rehearse. This theme became a signifying theme for the whole performance.

I also thought that it would be great to have a narrator since we had come across some interesting ancient writings, such as the "Great Hymn to the Aten" (a hymn to the sun god). One boy agreed to be the narrator. Two more boys in the class did not want to perform onstage but were very eager to work on the technology. They became the master technicians. Two brothers were not allowed to perform because of their religion. They wanted to be involved, however, and were happy to be stage masters.

This process of choosing roles and tasks among 35 students with diverse backgrounds, desires, and interests was challenging and time consuming. However, I believe that listening to each student is crucial in creating a meaningful learning process and a constructive experience for everyone. After this process of listening and encountering, it was time for me to change gears and become fully involved in the creative process myself.

Finding Connections: Teacher's Imagination and Creativity at Play

As the roles, ideas, and movement materials were becoming abundant, I started to focus on the structure of the piece. Now that the students were all involved in a task or a role that they desired, my job was to figure out how to connect all the sections and sequences together. At this stage, I became deeply involved with the mythology and the fascinating legends of that time. I read many stories and shared these stories with the students. They also studied the legends in their history classes, wrote papers and gave presentations on various related topics in their language arts classes, and became familiar with the visual arts of the time in their arts classes. Together we investigated the richness of the ideas and the wonders of the life in ancient Egypt. We realized that the everyday life was greatly affected by nature, especially by the sun and the Nile. We read the "Great Hymn to the Aten" together.

It then occurred to me that the sun could be the thematic core of the piece. I suggested to the class that our piece depict one day—one cycle of the sun—and that we organize all the sections accordingly: sunrise, morning, noon, afternoon, evening, and night. This dramaturgical decision seemed to make sense to everyone, and it created a feeling of continuity and meaning and a sense that everyone had an equal value in the piece. When one of the girls who I had persuaded to change groups asked me who had the leading role in this piece, I replied, "Everyone has a leading role in this piece." I genuinely felt that this was the case, and the hymn reinforced this idea of equality yet diversity.

Darkness and death are also significant in the ancient Egyptian mythology. Everyone who has visited Egypt remembers the sky at night and the amazing brightness of the stars. This image became the beginning and ending of the piece, reinforcing the idea of contrast between lightness and darkness and the idea that life is cyclical.

The students were a little worried about the plot being unclear to the audience and suggested that the narrator should explain what was going on. I assured them that the audience, like us, had imagination. I then explained that dance tells stories via body movement and gestures and that costumes, music, and lightning also help convey the message. Each student was involved in creating the costumes and headpieces with the help of a crafts teacher. Moreover, because we had advanced technology at hand, we were able to use background projections for scenery. The children's artwork was projected to the background to support the change of location and time of day. All the words that were used came from ancient writings.

Akhenaton, Nefertiti, Tutankhamen, and guests watch dancers perform for them in a feast for the pharaohs.
Photo courtesy of Helka Nurmi-Niemi.

To me, poetic words like those of the hymn are very powerful and can tell a story that does not need explanation. Learning through poetic or narrative language and stories is, to me, crucial in holistic learning and embodied knowledge. I can only hope that the performers and the audience members experienced the power of poetic language in some way. Poetic words were also used in the program, and the title of the piece bore layers of meaning: *Amarna—the Land of the Sun.* In the program the meaning of the word *Amarna* was explained as follows: "A modern name for the location, where Akhenaton moved his capital from Theba. The name of the new capital was Aket-Aton (the horizon of Aton). Amarna period means the short reign of Akhenaton (about 1360-1360 B.C.). Amarna art refers to the artistic freedom of that period." In addition, an excerpt of a novel by Finnish author Mika Waltari was printed in the program. This novel, *Egyptian: The Novel,* tells about this Amarna time and is a world classic. The excerpt described Pharaoh Akhenaton's views of equality and freedom.

During this project I was very involved in the creative process. I believe strongly that it is possible for the teacher or choreographer to be involved fully in a meaning-making process and still foster a collaborative creative process among the students or dancers. I think that the crucial moment is at the beginning of the meaning-making process. As I mentioned earlier, suspending your own ideas, visions, and plans in a performance project, or for that matter, any collaborative project, is significant here. By this I do not mean that teachers and choreographers should have no input in the creative work. Quite the contrary, it is crucial that they open their experience and imagination, just as they expect the students to open their experience and imagination. Maxine Greene has put it well: "The classroom situation most provocative of thoughtfulness and critical consciousness is the one in which teachers and learners find themselves conducting a kind of collaborative search, each from her or his lived situation" (1995, 23). In this kind of creative educational process, the teacher is also a learner and becomes surprised and changed:

> The surprise comes along with becoming different—consciously different as one finds ways of acting on envisaged possibility. . . . Moreover, to learn and to teach, one must have an awareness of leaving something behind when reacting to something new, and this kind of awareness must be linked to imagination . . . a kindred imaginative ability is required if the becoming different that learning involves is actually to take place. (Greene 1995, 20-21)

Shapiro speaks for pedagogy in which students can critically reflect on their personal experience and its relationship to the world and in which the teacher shares her own life experiences in the situation: "With the discovery of voice and relational and situational knowing, a realization is also made of the multiplicity and plurality of human experience" (Shapiro 1998, 10).

Life in ancient Egypt as a generative theme was very fruitful for a collaborative, multidisciplinary project. Using visual arts, language arts, history, crafts, music, drama, and dance, the students explored the roots of Western civilization. With each other and together with the adults involved in the project, the students invented new avenues for learning about our common cultural heritage. At the same time, they learned about themselves, expanding their capabilities as performers and learners, and their peers. Many students surprised themselves, their teachers, and their parents by doing things no one thought they could do, thus opening their personal growth and identity to new dimensions. Teachers, I believe, can do a great deal in supporting this kind of opening in their students (see Anttila 2004).

The idea that human beings are equal and free became the underlying moral of the project. We did not preach this message; instead, this project, involving the whole body and all the senses and arising out of collaborative work, may have developed another kind of understanding about these ideas. As an open-ended process, the project left the reasoning, decision making, and valuing for the students to complete in their active, curious minds—and bodies. As Freire wrote, "The teacher cannot think for his students, nor can he impose his thought on them" (Freire 1972, 50). The actual learning outcomes of this project were certainly diverse, but I truly hope that all the students experienced themselves as important, competent, and equal in the process. I believe that this kind of experience has repercussions in students' lives.

Conclusion

I have described this project in detail in order to give you a possibility to take part, through your imagination, in a process of holistic learning. In the closing of this chapter, I step into my researcher shoes again and gather some theoretical foundations for holistic learning.

The ideas of embodied knowledge and holistic learning are substantiated by scientific and philosophical findings that have all but falsified the notion of the split body and mind. A wide body of literature from phenomenology, somatic theory, and neuroscience has emerged in recent decades. Scholars from different domains have begun a multidisciplinary dialogue in an attempt to understand human consciousness (e.g., Damasio 1994, 1999; Fraleigh 2000; Green 2002; Hanna 1985; Lakoff and Johnson 1999; Merleau-Ponty 1945/1995; Parviainen 2002, Shapiro 1999; Thomas

2003; Varela 1991). These philosophical, psychological, and scientific breakthroughs in theories about human consciousness and embodied knowledge embrace a multitude of challenging and provocative views that depict a conception of the human being that differs considerably from conceptions that form the basis of modern pedagogy. Pedagogy based on cognitive and even constructivist learning theories emphasizes transmitting information and constructing meanings predominantly through linguistic, conceptual processes. These views are challenged by an alternative view in which prelinguistic, preconceptual, and sensory processes form the core of human learning.

Moreover, a new conception about language substantiates the need to reconsider *how* language is used in pedagogy and *what kind* of language is used in schools. Language is more than a linear and logical cognitive process that leads to logical thinking (Bruner 1996; Damasio 1994, 1999; Lakoff and Johnson 1980, 1999; Merleau-Ponty 1945/1995). Language is also a creative, narrative, poetic, and metaphoric process; such language connects directly to bodily and multisensory experiences. According to Bruner (1996), the role of narrative language in human development, learning, and pedagogy may be more significant for learning than the paradigmatic language.

A holistic conception of learning also means that learning is a collaborative process. The social construction of meaning is an important element in understanding how human beings negotiate meanings and build understanding through communal work (Gergen 1999; Greene 1995). Learning through collaborative action and reflection strengthens communities and builds understanding for others and respect for diversity. A dialogical approach in teaching and learning transforms the nature and meaning of these processes (Anttila 2003a, 2003b; Buber 1947, 1937/1970; Freire 1998). Emphasizing collaborative learning instead of individual performance and success leads to ethical contemplation. I am inclined to think that ethics are based on concrete experiences and that they are not just a matter of reason (Anttila 2003b). In collaborative, creative projects, students face each other in concrete action. They also face real-life conflicts, their own emotions, and others' emotions. Through these experiences they can learn how to deal with their emotions, how to communicate their desires and views, and eventually how to solve conflicts by negotiation and by respecting others' emotions and views.

Finally, holistic learning takes into account an aesthetic perspective. The idea that art is a basic human necessity is brought forth for example by Crowther (1993), who, following Kantian philosophy, states that there is an existential primacy of mental image versus thought and language and that imaging allows for creative interpretation of reality and this is the basis of personal identity and innovation. According to Crowther

(1993, 205), aesthetic experiences play an important role in harmonizing the "basic ontological reciprocity" between human beings and the world and that the aesthetic domain answers the needs of self-consciousness. Also, Elliot Eisner's thinking on the role of artistic practices in education is relevant here; he claims that "as we learn through in and through the arts we become more qualitatively intelligent" (2004, 5).

I consider these insights as foundations for holistic learning and embodied knowledge. I propose that this kind of conception of learning and knowledge has pedagogical implications because it appreciates the significance of bodily experiences, including internal sensations and concrete interactions with others and the world. The significance of multisensory experiences, the nature of emotions as bodily processes, a wider conception of language, and possibilities for collaborative learning need to be taken into account. This can be achieved, for example, through curricular developments that integrate arts and academics.

The arts, including dance, are central in this kind of pedagogy, in their own right as building stones of civilization and humanity and as avenues for embodied knowledge. The dualistic conception that separates sensing and feeling from knowing and that regards consciousness as being predominantly linguistic needs to be reevaluated from the viewpoint of the considerable developments in understanding the holistic nature of human consciousness and learning. This reevaluation may lead to considerable changes in pedagogical practices in all schools. For me, these changes toward dialogical pedagogy, holistic learning, and embodied knowledge are long overdue, and I hope that the thoughts in this chapter facilitate discussion among dance educators and classroom teachers about the possibilities that this change may have in supporting meaningful learning.

REFLECTIONS

When thinking about the teaching and learning experience and the roles we play as teachers, students, audience members, and performers, I am reminded of a phrase used by a famous U.S. theater director—the "politics of the room." In her context the director was referring to what happens among actors and between actors and audience members. The politics of the room address the interactions among the people within a particular space and describe how people within this space can experience a microcosm of the larger world where issues of power and status are played out. Eeva Anttila takes us through such an experience in which the authority of the teacher is purposefully shared with the students. Control of the final product was relinquished to a process of inclusion in which the relationships among all involved were paramount, including the relationship of the students to the material, the relationship of the students to each other, the relationship of the teacher to the students, the relationship of the students to the artistic product, and, finally, the relationship of the students to learning. This attention to a dialogical relationship, as Eeva reminds us, is essential to the process of becoming fully human and to becoming a greater part of our larger world. Incorporating Paulo Freire's work on critical pedagogy, Buber's concerns with authentic human relationships, the feminist pedagogy of Sue Stinson and others, and recent work in dance education that argues for an embodied pedagogy, Eeva suggests that it is within these frameworks that students, or participants, can engage in a meaningful pedagogy. Attending to imagination and creativity as well as to the relational and moral aspects of the curriculum deepens the human and social awareness of the students. It is here, within these kinds of meaningful learning experiences, that purposeful education exists.

Eeva also emphasizes the way that language limits and mediates our ways of knowing. She notes the role of the body as another way of knowing that is significant for any pedagogy or performance directed toward self and social communication. Recent discoveries in neuroscience have demonstrated how "mirror neurons" within our brains stimulate us to emulate the experience and affect of those we are observing (see Daniel Glaser's work *The Dancer's Brain)*. Though the research examined the neurological response to physical skills, such as a dancer observing another dancer, it demonstrates that we are made to respond to others, to their physical movement and to their affect or emotions. In other words, there is among human beings a powerful tendency toward an empathic response to others' emotional or physical states. People who are concerned with holistic learning might consider the following: (a) how to organize material and processes to empower students, (b) how to create a process for collaborative and shared learning, (c) how to draw upon students' life experiences, making them part of and connected to the larger curriculum, (d) how to uncover the moral and ethical dimensions of the curriculum, (e) how to engage students' imagination and creativity, and (f) how to assist students in drawing critical and ethical connections among themselves, others, and the global world. Within these kinds of critical and feminist frameworks the grounds for freedom and equality can be nurtured.

nine

Transferable Theory: Researching Movement Concepts in Different Cultural Contexts

Shu-Ying Liu

Associate professor in early childhood education
National Hsinchu University of Education
Taiwan

The arts have long been marginalized in many school curricula across the globe. Where they have been taught, they have traditionally been regarded purely as an art form. Dance has always faced particular challenges in that it is very much in the moment and has been often perceived as difficult to understand. Although permanent recordings can be made for later educational use, they are two-dimensional representations of a three-dimensional art form, four dimensions if time is included. However, the value of integrating the arts into the wider curriculum and of educating the whole child is now coming to be recognized.

The Taiwanese Ministry of Education took on this wider view in 1998 when they initiated some far-reaching educational reforms intended to make the school curriculum less fragmented. The resulting nine-year curriculum for elementary through junior high school was implemented in September 2001. It included a new subject, performing arts, that allowed for the possibility of developing dance as an art form in education.

However, theory and practice of dance education in general remains insufficiently developed. There are no dance education departments in universities of education with specialist training programs for teachers, so there is a huge gap between policy and practice. The six universities with dance departments focus on vocational training for professional artists. Although a few offer courses in the theory and practice of dance education, they are not officially recognized for teacher certification.

Within kindergarten education, both specialist and generalist kindergarten teachers typically copy productions, or steps and sequences from commercially published books, DVDs, and videos, and then teach dance routines to children by rote (Liu 1998). The absence of teacher guidelines that translate government policy into practice means that there is a need to develop and test strategies that help teachers integrate dance with other art subjects.

In an attempt to achieve such integration, a recent collaborative research project asked how drawing and painting could be used to motivate dance and help young children reflect upon it. In doing so, it also aimed to provide a better understanding of how children connect learning in drawing and painting with action in dance. The project developed strategies for kindergarten teacher training in Taiwan to develop young children's abilities to make, perform, and appreciate dance. It applied Davies' movement framework (Davies 2003; see table 9.1), which prioritizes body, space, dynamics, and relationships, as a basis for dance learning, and it developed and tested related learning and teaching strategies at the kindergarten level. It also contributed to Matthews' theories of figurative representation and action representation (2003), as well as his suggestion that young children's drawings and paintings not only capture shapes and structures of objects but are also associated with the way they move.

Three cycles of collaborative action took place over six months in 2003 and 2004, underpinned by Elliott's model of action research (1991). They included a professional development workshop followed by two series of classroom experiments. The research team consisted of qualified Taiwanese kindergarten generalist teachers assisted by student teachers, an art specialist, and myself as a dance specialist. Teaching strategies were developed and evaluated, and conclusions were drawn about the contribution of the research to kindergarten teachers' professional development and to integrated dance and visual arts curricula at this level.

This chapter focuses on cycle 3, which took place over four weeks in two classrooms, each with approximately 30 children aged four and five, a qualified teacher who taught the lessons, and a student teacher who recorded the activity using electronic media. The teachers experimented with two stimuli for facilitating young children's dance and drawing: movement concepts based on Davies' movement framework and Beijing opera masks. The lessons were observed by myself and fully documented, and the stimuli, strategies, and learning outcomes were reviewed and compared in three team evaluation meetings.

Table 9.1 Davies' Movement Framework

Main category	Subcategories	Further divisions
Body (What takes place)	Action	Traveling (e.g., crawling, stepping, running, climbing, sliding, balancing)
		Weight taking and transference (e.g., rocking, rolling, tumbling, swinging, handstands, cartwheels)
		Flight (e.g., hopping, jumping, leaping, vaulting)
		Handling (e.g., kicking, throwing, catching, hitting, rolling)
	Design	Symmetry
		Asymmetry
	Articulation	Parts leading the movement
		Parts highlighting the movement
		Parts limiting the movement
	Shape	Long and stretched
		Wide and stretched
		Curved
		Twisted
	Fluency	Successive
		Simultaneous
Dynamics (How movement takes place)	Weight	Strong, firm
		Light, gentle
	Space (qualitative)	Straight, direct
		Flexible, wavy
	Time	Quick, sudden
		Slow, sustained
	Flow	Controlled, bound
		Ongoing, free
Space (The medium in which movement takes place)	Size	Big
		Little
	Zone	In front
		Behind
		To the side
		Above
		Below

(continued)

Table 9.1   *(continued)*

Main category	Subcategories	Further divisions
Space (continued)	Extension	Near Far
	Level	High Low
	Direction	Forward Backward Sideways Upward Downward
	Pathways and patterns	Straight Zigzag Curved Twisted
Relationships (How the moving body interrelates)	The body relates to itself	One half with the other half Body parts meeting Body parts parting Body parts staying in contact
	The body relates to objects	Handling Maneuvering Wearing
	The body relates to other people	Alongside Doing the same Copying Leading Following Cooperating Competing against

Created from text in M. Davies, 2003, *Movement and dance in early childhood*, 2nd ed. (London, England: Paul Chapman Publishing).

Using Davies' Movement Framework

Many dance educators and organizations worldwide (Chang 1997; Davies 1995, 2003; National Dance Education Organization 2006; National Dance Teachers Association 2006; Smith-Autard 1994) organize dance learning into the three curriculum domains of creating, performance, and appreciation, although the emphasis given to each varies. In Taiwan, Chang (1991, 1997) researched a creative dance model for elementary schools that integrated other subjects, considering that Taiwanese children's creating, performance, and appreciation in dance learning also had benefits for their general educational development and Taiwanese cultural understanding. However, her model was never empirically tested. As a teacher focused on early childhood education, I wanted to conduct a research project that used the three-domain model in a Taiwanese kindergarten context with the aim of understanding how young children's dance knowledge can be developed.

Davies (1995, 2003) provided a conceptual movement framework for dance learning and teaching, which stems from Laban movement theory (Laban and Ullmann 1988). It prioritizes body, dynamics, space, and relationships as the key movement factors relevant to dance learning in primary education settings. It can be used to develop young children's abilities to make and perform dance by focusing their attention on particular movement concepts within the framework, such as what the body does, where it moves, the dynamics involved, and the relationships it makes within itself, with other people, and with the objects with which it comes into contact. The framework can also provide teachers with tools for assessment and a common specialist language for discussion and appraisal of research.

Davies (2003, 158) claims that, in early childhood, "dance is dancing and dancing is the dance." Thus, the moment of the children's dance making could be deemed dance performing. In this research, dance was defined as intentional movements aimed at and carried out for the purposes of creative expression and interpretation.

Figurative Representation and Action Representation

"Dances cannot be made from nothing" (Davies 2003, 161), so teachers have to encourage children to create them using varied stimuli, one of which could be drawing. Matthews (2003) noted that young children's drawings and paintings are not just figurative representations that capture the shape or structure of an object but are often associated with movement. He used the term *action representation* to describe how young children represent the movement of an object or the actions within an event in their drawings and paintings.

Four working hypotheses, derived and developed from Matthews' theory of figurative representation and action representation, explored ways drawing and painting can be used to motivate dance making, performance, and appreciation and to help young children to reflect upon the process:

1. Encouraging children to draw their own or others' body movements in space will help them to improvise dance.

2. Encouraging children to record their own or others' movements through drawing will help them to compose dance phrases.

3. Displaying children's drawings of movements will help them to memorize dance phrases.

4. Encouraging children to observe each other's dance performances and then draw them will facilitate their reflection on and appreciation of dance.

Object-based teaching, or providing relevant sources for looking at or materials for handling, maneuvering, or wearing in dance activities, was also used to stimulate the children's improvisation and composition of dance in a playful learning environment. Other visual arts resources such as abstract artworks were used to develop teachers' and children's artistic awareness and symbolic representation abilities.

Cycle 3 Design

In the research just described, the analysis of data from each cycle led directly to planning the action in the following cycle. The classroom experiments in cycle 2 showed that the teachers were able to work as a team and design and implement dance lessons using action words derived from the concepts within Davies' framework as basic vocabulary. They also showed that most of the children were able to improvise movements in response to teachers' action words and visual stimuli such as artists' drawings or paintings. Their spontaneous dance drawings mainly represented body shapes, but with teacher guidance they also depicted a variety of floor patterns and movement pathways. However, the diverse themes of individual lessons were unconnected and the learning was fragmented. In cycle 3, therefore, a single theme was used, one that allowed the children to "feel connected with and make sense of the world we live in" (Stinson 1991 , 137).

The lunar year of 2004-05 was the Year of the Monkey. In Chinese literature, many monsters are involved in stories of the Monkey King. Some examples are shown in figure 9.1; the mask of the Monkey King is represented at the top left in the illustration. It was therefore agreed that cycle 3 would use Beijing opera masks in a Lunar New Year monsters theme. It was hoped that the use of concepts from Davies' movement framework with visual arts would encourage the children to devise longer and more complex dance sequences encompassing bodily, dynamic, and spatial factors. The combination of stimuli also allowed for the creation of a range of imaginative monster characters and motivated the children's emotional, physical, cognitive, and social interaction in dance and visual

Figure 9.1 Beijing opera masks.

arts learning. The conceptual framework for linking dance and visual arts in this cycle is shown in figure 9.2.

Project Zero is an educational research group at the Harvard Graduate School of Education whose mission is to understand and enhance learning, thinking, and creativity in the arts, as well as humanistic and scientific disciplines, at the individual and institutional levels (Project Zero 2006). In a collaborative project with the preschools of Reggio Emilia, Italy, Krechevsky and Mardell (2001, 285) defined a *learning group* as the following:

> A collection of persons who are emotionally, intellectually, and aesthetically engaged in solving problems, creating products, and making meaning—an assemblage in which each person learns autonomously and through the ways of learning of others.

In addition to using movement concepts and paintings as stimuli, collaborative learning enabled the children to learn from each other, the teachers to learn with the children, and the teachers and arts specialist to modify, extend, clarify, and enrich their dance teaching strategies for formative evaluation. Figure 9.3 shows an overview of the action research activity in the cycle and the relationships among participants.

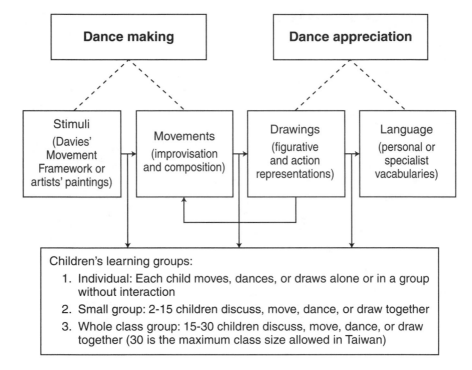

Figure 9.2 Links between dance and visual arts in cycle 3.

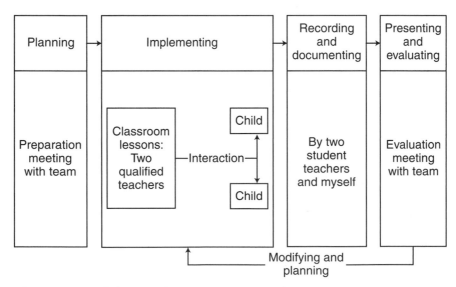

Figure 9.3 Collaborative learning groups in cycle 3.

Examples of Lessons

Cycle 3 consisted of 15 lessons divided between two classes over four weeks. The following describes four of the lessons, all of which used masks and the concept of Lunar New Year monsters to facilitate activities.

Class A, Lesson 1: New Year Monsters Are Coming (Shadow Dance)

Activity 1: Introducing New Year monsters (dance making and performance). Teacher A took the children to the dance studio and told them the familiar children's story "Little Red Riding Hood" but revised it to include hungry New Year monsters. She asked one child to improvise a monster's movement. When he moved forward, she reacted by immediately stepping back as if afraid. After three more children had improvised monster movements, she asked two to demonstrate their movements side by side so the other children could compare the levels and dynamics. The whole class then improvised monsters traveling around the space.

Activity 2: Painting body shapes (dance appreciation). Using the light from an overhead projector, one child created monsterlike shadows on a large sheet of paper that was hung on a wall. Another then used a sponge brush and black ink to paint the monster shadow in outline. Teacher A asked the children, in groups of three, to paint other monsters as a warning to villagers, one child creating the shape and the other two painting it. At the end of the class, the children lay on the floor with their eyes closed and mentally reviewed what they had done and seen.

Class A, Lesson 2: Different New Year Monsters (Monster Dance)

Activity 1: Introducing abstract paintings and monster masks. Teacher A put on a Beijing opera mask and pretended to be a New Year monster that had lost her friends. She said they all had different faces and the only way the children could help her find them was to draw masks showing their faces.

Activity 2: Drawing monster masks. The children drew various shapes and sizes of monster masks with colored pens on paper and then cut them out. The teacher helped the children punch holes in the sides of the masks for rubber bands so they could wear the masks.

Activity 3: Creating monster shapes and dynamic movements (dance making). Teacher A asked the children to express the lines, forms, and shapes they had drawn on their masks as dances. They all put on their masks and made monster shapes. The teacher put on her mask again and said, "You have found my friends!" The teacher then took a hoop and framed individual and group monster shapes as if taking a photograph. Finally, a monster reunion party took place, with the children moving all around the classroom.

Activity 4: Talking about masks and dances (dance appreciation). The children worked in pairs, talking about each other's masks and dances. Teacher A walked around the classroom listening to their discussions.

Class B, Lesson 1: Introduction (Monster Dance)

Activity 1: Introducing New Year monsters (dance making and appreciation). Teacher B showed the masks, told the children the Lunar New Year monster story, and asked them what the monsters looked like and how they moved. The children used their bodies to create monster movements individually, in pairs, and in small groups. The teacher kept adding movement vocabulary, such as *timid, sharp, strong,* and *big,* in order to stimulate the children's movement development. Finally, she asked the children to describe their movements in their own words.

Activity 2: Drawing monster movements (dance appreciation). Each child was given a sheet of paper and crayons to draw a favorite monster movement. Most were realistic representations; very few were abstract.

Class B, Lesson 3: Creating New Year Monsters (Dances With Objects)

Activity 1: Trying on monster skins (dance making and performance). Teacher B placed four colored hoops in the performance area to represent caves. Referring to some Beijing opera masks hanging on the wall and a bag containing different types of clothing and fabrics that she was holding, she explained that the monsters had gone to bathe and she had collected their skins from their cave. She said they came from pregnant monsters, twin monsters, and itchy and stretchy monsters. The children dressed up in the clothes and masks and created new dance steps for each type of monster, with the teacher highlighting different movement concepts such as *heavy, wavy, twisted, long,* and *stretched.*

Activity 2: Drawing dances (dance appreciation). The children were divided into four groups, each drawing the monsters in the dances using crayon on large sheets of paper. Teacher B told them, "The monsters are afraid of red. If we use this color, they will not escape." She asked them to apply red watercolor to their previous monster drawings, which were then displayed in the corridor.

Interrelationships Between Children's Dance and Visual Arts

Although the teachers used drawing and painting with dance making and performance, they were mainly used to encourage dance appreciation. According to Matthews (2003, 23-26), when young children represent dancelike forms and processes, bodily dynamic action stimulates figurative representation. The data in this study showed there is a kinetic-visual relationship between two-dimensional drawing or painting and the three-dimensional body movement it represents. Vice versa, Matthews' ideas support the idea that visual images provide a means of creating, composing, remembering, and reflecting on previous action and that young children's drawings of body figures and movement can have a significant influence on their dance learning.

There were five types of drawing and painting activities:

1. Kinetic dance painting on life-size paper (see figure 9.4). This was used to motivate simultaneous action-representational drawing and painting, as well as dance movement.

2. Figurative representational art with proprioceptive information (Matthews 2003, 171) about the positions of joints and limbs, balance, posture, and stress. In figure 9.5, the child's figurative painting exaggerates a long, stretched body shape mainly represented by nonlocomotor movements in the dances. The teachers sometimes used such drawings or paintings to encourage the children to reflect on, remember, and compose longer dance phrases from the body shapes.

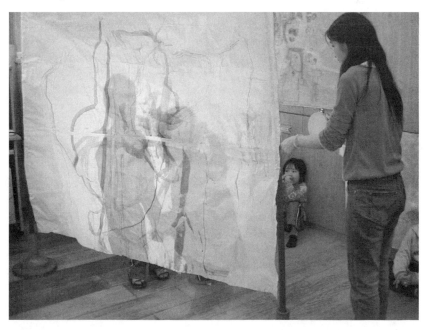

Figure 9.4   Child kinetic dance painting showing body shadows of two girls.

3. Action-representational drawing of pathways or floor patterns (see figure 9.6). These drawings or paintings illustrated dance in time and space, and they mainly represented locomotor movements. The teachers sometimes used them to help the children recall dance pathways or floor patterns.

Figure 9.5 Painting showing an exaggerated body part (long, stretched leg).

Figure 9.6 Drawing of dance routes.

4. Drawing of monster masks or costumes (figure 9.7). These drawings on paper and fabric expressed monsters' movements and characters. Class A made masks from their drawings and class B's drawings were sewn on clothes or fabric for use as costumes in the performance.

5. Painting of traditional *chun lian* banners (figure 9.8). These banners showing traditional lucky phrases are hung from buildings at the Lunar New Year. Class A painted simple words directly on the banners, whereas teacher B sewed her students' drawings on the banners. They used the banners as a stage set for the performance.

Figure 9.7 Drawing of stretchy movements in the monster dance.

Figure 9.8 Children's artwork used as scenery.

Action Representation and Meaningful Scribbling

Action representations are "dynamic modes of representations recording or monitoring the movements of events or objects, often seen or imagined" (Matthews 1999, 155). In cycle 2, the children in class B did not know how to draw actions until they received teacher guidance. In cycle 3, student teacher B's reflections and summative evaluations referred to a four-year-old boy's drawing of an aerial pathway of a ribbon. She noted, "Others might think this drawing is just scribbling, but in our view this boy has drawn the actions the teacher and I were looking for, clearly showing a sequence of movements." This was confirmed next day when he looked at the drawing and repeated the forms and sequences exactly, suggesting that the drawing itself contained the rhythm and dynamics of the movement. Kapsch and Kruger (2004, 72) similarly suggest that drawings can prompt a "metaphorical interpretation of rhythm and movement as it is experienced from the inside [of their body]."

These children were able to use drawings of dance pathways to recall dances they had created. Although the drawings did not contain concrete body shapes, they were intentional and functional, and they captured the moving pathways of the ribbons, thus confirming Matthews' (2003, 197) claim that in the development of visual symbolization, "sensory-motor patterns become the structure for further layers of meaning."

Drawing dance pathways proved highly effective in reinforcing children's memories of their dances so they could be repeated and developed later. This kind of child-initiated dance notation was also useful in enabling them to share dances and help other children to read, understand, and

learn them. For example, figure 9.9 shows a girl's drawing of pathways in each of the four eight-count bars in her ribbon dance. They included short and long traveling zigzags (numbers 1 and 4), a plantlike pathway with a spiral end (2), and vertical tiny loop (3) in the ABA dance composition form (Humphrey 1959/1987,

Figure 9.9 Child's drawing showing pathways in a dance.

150-151). The contrast between the spiral and the vertical tiny loop showed an energetic and rhythmic dance form. The drawing showed the child's ability to compose the dance and deliberately draw movement actions through careful observation. This kind of visual documentation can help teachers make sense of young children's scribblelike symbols and better understand their development in action representations and dance.

Given this, the question arises as to whether symbols should be included in the representational domain. Matthews (2003, 144) calls them "visual or pictorial symbols" that capture something of the shape of represented objects or scenes. In some drawings there is evidence of symbolic representation of the children's own and each other's dance movement. This data showed that scribbles can be beneficial for dance learning. They are dance notations that can be simultaneously realistic and symbolic.

From Realistic to Symbolic Representations

When the teachers only used movement concepts, most children responded with static representational movements and drawings, for example by drawing biceps to symbolize *big and strong*. Figures 9.10 and 9.11, for example, show conventional realistic symbols that children easily

Figure 9.10   Showing off strong biceps.

Figure 9.11 Figurative drawing of the strong biceps dance.

understood. Their narrative movements were directly translated from movement vocabulary. Although these movements and drawings served a communication function, facilitated the child's development of imitation schemas, and fostered a sense of belonging, they lacked individual story character development and creative expression.

However, the children became more imaginative once objects (such as clothes, fabric, and masks) were introduced, and they drew and danced more abstract and complicated forms. In a twin monster activity, two children wearing a single tube of fabric were asked to show different stretching movements away from (figure 9.12) or toward (figure 9.13) each other. Afterward, one child drew both realistic and symbolic drawings (figure 9.14) showing how the dance and mask actually looked, whereas the other drew only the mask (figure 9.15). Although the

Figure 9.12 Stretching in opposite directions.

Figure 9.13 Stretching inside fabric.

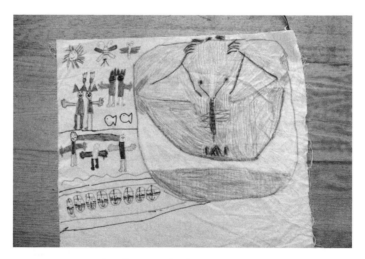

Figure 9.14 Drawing of wide, stretched movements in figure 9.12.

two mask drawings were abstract, they hinted at relationships with the dance. Figure 9.14 shows a drawing of two-way stretchy dancing figures with a wide, round mask representing the wide, stretched movement. In figure 9.15, the mask is narrower and longer, and the dark color on both sides of the chin emphasizes this. The upward lines and curved shapes at the top represent a stretching movement from inside the fabric.

Figure 9.15   Drawing of long, stretched movements inside fabric in figure 9.13.

The data suggested that children do not need to draw realistic human figures to represent Davies' concepts since they can represent them using symbolic forms. Although the forms may differ, their interpretation is the same. This echoes Matthews' suggestion (2003, 194) that children may use drawing images as "metaphors for ideas, feelings, and concepts" and begin to consciously manipulate imagery and further their artistic development.

Combining Realistic and Symbolic Representations

According to Zelazo and Lourenco (2003), when children imitate, they are not merely copying but are doing something more deliberate. Vygotsky's theory of the zone of proximal development (ZPD) (1978) says that when younger children work with older or more experienced ones, it promotes their cognitive development. This happened in the pregnant-monster activity. The mother and baby monster combinations were composed of an older girl at the back with a younger one in front. They wore a single baggy piece of clothing and thus could only move together (figure 9.16). Figure 9.17 shows the first drawings after the collaboration, the younger girl (left) imitating the mask drawn by the older one (right). In Zelazo and Lourenco's transfiguration theory (2003), such imitation is a positive act that consolidates the follower's configurative ability and allows further development. Bruce (2004, 57) also argues that imitation means "taking an idea and interpreting it to suit another context."

Zelazo and Lourenco (2003) also suggest that external support for children's imitation stimuli should be subsequently diminished, allowing them to motivate their own kinesthetic and representational schemas. The children were more skillful in their transfiguration in cycle 3 than in cycle 2 and moved beyond imitation, transforming ideas into personal symbols. Figure 9.18 shows a drawing by a girl aged five years, six months. The drawing is of her and her partner's bodies in the pregnant-monster activity and how they overlapped when seen from the front. Her younger partner, who was four years, six months, drew herself inside her mother's round body (figure 9.19). These X-ray

Figure 9.16 Mother and baby monsters.

images were based on what the children saw, knew, and felt in the dance; this strongly suggests the younger child's feeling of being inside a womb, even though her legs can be seen. The art specialist and I both thought

Figure 9.17 Drawing of a mask by a girl aged four years, six months (right), imitating one made by a girl aged five years, six months (left).

Figure 9.18 Drawing of overlapping bodies by girl aged five years, six months.

Figure 9.19 Drawing of overlapping bodies by girl aged four years, six months.

this drawing was full of meaning and evidence that younger children's artistic sensitivity is not necessary less developed. Both the older and younger children could interpret and represent their dance in drawing creatively. The pairs in the pregnant-monster activity remained the same throughout, their enjoyment of working together and close relationship showing all through the rehearsals and performance. The drawing in figure 9.20, meanwhile, shows how the pair combined their two dance characters and previous drawing styles in one mask.

According to Whitebread (1996, 12), children do not passively receive the information that teachers provide; rather, they are "active information processors." He suggests that "hands-on experiences" (14), in which children gain information directly through their senses, are always likely to be a more effective way of processing their symbolic understandings. Matthews (2003, 97) argues that children's drawings and paintings "combine many sorts of information deriving from different perceptual channels, including touch and movement and also involving language and concepts." I thought the final dance drawings were strong evidence of how their interaction and collaboration facilitated emotional, social, physical, cognitive, and artistic development all at the same time.

Figure 9.20 Drawing showing how one pair combined mother and baby monsters in one mask.

Conclusion

The children and teachers constructed the meaning of movement concepts and thus developed an understanding of Davies' movement framework in relation to the New Year monsters theme. Using visual arts as stimuli together with everyday objects can motivate children to create more personal, symbolic representations in their dances, drawings, and paintings. Dancing and painting, where children both perform and view, are "reciprocal processes" (Davies 2003, 172), where one stimulates the other. Children's dance drawings and dance paintings contain proprioceptive information about dance and exaggerated limbs or body parts, and they express the main movement characteristics. Some children's scribblelike dance drawings and paintings are meaningful symbolic representations of dance and can be useful in later dance composition. Through discussion and interpretation, they become dance notations that other children recognize and understand.

The research data supported the argument by Sahasrabudhe (2005, 19) that visual realism should not be viewed as the end point of children's artistic development. It is more important to consider the ways they use, perceive, respond to, and transform abstract aesthetic forms in visual arts and dance. This research produced evidence that the use of external visual stimuli combined with internal kinetic experiences positively affects children's artistic development in that they are able to transform their experience of dance and communicate it in a visual, symbolic mode. Although the children in the research used different kinds of visual representational modes and combined or developed realistic figurative representations with symbolic action representations, all of their drawings were intentional responses to the dances they created, saw, felt, or knew.

Although developed in the United Kingdom, Davies (2003, 157) claimed that her conceptual movement framework and three curriculum domains of creating, performance, and appreciation of dance learning could be applied to different cultures, styles, and client groups. This research confirmed it could be applied in Taiwanese kindergartens. But what of other cultural contexts?

Since the research project in Taiwan, I have collected and analyzed children's dance drawings and dance paintings from workshops for children aged 4 to 11 in the United Kingdom, Portugal, Angola, and Macao, as well as further examples from Taiwan. These workshops used the same dance materials as the original research, including the stretched bags and ribbons. As before, the children were asked to dance with the materials and then draw their impression of the dance. The results were remarkably similar. The children's drawings often showed body shapes inside the stretched bags as if they were transparent or had used an X-ray machine. They were aware of what was happening physically inside them. Most also drew pathways and patterns of their kinetic and visual experiences in the ribbon dance without guidance. This suggests that Davies' framework and Matthews' drawing theory are transferable and that children in different cultural contexts have similar figurative and action-representation abilities.

There were, however, subtle differences between boys' and girls' outcomes. In general, boys prefer to use strong, straight, quick but controlled dynamics and to draw body shapes with proprioceptive information imbued in limbs. Girls' drawings, on the other hand, tend to show showed gentle, wavy, sustained, and ongoing dynamics, especially in relation to the space created by ribbons in the ribbon dance.

There remains much room for further research. The children's movements and dance drawings tell us a great deal about their understanding of their bodies' dynamic relationships with personal and general space in time, as well as their cultural understanding. However, would the use of other cultural constructs or contexts encounter different results? Although this research focused chiefly on the pedagogical possibilities, there are exciting opportunities to compare the ways individual children express cognizance of certain concepts at different moments in the learning process and in different cultural contexts.

REFLECTIONS

Many of us have experienced the nuances of cultural difference in the field of dance. Whether learning about these differences while studying dance history or appreciation, performing a different cultural dance form, performing anthropological research, or embodying the movements through a choreographic project, we recognize that dance is a migratory art form created from a diverse collection of traditional and multicultural dance forms. Our tradition in dance has been to adopt techniques, notation forms, and movement frameworks from one cultural context and use them in another without much thought. Shu-Ying Liu has guided us through a project that engages us in thinking about how children can create visual images of their movement and use their drawings as a form of notation for their movement that they can then read and recreate in movement. Her research brings to the fore questions such as, what in dance can be universalized or adopted for cross-cultural use? What kinds of different information might be revealed using the same tools in different cultures? What might need to be changed in order to preserve or respect the diversity of cultural values, attitudes, and beliefs?

Some issues, however, might need to be excluded for cultural or political reasons. Culturally, we would be unable to have students imagine themselves as being pregnant if we were working in North Carolina schools in the United States. As educators, as we choose theories, frameworks, techniques, choreographies, or any educational material or processes, we find ourselves negotiating between cultural values and dance traditions, local and global cultures, and what our educational systems value. Our educational choices, whether directed toward formal or informal education, demand sensitivity to the child's life, to the cultural and historical location where the learning is located, and to the direction or course that we are offering our students. As Shu-Ying reminds us, we engage in creating our world with our students, whether in the classroom, studio, or stage; this is where our wisdom is needed to nurture the creative soul, to listen for the authentic voice, and to make a space for that which is barely imagined.

PART III REFLECTIVE QUESTIONS

- Does dance have the unique potential to increase understanding and sensitivity toward cultural differences?
- Do those involved in dance have a responsibility to assist in the development of a more globally sensitive and aware student?
- Have you experienced dance as a process that has increased your empathy and understanding of people who differ from you in their culture? What distinguished those experiences?
- Should we have concerns about transposing concepts, theories, or techniques from one cultural context into another?

part IV

Transcending Differences:
The Commonalities of Dance

ten

My Body, My Life, and Dance

Adrienne Sansom

Senior lecturer in dance and drama
University of Auckland, New Zealand

In this chapter I explore the relationship between dance, or embodied knowing, and humanity through recounting a personal story in which, through a kind of experiencing, there is a new found understanding of being human and thus connecting to others, humanity, and issues of social justice. The telling of one's own story draws on multiple layers of being and unearths the deeply embedded emotions that lie within, thereby exposing something about who we are and what we care about. In a sense, this type of narrative or autobiography of the self invites others to recall their own stories or lived experiences, which have also been experienced in and through the body in similar ways. I want to reveal the persuasive sway that one's lived experiences can have in connecting to other areas of life while also showing how dance education can be a powerful tool for addressing who we are as people and acting as a conduit through which we might contribute to a better world.

This story comes from a time when I was facing perhaps some of the most difficult moments a person can experience. I have experienced profound moments in my life, but few have been as overwhelming or as intense as facing my own mortality, or the sudden realization of my limited time on this earth. It is my intention in this chapter to focus on that aspect of our common humanity and to illuminate how dance can become powerful not only as a holistic embodied experience but also as a way to understand ourselves and thus connect to others and to provide meaning in our lives as we help create a better world.

What Has Brought Me to This Place?

Long before I ever entertained the thought of pursuing a career in dance, I had the need to be physically active. As a young child, I sought adventure and ventured into regions outside the parameters of my garden gate. My first foray into the wide unknown was as a toddler when I loaded my push-chair (stroller) with toys and walked out my gate and up the road, pushing the push-chair. My wandering did not stop there; I continued throughout my childhood to venture into other territories in and near my neighborhood, seeking adventures and discovering new or imagined worlds.

The dramatic world of play was very much a companion of mine during my childhood years. It was not until my teenage years that dance officially entered my life, although it was evident on the margins of my childhood as I invented and reinvented myself as a dancer in my imagined world. Although I always wanted to dance, dancing as a formal pastime did not exist until I was offered free ballroom dancing lessons by a studio canvassing homes to boost their business. I soon became enamored by the possibility that not only could I learn to dance but that I actually liked to dance. Because being physical had always been a large part of my life, it was not surprising that I embraced this opportunity to use my body in the pursuit of learning something new that also complemented my social life. As the years progressed, ballroom dancing soon made way for other forms and my world became focused on dance.

These experiences in dance ultimately led to my involvement in dance education, when I commenced my career as a kindergarten teacher. It was during my early years of teaching that I adopted an experiential approach to exploring dance with young children. I discovered that because I could create dance when working with other adults, this process of learning could be transferred to my students. The receptiveness of the young children was refreshing and the experience forged many relationships between the children and me that may never have been experienced if it were not for dance. This was the opening I was waiting for. It was the doorway to the future, to the possibility of dance education as an enriching but untapped and undervalued area of learning.

My burgeoning interest in dance inspired me to search for more information. It was during this time that I discovered daCi (Dance and the Child International), which was a community of dance teachers, some of whom researched and wrote about dance for children. This was the initial seed that blossomed into an ongoing exploration of dance for children. The pursuit in dance related to children continued over many years as I traveled to different places to study dance. Throughout this pursuit, which continues today, I realized that there was something more pressing than just the study of dance. This something was about being human, and although my initial foray into dance was not consciously focused on issues of humanity, I began to realize that the humanitarian concerns that affect who we are as people were inextricably linked to why I danced.

Regardless of where this journey has taken me, I often look back to where this underlying connection to issues of humanity first materialized, and I recognize that it materialized because of the aspirations I had as a young child for some form of hope in the world, albeit a limited world restricted by the confines of my geographical location. These childhood aspirations or imaginings came from an expansion of my little corner of the world into an ongoing sojourn into literature with books that I borrowed from the library. The time spent reading books enabled me to travel to many different lands through the eyes of children from other cultures. I was fascinated by the different lives of these children and often attempted to replicate their lives in my imagined worlds of play.

Little did I realize that these imagined journeys into the lives of others would become pivotal in my life as I continued to pursue what it means to be human. Perhaps it is still this child within that spurs me on as I recall the significant times in my life that were experienced viscerally and emotionally, whether joyous or painful. The empathetic connection I formed during those early years has remained a central component of who I am today, and it reminds me of the empathy I have witnessed in young children; their feeling for the well-being of another. In my present role as a lecturer in dance education, I am reminded of these initial encounters with the stories and plights of others. I am also cognizant of my responsibility in this role within teacher education to not only expand the horizons of those I teach but also help students become conscious of their role as it relates to the world in which they live.

Facing Criticality, or Is Ignorance Bliss?

This aspiration to find ways to link to others and thus, humanity in and through dance, however, is no easy task. It is perhaps the area that I am least familiar with, or that is least evident in my practice, and yet it is the underlying motivation for much of my work. I have scarcely skimmed the surface of what it means to address issues of being human, especially from a critical perspective, let alone what a critical approach to concerns about life and dance might be like in actual practice. I am concerned that an aspiration of this proportion can all too easily fall into the syndrome of hollow rhetoric. If anything, I have savored my time in dance and viewed it as a refuge from the storm; up until now I had thought little of being critical not only of the field of dance in which I had found a home but also of using dance pedagogy as a conduit to address the injustices in our world. Did I really want to burst my bubble?

As indicated in the abstract for her paper "Re-Membering the Body in Critical Pedagogy," Shapiro (1994) draws on "feminist and postmodern critiques . . . to focus on the body's role in the process of knowing and the praxis of freedom" (61). Shapiro's viewpoint, therefore, is about placing the body in the center of an approach to critical pedagogy. For Shapiro, "critical pedagogy is a philosophy of praxis concerned with emancipation and committed to a process which connects self-reflection and understanding to a knowledge which makes transformation of the social conditions we live possible" (Shapiro 1994, 65).

Furthermore, Shapiro (1998) states that an education that focuses on "the thoughtful and conscious struggle to reshape our world into one that is more just and compassionate . . . [needs to be] joined to a feminist pedagogy that insists that education must start from the lived experiences of our students' lives" (9). Because much of our lived experience is housed in the body, the body needs to be central to a feminist and critical pedagogy and, ultimately, to an understanding of being human, or a humanitarian approach. This has huge implications for me as a dance educator, for the body is central to my teaching and it is on and in the body where students' stories are housed. If, as Shapiro (1994) suggests, our bodies carry the memories and signs of our culture, we can examine the "relationship between ourselves, others, and the world in which we live" (65), which give insight into social issues of justice and equality, relationships, and freedom from a critical perspective. Thus, the body can become a site for critical pedagogy, which calls for a different approach to teaching dance, especially in education.

My World Today: Dance for All

As a dance educator in New Zealand, I work with generalist student teachers for the purpose of teaching dance in educational settings. Within the desired objectives of dance education an emphasis is placed on the thinking involved in the creative development of ideas in dance. For this to occur in a meaningful way, one's personal life and culture are also crucial components in the process of making dance and expressing meaning.

Regardless of all this, however, I struggle with the majority of the student teachers' apparent lack of acceptance of the body as a viable means of thinking and expressing in education. This has, without a doubt, come about because of the repressed and almost invisible use of the body in the more traditional areas of education that the majority of students have received and the limited venues where it has been appropriate to use the body. As a consequence, to reactivate the body in order to realize its presence in education is an overwhelming thought. The additional component of dance as critical pedagogy from a postmodern, feminist, sociopolitical, and cultural perspective for the purpose of pursuing a humanitarian objective is a further factor to consider.

This alienation or disdain of the body as a viable entity in the hallowed halls of academia should come as no surprise. McLaren (1999, 277) provides a damning report about the place of the body in education:

> In their steely resolve as custodians of reason, educators have hacked away at the tendons that connect meaning and the body. They have done so to the detriment of their pedagogies and at their own peril as producers of historical agency. This is most damagingly evident in "official" school practices where we witness in oppositional student behaviour what Terry Eagleton (1990, 13) calls "the body's long inarticulate rebellion against the tyranny of the theoretical."

For this reason, educators need to address the absence of the body and, in turn, the ignoring of historical determinants so as to render such pedagogies problematic and to eventually "find ways of transforming them into a larger political project and social vision. Only in this way can liberating pedagogies be developed that will enable students to construct meanings that are lived in the body, felt in the bones and situated within the larger body politic in the form of public meta-narratives . . . aimed at increasing social justice and emancipation" (McLaren 1999, 278). This means not only reinstating the body just for the sake of it in education but also reinserting the body forcibly for the purposes of social critique.

As educators, we need to address the issues of race, class, gender, sexuality, age, and ability that are inscribed upon the body as cultural and social constructions and lived in multiple ways. As a dance educator, I need to heed the charge of the pedagogy of the body and take seriously the importance of including the many different lived experiences and diverse cultures that shape the identities of the students I teach. This means that I place myself in a position of receivership so as to invite the lives and stories of the students I teach. It also means that I prepare myself to face the less-than-desirable or confrontational perspectives that arise as a result of this process, because it is the opening up of contentious issues that is pivotal to a critical pedagogy. Finally, it means that I share my own life in a candid and authentic way so as to present myself and my stories as equally viable and vulnerable in the process of interrupting or interrogating the construction of personal as well as public meaning.

Indeed, it is my responsibility to act as the protagonist in this process so that the necessary disruption occurs.

Therefore, in order to invite the lived experiences of my students into the dance process, I face not only the difficulty of sharing personal experiences but also the problem of involving the body in the process of expressing those lived experiences from students who have little or no experience in dance. This is not to say that it is impossible; it is more about how I should go about it. What do I need to change in my teaching approach in order to extend this invitation to the student teachers I teach?

Although we talk about the disappearance of the body in education, little is written about how the body can be reinstated in education for the purposes of creating embodied learning. As stated by Shapiro (1994), although we "have given attention to the absence of body knowledge in this pedagogy, there are still few examples that really illustrate what this might mean" (65). It is all too easy to use the rhetoric while neglecting the actual practice or application that is so vital in promoting the body in learning, particularly from a critical perspective. This is still a dilemma for me. I have been involved in bodily learning for most of my career, yet until now I have given little consideration to what this bodily involvement means from a political and socially conscious perspective.

Another aspect that is significant in pursuing the role of the body in education is connected to history. I believe that students need to know what has been in order to face the bruises before they can become part of a movement for change. If there is no recognition of previous struggle, there appears to be an attitude that everything is fine. There is a need to reinsert those areas of knowledge that have been neglected historically, politically, and culturally because it is knowledge of both the limitations as well as the possibilities that can help create a liberatory praxis. This requires looking at the pedagogy of the body from a critical perspective as well as viewing the body as a site of knowing. I am interested in exploring the notion of how dance can become a catalyst for communicating about the humanitarian aspects of life and consequently how this might contribute to a reconceptualization of dance as an agent of change.

The Body as Voice: Finding New Expression

Focus on the body invites a visceral approach to knowing, and knowing in this way evokes a powerful form of engagement that has the potential to connect to the inner sanctums of our bodies and the deeply ingrained range of emotions that our bodies possess. It is my contention that when we feel—when we experience the pain, the atrocities, the anguish, as well as the desires, the joy, and the ecstasies of life—we also think differently. This connects to something that Shapiro and Shapiro (2002) said when referring to the visceral nature of embodied knowledge: "It is the return of an aesthetic language, that is no more the marginal or fantastical stepchild of modernity, but one that takes us to the heart of being itself" (30). This is the existence of life, or of humankind. If we didn't care, why would we bother? And what better way to care about something than to invite it into our lives, into our bodies, so that we can embody it, examine it, nurture it, or change it?

Shapiro and Shapiro (2002, 31) link this focus on the body to the pedagogy of the body "as a lived medium [who] becomes a part of the curriculum." This focus is true of dance education, which is not surprising since dance uses the body as its primary medium, although most of the dance forms adopted by Western societies have focused on the aesthetic of the female dancer to be objectified in a male-dominated ideology and thus can be, "as far as females are concerned . . . a highly repressive aesthetic practice " (Shapiro and Shapiro 2002, 31). Dance education has also suffered from misnomers, such as *creative dance* or *free expressive dance*, which, while perhaps enabling one to find some personal and spiritual pleasure, do little for the art form as a way of responding to and commenting on the world we in which we live from a sociopolitical standpoint. As stated by the authors, "There is, typically, little here that connects dance education to a critical apprehension of culture or a socially constructed subjectivity" (Shapiro and Shapiro 2002, 31).

It is important to see that dance can be used as informative and political literacy, where the body becomes the site of social commentary using memories of personal experience and social construction through both an affective and a cognitive cultural process (Shapiro and Shapiro 2002). When people are able to create movement drawn from their own reflections and dialogue to explore designated themes, the resulting choreographic process is clearly political as well as personal. Thus it becomes dance created beyond the constraints of predesigned and prechoreographed dance, which is instructed to, and digested and regurgitated by the performers with little personal or intellectual input from them.

Dance education does not need to be that way, but although hindrances (marginality, designated language, prescribed outcomes and purposes) exist in education that limit the accessibility of dance as a critical pedagogy, the traditional behaviorist modes of learning remain the preferred teaching methodology. This is not dance education; it is dance training, and there is an important distinction. Dance education is not just about learning the elements and language that constitute the dance process—it is about addressing who we are as people, embracing difference,

Kilda Northcott.
Photo courtesy of APN New Zealand. Photographer: Jane Ussher.

encountering numerous cultures, interacting and collaborating with others, and inviting response.

The New Zealand dance curriculum exemplifies these values in the strands identified in the curriculum document. These strands are understanding dance in context, developing ideas in dance, and communicating and interpreting in dance, together with developing practical knowledge in dance (Ministry of Education 2000). As a performing art, dance is about audience reaction, visual reading, and thinking based on the context in which we live. Although the curriculum espouses such aspirations, it is important that these ideals are put into practice. These desires may become empty promises unless serious consideration is given to the larger purpose of dance from a sociopolitical and cultural perspective. This is where I reflect seriously on my role as a dance educator so as to have the chance to realize these aspirations in order to influence the reconceptualization and hopefully the progress of dance education in New Zealand.

Although dance may be a reflection of a culture, it can also stir the imagination, which can then motivate a community to work toward change or the amelioration of social injustice. But first and foremost there is a need to establish dance as a valid area of learning, one that is recognized as academic and not just as personal or public recreation. However, dance must also adopt progressive and postmodern educational principles so as to no longer replicate what has been handed down as dance education from a Western or Eurocentric perspective, to ensure that dance today reflects the multiplicity of cultures. That requires bringing in different voices, languages, and approaches to teaching in dance.

Having espoused these ideals for dance education, and to make some connection to my thesis of dance as a way to address humanitarian concerns, it is important that I face my own uncertainties. I have chosen to do this in the form of a reflection so as to confront the question of whether this epistemological ideal in dance education is a possibility, as well as to provide an example of what it means to delve into one's own body and life for the purpose of exposing those bodily sensations—emotions—that connect us all to the frailties of humanity and inextricably link us as human beings. This behooves me to enter the terrain of the unknown, albeit through something I once thought I knew so well: my own body.

Entering Unknown Territory: My Body, My Life, My Dance

One of the ways I thought of approaching this area was to recall a bodily experience in which I remembered the inscriptions, or body knowledge, that were etched into the body as a lived experience. These inscriptions or body memories simulate, to some degree, an experience of oppression as well as liberation and transformation. In other words, I want to relive an embodied experience through an autobiographical approach. Through doing this, I hope to replicate to some extent what it might mean for others to delve into their own lived experiences and to recall something of their visceral responses to oppressive aspects of life in order to place these experiences as central areas of exploration in dance. I am continually reminded that knowledge of the body is often relegated to second-rate status and is also, as stated by Zandy (2000, 183), "not easily articulated and not often part of bourgeois intellectual circles." For this reason, and because the body is central to my pedagogy and consequently my narrative, I want to resituate the body as a viable source of knowledge and as an acceptable part of educational practice.

The hardest part of this process is deciding which lived experience to unravel and delve into, but the one that comes to mind is still central to who I am today and how I live my life. It occurred during my earlier graduate studies in dance and for this reason was an incredibly somatic experience. Furthermore, it occurred during a time when I was keeping a journal in which I recorded the unfolding events, encapsulating my raw emotions, bodily responses, and deeply ingrained thought processes.

A Somatic Sojourn

In 1997, I was in the second year of my graduate study in dance, enjoying stimulating subject matter, enduring demanding technique classes, and indulging in a course focusing on somatic practices. This latter course provided an antidote to some of the stresses I was subjecting my body to as it moaned and groaned through endless days of physical work, though there were also times when it soared with great glee as I participated in the sheer delight of moving. I found that my body, and, consequently, my emotional self, was on a constant pendulum, swinging high and dipping low as I lived my life as a dancer. There was definitely physical pain, especially in my neck (a site of an old injury that always plagued me when under strain), but also in my legs and lower back. The skin on my feet was having a hard time staying intact as it was constantly churned on the floor.

Sometimes it seemed as though all the feelings, injuries, and daily insults on the body would erupt into the head, as if it wanted to push forth like a volcanic eruption. These types of feelings are relatively usual for a dancer, particularly an aging dancer, because the body is subjected to a great deal that the body would not experience during the normal course of daily events. The body is twisted, bent, stretched, curved, and straightened; it writhes on the floor, soars through the air, pounds the ground, or caresses the sky as it travels, turns, jumps high, and falls.

Twice a week I attended a morning class that explored somatic practice. In many ways this class turned out to be a moment of re-gathering the self, as if I had become dismembered or disconnected from the self as it navigated the highways and byways of life. Each session introduced us to different mind–body practices in which we had the chance to reconnect to our breathing; to our bones, muscles, and flesh; and most of all to the inner sanctums of our mind and spirit. Most practices were slow and deep as our bodies settled back into themselves through guided visual imagery, meditation, and breathing exercises. I luxuriated in the experiences, and I came away from each session feeling a little more connected to the self, although sometimes I felt even more aware of those parts of the self that were out of sync or hurting. The somatically induced awareness, however, of certain parts of the body helped me take more care of how I treated my body.

Little did I know that one of the greatest challenges I have ever had to face was just around the corner. I had no inkling of something else that was lurking inside my body at that time that was insidiously growing and would eventually erupt through the flesh. I had no idea that I was about to go through some of the most invasive experiences my body would ever endure, compounded by even greater despair with the about-to-be-discovered loss of a loved one. Life could not have been more tumultuous for me. I was about to feel as if the earth had swallowed me up and the sky had fallen in. This was a time when I needed to pull on all my reserves bodily, rationally, emotionally, and spiritually so as to survive what lay ahead.

My Body, My Life: Inner and Outer Journeys

At the beginning of the somatic course we were encouraged to record how we felt, drawing on awareness of our bodies and all the nuances embedded within. My first journal entry read as follows:

> I am immediately struck by the dichotomy in which I exist daily; the need for care of the body—nurturing and feeding, rest and relaxation—versus the requirements set by the world I exist in—reading material, course work, timetables. . . . There are things that appear to be outside my control, such as an inadequate bus service, the cold days waiting outdoors at the bus stop paralleling the much warmer internal environments that play havoc with my body.

> I guess I could also view these things as the challenges of life—because do we become flaccid, uninterested souls in the universe if we are not questing, seeking, continually striving for some form of aspiration—something better in life, or something to make life on this planet better? I would like to think so, but at the moment I only know that these are the present realities of my life.

> I fear things before they happen. I want to do my best, produce high quality, A+ work. I face disappointment (definitely a masochist for that) when I do not reach my intended goals.

> Although I experience these dichotomies, I am also reading about the dichotomies others experience. This appears to be a human condition—and this is where I need to look inside myself and recognize those things, which are part of me, shaped by who I am and how I grew up. I need to take a good look at myself not just physically

but at my entire self, body, mind, and soul, inside and out—which is a manifestation of my state of being.

As the course progressed, further journal entries demonstrated something of my thought processes in relation to the material we were reading. I used this time to concentrate on the sensations my body felt from day to day:

> Sometimes I feel that I am blind to the messages my own body is sending to me and I need the objective observation of another person to alert me to my own state of being. When we live inside our bodies all our lives they become familiar territories, and with that familiarization habitual patterns develop that we begin to take for granted.

> Chronic pain persists—this is my reality, even though I have sought ways to recognize it, release it, live with it.

> Yet I want to dance, I want to use my body—to experience the feeling of physical goodness—the excitement of dancing well, full out—it is somewhat an addictive feeling—exhilaration!

A later journal entry begins to reveal something that was looming on the horizon, something that was going to test my body in every way and take me on the journey of my life:

> Something has ballooned out of my body—what is this? Cancer! Why? What is it? What type? Is it invasive? Did we get it early? Is it treatable? How? What's the prognosis? What will I do? Will I be sick? Will it be painful? What about the side effects?

> I feel empty, nauseated—butterflies in my stomach, definitely nervous—scared. My emotions are mixed and jumbled—my body is lacking sleep as I also harbor another despair!

> I don't know whether I am trying to face everything bravely or whether I should let the emotion pour out, which I know is swirling around inside me. How will I be treated—will I be treated as a whole person?

> I feel as though I am sitting on the horns of a dilemma while I pursue the process of an uncertain medical diagnosis—it is somewhat scary not knowing what the answer or outcome is yet. My breathing becomes affected—it feels rapid and shallow—as my nerves erupt like a prickly pear!

This was also the time when I received the devastating news of the loss of my godson at sea. I continued by writing:

> I feel as if I am squeezed between two drastic situations, I feel out of sorts—my body and my mind are definitely out of kilter! I feel as though my emotions are in a state of turmoil.

> With a lack of appetite I feel as though I am in a state of fasting, cleansing my body—to allow my body (and mind) to be open to what lies ahead. I could not get the real benefit of breathing deeply today because there would be this kind of shattering effect, as if my life had begun to slip away and I had to take quick but shallow breaths so as to come back to life. What a metaphor!

> The other trauma I face is irreconcilable and only time will take away the deep and immense pain I feel at the moment.

At this stage in the proceedings, I was facing my first surgery (the initial biopsy to confirm what was already suspected). In response to this situation, I wrote the following:

> I have been thinking how ironic this situation is for me, where I have to give my body over to another person (the surgeon—a woman nevertheless) to take care of the problem. Even though I have been exploring a form of healing the self through this course, I do not think I can take care of my present issue through my own means of healing or via an alternative somatic practice. I am well aware that an understanding of my body has led to the detection of the problem and my continued understanding of how the mind and body interconnect will, hopefully, contribute to the healing process.

The results of my biopsy were positive and I was diagnosed with an invasive form of breast cancer. This promoted further visceral bodily responses:

> My emotions have always played a large part in everything I do, so they are at full speed right at this moment. Not only do I have my cancer diagnosis to deal with, I have also received confirmation that my godson is lost at sea, presumed drowned, and this has hit me so hard that it is like a large rock inside of me that just won't resurface. I don't know what to feel (except the deepest pain) and what to think—but whatever it is, it is so deeply entrenched inside me, it almost feels as if it is unreal. I want to push it to the deepest, darkest reaches of my thoughts—but my feelings loom large and

will not go away! I feel both pushed and pulled at the moment, as if I am internalizing, or trying to find a safe haven from my vulnerable feelings, which can be seen in a metaphoric sense as well as a literal sense where we often move backward before we move forward—while I am reaching forward, sometimes moving rather quickly through all the steps required to deal with the procedures, I also find myself going backward from time to time, often right back to the time before the prognosis—this, I presume, is my safe haven where I can return to a more secure world—it is almost as if this invasion in my body is not real, and I am living in some sort of fictional world.

It was interesting to note in my journal entry toward the end of the course, when I was facing major surgery, that I acknowledged the significance of this somatic course, which concentrated so strongly on knowledge of the whole body, while also connecting to a feminist research course I was doing concurrently. This provides evidence of the effective interrelationship between the pedagogy of the body and feminist theory. Equipped with the knowledge from both of these courses, I found that I was empowered to handle the situation, to have some authority over what happened to my body, and to become an active collaborator in the overall process with the belief that it would result in a positive outcome.

This somatic sojourn was an experience that I lived through from a visceral perspective, and although I was not experiencing oppression in the usual sense of the word, my body was definitely under siege. This was one of the ways in which my voice, and my body, could be expressed at a time when my feelings were at their most raw. I was open and vulnerable; I was scared and felt powerless. I learned, however, that I did not have to remain powerless; I could find my own sense of agency and, in turn, affect the way I responded to my situation. This is the power of the body and of the mind, of the body memory and all that is inscribed on the body by outside influences, which can be used to oppress or, alternatively, used to empower and, in turn, can ameliorate oppression and tyranny. We have in our hands (body) the agency to take back our bodies, our lives, for the purpose of working toward release from oppressive regimes that seek out the body and, consequently, the lives of people so as to keep in place those who have power.

My Dance: Finding My Feet

Following the surgery and during my ongoing treatment for cancer, I returned to dance classes and found yet another avenue to express my feelings about my body and my life through dance. I am attempting here to write what my body was performing so as to capture something of the dance I created at that time. This can only be an approximation of the totality of my experience because the body tells and feels much more than my words can convey.

> Heart pounding, feet floundering—I beat out my dance on the grate; my body is viscerally present yet distantly absent as I recall and relive my pain. The feet gather speed as they pound on the ground and my upper body extends skyward as I look and reach beyond the sun to a place unknown, far beyond the confines of earth. Others gather around me and join in a chorus of stamping feet and quivering bodies; arms embrace in a united coalition of shared pain, grief, and love. My body senses relief as the feelings rise and are released; then my body yields and relinquishes all its power and energy as I fall limp to the ground. I am breathless but exhilarated; I am depleted but completed. This was a dance for my godson lost at sea; this was a dance about my cancer soon to be eradicated from my body; this was my dance, my dance of life. I became a stranger in a familiar and yet strange land.

My body, my dance, and my life all become intertwined through the process of performance. It is through this performance that I am able to harness my own energy and agency for transformation. In a sense, I enter a new realm of being, in a place that is familiar and yet unfamiliar because I have never experienced this situation before. I have entered the unknown, but it is the unknown that frees me. This reminds me of what the Brazilian educator Paulo Freire (1988) says about how our destinies are not set in stone and therefore are not prerequisites for the way we are destined to live our lives. We have the power to change our destinies once we realize our potential, or once we self-actualize by actively raising our consciousness, where opportunities for hope and action can be manifested.

This is the power of the body, the power to be transformative,[1] the power to transgress the restrictions placed upon the body, the power to liberate through critical reflection and dialogue, and the power to have an effect on others and on the world. If the body is left out of this process, we will never fully realize the strength of the individual and the potency of the collective, as well as the ability to truly change what is, because an enormous part of who we are will be missing. The stories and experiences that are etched onto our bodies remain one of the most valuable resources we could ever use in the ongoing struggle for social justice. Dance, therefore, can become a influential adjunct to critical pedagogy with a common goal toward the amelioration of injustice, but "art must be given broader significance, to help us understand something about the 'what is' of our concrete lives, and to imagine and/or experience kinesthetically the possibilities for 'what could or should be'" (Shapiro and Shapiro 2002, 39-40); to imagine "what might be, what should be" (Greene 1973, 7); to discover "alternative possibilities" (Greene 1988, 119); or to imagine "what we might become" (Freire 1988, 120).

This connects to my belief in the need to seriously consider what it means to be human as well as to my area of teaching in dance education. Dance, as well as other art forms, is part of the humanities and as such can embody a diverse range of learning styles so that the lived experiences of our students can become central to a critical pedagogy of difference. Through the creative process of the arts, we have a "means of exploring, and of reshaping, who we are and how we live together" (Greenwood 2001, 199). The arts link to the human condition, and the human condition links to diversity, which can give us the opportunity to explore multiple forms of human experience. Diversity encompasses all people in our pluralistic societies today, and this in turn affects my role as a dance educator in New Zealand. In this union of difference we are able to find new meanings, meanings that emerge from an alliance, albeit sometimes a less-than-comfortable alliance, that produces profoundly deeper and more enriching understanding.

Conclusion

If we begin to recognize dance as a viable avenue to explore human and social issues, I believe that we have yet another opportunity to rejuvenate the connective tissue of humanity and, thereby, further open the portals that link us. Dance has the potential, through the opportunity of full bodily engagement, to delve into the embodied experiences of our lives so as to connect to what it feels like viscerally and emotionally to be human. For this reason, I believe dance can enhance the opportunities to make connections to others and thereby increase the possibility of ameliorating oppression and injustice because it makes possible an expanded empathetic understanding of the human condition.

In relation to the human condition, I often reflect upon the fact that we are mortal beings and exist within a body that inhabits both wellness and sickness, which manifests itself in either energy or apathy. This can set a precedent that life is hard and that continual struggle toward an ideal is a difficult thing to do. I saw it as a factor in my life when recognizing the reality of my own mortality, which can prevent me from completing the action I need to take in order to pursue freedom or justice. This, I believe, is part of the human condition, something we all have in common. If anything, life teaches us that we have but a short time to do things and, therefore, time is precious. It is time and experience that bring us closer to this realization. As Greene (2001) states in a film about her life, "One is never done on this earth and . . . 'wide-awakeness' and conscious raising are pursuits of a lifetime with no end in sight." These types of realizations or awakenings correlate with the emotional lives we all embody, which cannot be ignored. I also recognize how painful real issues in education can be when we come up against different points of view, conflicting interests, or undeniable anger, but, if I am to seek the unfamiliar (the critical) within the familiar (dance), it is imperative that I allow for both the pain as well as the elation such experiences can bring. Greene stated the following with reference to Buber:

> I recall Martin Buber speaking about teaching and about the importance of "keeping the pain awake" (1957, p. 116); and I suggest that the pain he had in mind must be lived through by teacher as well as student, even as the life stories of both must be kept alive. This, it seems to me, is when real encounters occur—when human beings come together as beings living in time. (Greene 1995, 113)

With this in mind, I see my role in dance as a way of expanding horizons, overcoming the apathy of a society that is conditioned to see things in a dehumanized way, and promoting new possibilities. This requires imagination, arising from the premise of critical thought and moral aspirations for a better world.

The word *imagination* means a great deal to me because it is imagination that helps us create new worlds, new ways of thinking that enable us to go beyond what is and to imagine what could be. It was because of my fertile imagination as a child that I ventured forth on this pedagogical endeavor. Dance provides an approach to learning and thinking that is often avoided in other areas of learning: the embodiment of learning. Greene (2001) talked about "embodied perspectives, knowing the world with my whole being, the body." Consciousness is an embodied consciousness, not a mind–body split, which has shaped the way education progressed for numerous years. It is my role in education to alert those I teach to think about issues in the world, particularly the concept of freedom from oppression. The obstacle, as I see it, relates to "the inability to name what lies around" (Greene 1988, 125), to label the oppression. We are generally silenced during our learning and become numb to the desire to ask questions in order to seek meaning that relates not only to our circumstances but also to the circumstances of others. It is because of the collective mind that the individual can work toward freedom for the greater good, and this is where a reawakening must occur.

This is also where imagination is key because, as Dewey (1934, 283) states, the imagination "is the only gateway through which these meanings can find their way into a present interaction; or rather . . . the conscious adjustment of the new and the old *is* imagination." The awakening or raising of consciousness is an important step in the pursuit of freedom. To imagine the possibilities (or to be able to identify the obstacles) sometimes comes from others' prompts. This is the action the educator must take. Greene (1988) reminds us that "education for freedom must clearly focus on the range of human intelligences, the multiple languages and symbol systems available for ordering experience and making sense of the lived world" (125). It is then that we can find ourselves in a position to see things differently or placed in a situation that we can deconstruct and transform. This is the imagined world that takes us beyond who we are and hopefully awakens a new way of seeing things with the purpose of influencing the social conscience in order to work for change. This is what I chose to do when I faced my own obstacles and eventually let the power of the imagination and somatic experiences guide me.

For me, it is through the art of dance that both the critical and the imaginative can be used as a new way of looking at things by using multiple or embodied approaches to thinking and seeing. Of course, as Greene reminds us, the potential the arts have in transforming our thinking cannot alone be relied upon to "educate for freedom" (1988, 131). The arts have not and may never be given the credence they deserve in education, because they are perceived as decorative, works of little value in a society concerned with money and commodities. However, as Greene (1988) emphatically states, the arts "ought to be, if transformative teaching is our concern, a central part of curriculum, wherever it is devised" (131).

I would like to conclude with a passage that I believe is important for us to remember as educators.

> Teachers, like their students, have to learn to love the questions, as they come to realize that there can be no final agreements or answers, no final commensurability. And we have been talking about stories that open perspectives on communities grounded in trust, flowering by means of dialogue, kept alive in open spaces where freedom can find a place. (Greene 1988, 134)

To act consciously in this world is to induce change through both critical and mindful practice for the purpose of social justice and liberation. As a dance educator, I continue to reflect on my actions in order to activate dance as a conduit for social change and as an agent for humanity.

REFLECTIONS

I often ask my dance students who will be teachers, "Why do you dance?" They most often respond, "Because it makes me feel good." Adrienne Sansom helps us to connect these good feelings to an empathetic understanding of others in our world. Her work reminds us of the choice we have between retaining dance as a safe place where one can escape from the world and using dance in a way that connects us to the world, with all of its suffering and injustice. This is not an easy choice for most of my students. They do not want to give up the one place they have found where they can forget their problems, where they can focus only on themselves, and where they experience a therapeutic response. Coming to know the body as a repository of life experiences, as a site for both oppression and liberation, and as something that can be drawn upon to help us make meaning for ourselves and in our world challenges the more acceptable use of the body in dance, which concerns only technical skill and escaping from life.

To take the body seriously as a site for self and social understanding would indeed mean, as Adrienne suggests, that questions of pedagogy and curricular objectives in dance education would necessarily change. Using the body as a site of knowing and understanding could deepen our aesthetic processes in the classroom—our work would be directed toward the tasks of self and social understanding. Recognizing that dance has historically been used to transmit cultural values, attitudes, and beliefs is an important first step. Going beyond this, it would deepen our appreciation of the way cultural values become embodied. This kind of embodied understanding can lead us to appreciate dance as a means for uncovering the ways that cultural dispositions, values, and beliefs are instantiated in our somatic being. Bringing body knowledge out of its "second-rate status," as Adrienne states, is to "resituate the body as a viable source of knowledge and as an acceptable part of educational practice." Making the body central to knowing brings our aesthetic attention to the way the world enters into our muscles, bones, and organs. Connecting this kind of embodied knowing and dance to a framework of critical dialogue, moral questioning, and imaginative vision is what makes possible an education directed toward understanding and changing the present human condition. The question remains: Do we want to?

Note

1. Here the body is seen as "the primary site for a transformative type of knowing, one that arises through physical action, through a type of praxis" (Freire), as a revolutionary practice (Cruz and McLaren 2002, 198).

eleven

Holds No Memory: A Proposition as a Way to a Proposal About Dance Through Dance

Ana Sánchez-Colberg

Artistic director for Theatre enCorps
Senior lecturer, Central School of Speech and Drama
University of London

Holds No Memory, Helsinki, December 12, 2004[1]

no time no space no inscriptions nor etchings in cave walls no markers no anchors no compass nor compass points no constellations no footprints in the sand no line of breadcrumbs to show me the way back home no broken twig left as a clue no ribbon tied around a tree no chain of DNA no mitochondria nor nucleic fluid all is wiped clean blink so that everything disappears the only way to stop [the anger] to become again stellar dust to be origin not history but beginning [I dreamt about you like I had never done before, You a force field, enveloping. And I did not want to wake up, but I did. And the morning that refused to welcome me was grey. And as if mourning the loss of the dream, I wore black.] no lineage no heraldry no heredity no bloodline no heartstrings nor apron strings no hearth no home fire no oil lamp left at the window sill no baggage no luggage no photo album no postcards no letters kept no Valentines no calendars no agendas nor Happy New Years no anniversaries no appointment cards no souvenirs no photos left in the wallet nor locks of hair in a treasure chest no birthday candles blown out by a single gulp of air no bone ash collected in an urn nor twenty-one gun salute to remember who I was or where [nothing] but timeless darkness Eve without a paradise not first but only what then? Alone holding chaos inside to hell and back.

The point of departure for this writing is the creative process toward the dance event *Holds No Memory*. Devised as a dialogue in art through art, the creative process has brought together two women who are dance artists, performers, choreographers, teachers, and mothers: Efva Lilja, director of the internationally renowned Swedish dance company ELD, and Ana Sánchez-Colberg, artistic director of British dance theater company Theatre enCorps. I, Ana Sánchez-Colberg, offer the primary voice throughout the writing.

The thoughts contained in this writing constitute my reflection on the process so far and bring to the page, as much as memory can allow, the content and spirit of the dialogue with Efva. This dialogue has taken place in two stages of artistic research. The first was a studio-based exploration that took place in London from July 30 to August 13, 2005, as part of The Place Theatre Artistic Research Programme Choreodrome. The second stage took place in Stockholm from September 30 to October 3, 2005, when I visited ELD. For the purpose of this writing, I focus on the first part of the project, what I later refer to as the *local story*. At the time of writing, the final, public piece, the global story, is still in the making.

By proposing the process as a dialogue—originally in the studio, and now on the page—the research is attempting to move toward a different relationship between concepts and practice. A primary aim of this essay is that it should exist side by side with the event as it is being generated; the thoughts may change in time and through time as the art is engendered. Through related outputs in performance and critical writing, I am trying to find a mode of dissemination that will make available what Melrose (August 23, 2002) defines as "the operations of performance-making intuition, their moment of emergence, and their identification and exploitation of contingent factors." It is the particular story of this process that I want to expose in a manner that remains within my command as an artist and a writer. I am attracted in this way to the notion of "knowledge through intuition and knowledge through the construction of concepts within possible experience" suggested by Melrose (August 23, 2002). I would perhaps juggle those words further and propose that my interest is in *possible* concepts within experience that remain tentative and always propositional.

This aim has a political implication. It defines an attempt to return ownership of concept and practice to the artist (and in this case female artists) and allows art to be voiced and validated at the source. In pursuing this, I am seeking a status for artistic research that clearly locates it outside modes of validation associated with the scientific methodologies and structures embedded in academia. Notwithstanding progress made into articulating practice as research, scientific method cannot help but filter through, like a bad habit we cannot shake, bringing with it an inherent desire for singular truth—effective when dealing with the function of things but not their existence.

This writing is an attempt to destabilize notions of objectivity where art is concerned. I suggest, awkwardly manifest, in the exposition of this process, that to be objective when faced with art (or any opinion and decision made about art, including those of criticism, funding, programming in venues, and development of curriculum) misses the point. The nature of art is rooted in subjectivity: Art speaks of the moment; it is symptomatic of the strengths and weaknesses of those who made it, and, as part of the life that spawns it, it should die rather than perdure. What remain are traces, never works, and their reconstitution within any process of history, equally conditioned by those selves that retell, recount, refashion, and rearticulate. Therefore, by its nature, art relates to the particular beings that gave rise to its (and their) uniqueness within a field of probabilities, variations upon the theme of what being human is all about. In the case of *Holds No Memory*, the personal, political, and the poetic intertwine. Here is where our art lives, in the questions, not answers, that we publicly betray, contributing to historical thought a perpetual enigma, not a theory.

Dialogues in Dance, Dialogues About Dance

Looking at my past work, I can see that the idea of dialogue has defined a central preoccupation with the relationship between words and action and the manner in which interrelated but not always congruent dimensions of experience are revealed. In *Family Portraits* (1993), a dialogue or perhaps antidialogue was the key devising strategy of the story of the couple that was told and retold, never arriving at a cohesive end. Any notion of truth escaped either or both of the characters. In *En Viva Voz: And the Word Became Flesh* (1996), the title revealed the concern with the relationship of words to bodies, and in particular female words to male bodies, as a single female on stage struggled to understand the ever-changing world of five men evolving in front of her, in which she could only engage marginally, speaking with borrowed words. *Futur/Perfekt* (1998-2002) used the structure of a dialogue to generate a work, across continents and across companies who met, talked, prepared meals together, made work, and performed versions of the history of the work itself as it accumulated three years of performance history in the making.

In *Mahler's Fifths* (2004), I began to formulate the thoughts that bring me here today, a dialogue with another to consider who we are as artists and who we become in and through the making of a work. Since the early stages of the project, *Holds No Memory*, I found myself thinking of it as a dialogue with Efva. I presented it to her as such, we have structured the creative process as such, and we have continued to engage in all aspects of its development. In time, the significance of that first intuitive decision has come to flourish. This writing is an attempt to make the effects of that first utterance explicit in the hope of articulating new ways of being and doing dance.

In today's world of reality TV, talk shows, and information overload where talk is trivial, the fullness of the concept of *dialogue* may be easily forgotten. I am drawn to the original meaning of the word, from the Greek *dia* (into) and *logos* (knowledge): a conversation, a debate, an argument at the end of which there is the potential for new knowledge, the philosopher's preferred method toward an understanding that would then affect a way of life. In trying to unpack the idea of dialogue in relation to dance theater as a way to contextualize *Holds No Memory*, I have revisited the Platonic model and begun to trace a compatibility with dance theater choreographic strategies. Plato's dialogues have been described as

> intellectual, noetic experiences; as dramatisations of communicative interactions, they bring into exhibition claims and arguments in active confrontation with each other. The dramatised encounters hold in suspension the question of the validity or invalidity of the counter-claims and arguments, while yet allowing the reader-auditor to feel their force. (Fortunoff 2002)

A dialogue is purposely intended. It is not just conversation, but a debate, framed and enacted to arrive at new knowledge. There is an acknowledged theatricality in that

> they are staged interactions in which readers and listeners—like the dialogical participants themselves—become immersed, and absorbed in the scene. It is a tribute to the effectiveness of Plato's dramatic craftiness (poietikós) with the dialogue-form that, engulfed in it as we become, we can actually forget that the speakers exhibited are under observation by us, not talking to us. (Fortunoff 2002)

The dialogue as a theatrical literary event was both an exercise in method as much as a search for a particular content:

The subject matter is, therefore, reflexive. A dialogue is about itself in the sense that the tacit lesson (practising the dialectic) will be remembered after its ostensible subject (some philosophical problem) has ceased to be debated. (Fortunoff 2002)

The method was linked to the people engaging with the exercise. It was not simply shown to an audience for consumption (as today's creative industries demand). As mentioned earlier, spectators and participants were immersed in the scene that, according to Fortunoff (2002), has a maieutic function. The word *maieutic* comes from the Greek root of "mother" and means to elicit and clarify the idea of others as it exhorts "interlocutors into stating and reflecting upon the implications of their uncritically held opinions" (Fortunoff 2002).

The Socratic method is creative insofar as it produced cognitive gain or a changed perspective. It guides us anew each time to just and right human responses. It provides the guidance for initiatory responses demanded by each uniquely evolving occasion one faces. (Fortunoff 2002)

As I consider dialogue in relation to dance theater, I remember attending a question-and-answer session at the Brooklyn Academy of Music on October 20th, 1984, following the performance of *Seven Deadly Sins* by the Tanztheater Wuppertal. During the discussion with the audience, Pina Bausch made a significant statement after an audience member asked, "What is the work about?" Bausch shook her head in disbelief, and expressing more a sense of frustration than an explanation, she replied (I paraphrase from my notes): "Why should reality be understood intellectually, I don't understand . . . look at the work, it is all in the work." The statement became a kind of sense environment that has remained part of a latent ecology that I carry with me, a conceptual and affective kinesphere. I have tried to consider possible meanings, to uncover the relevance of the statements in dance generally and to my own dance specifically. From where I was sitting that afternoon, Bausch seemed to be asking us to reconsider our engagement with the work, not to seek what she had to say to us. She seemed to be questioning us about the knowledge coming out (of ourselves) in the process of witnessing, not unlike Platonic interlocutors and audience, the unraveling of the events on stage. She kept referring the questions back to us: What do *you* think? This is a more complex approach than the facile postmodernist attitude that the audience will make of it what they will.

Ana Sánchez 1.
Photo: Håkan Larsson, extremeproduction.se

However, in clear difference to organicist attitudes toward the body, Bausch avoided the naive, essentialist attitude toward the body that pervades so many pseudotherapeutic training methods fashionable today. With a sense of irony, Bausch stated that a reality that is only danced would be equally incredible and ineffectual (Gubernatis and Bentiviglio 1986, 10), whereas the Platonic dialogue engages us with "all three modes of human judgement: doing, making, and saying" (Fortunoff 2002). Dance theater engages us with the complexity of human corporeality where the body is subject, material, and tool. Currently, I am interested in the implications of proposing that there is a compatibility and a comparability between the body as a 'subject' body as a subject (corporeality), when the body is used as a the body makes as a material (flesh), and when the body is employed as a tool at the body does as a tool (physicality). In "An(n)a Annotated," (Sánchez-Colberg, December 9-12, 2004) I suggested that the complexity is conditioned by "the impact of the world's reality upon human existence felt and received as a conditioning force" (Arendt 1958, 9-10). I would propose that this is a central concern, viewed and reviewed in each work. As a consequence, I have come to suggest that contemporary dance theater (Tanztheater) is an umbrella, generic notion. It demarcates a process into performance that explores

> the relationship between ineffable aspects of our humanity—our interior psycho-physical landscape—and the external world of action, the realm of the theatrical, within a performance frame that places, what is normally viewed as a private domain within the context of the public realm, the realm of plurality, of human exchange. (Sánchez-Colberg 2004, 198)

I no longer think of Tanztheater as a style or genre, or a historically defined -ism but rather as a method that serves a particular questioning as to what dance is and how it is. The world of dance theater emerges in the space in between, in the interstice of two dimensions, that of action and that of words. The dance is the result of the dialogic dynamics of self in interaction across the two spheres. The transit between the two is movement—dance. On stage it takes the form of exchanges of stories as dancers address each other and the audience across the fourth wall. The scenes are framed dialogues, sometimes spoken, sometimes danced, but always moved.

I now find myself rethinking the statement "What moves us, not how," repeated by so many critics when discussing Tanztheater yet the fullness of its theatrical implications so little examined. This is in a different territory than the idea of Lange's virtual force, the philosophical albatross that continues to dominate the manner in which so much dance composition is produced, performed, and reflected. In "An(n)a Annotated," I discussed in detail the educational implications of this with regard to dance training, reassessing the Laban-Wigman-Jooss approach to technique training vis à vis Hannah Arendt's concept of the vita activa. As a complement to that proposal, I would now suggest that dance theater is like a dialogue:

> [It] has great communicative power for teaching [the dialectical] art as a practice, since it is the generic of its type . . . And by virtue of this dynamism, liveliness, progressiveness, openness, and revisionary nature, dialogue is a . . . form for capturing—but not arresting—the inherent movement of the dialectical method and of the human interactions framing it . . . [it] is a means of inspiring renewed self-discovery. Whatever their ostensible subject-matter, each is about the functioning of his Socrates . . . a phenomenon we shall identify as Lebensphilosophie. . . . (Fortunoff 2002)

This is evident in the manner in which choreographic content is discovered through a choreographic method resembling more a theatrical laboratory than the conventional and favored method of modernist and balletic systems that focus on shaping bodies through space. Choreography is pursued as a question, similar to a theatrical étude in which the what-if sets up a context for investigation. It comes as no surprise that as early as 1940, dance theater was being described as "living philosophies" (Storey 1940, 596). Laban described Kurt Jooss' work as that of a "dancing philosopher" (Storey 1940, 596), offering observation of human expressive essentials through works that mirrored, magnified, enlarged, and parodied familiar objects (Storey 1940). In a manner that echoes the Platonic dialogue in which the philosopher "is not going to decide which among them is the true one, but to reveal the insufficiency of them all—including his own," works in dance theater are open-ended (Fortunoff 2002). Jooss achieved this through the use of alienation devices—repetition, magnification, and parody. Bausch adopts a multi-perspective attitude to the work:

> I just can't say 'that is how it goes'. I am watching myself. I am as lost as all the others . . . You can see it like this or like that. It just depends on the way you watch. But the single stranded thinking they interpret into it simply isn't right. You can always watch the other way. . . . (Hoghe 1980, 71-72)

A Particular Kind of Dialogue

The idea of calling *Holds No Memory* a dialogue was an intuitive response to my desire to address the processual focus of dance theater, away from a thing made (a dance work) to a process between people. However, as I tend to do, I utter these statements and then throughout the course of the process figure out what I actually mean by them. In the case of *Holds No Memory*, it is not only relevant to note that the idea of a dialogue served as a structure to shape a process and give content to a work, it is also significant that the dialogue is a particular kind of dialogue. It is by and about two women.

In *Relating Narratives: Storytelling and Selfhood* (2002), Cavarero suggests that "communication between women unfolds as the comparison of life stories, rather than the reciprocal exchange of ideas" (Cavarero 2000, 54). acknowledging the Platonic inheritance, Cavarero suggests that dialogue among women "repudiate[s] the abstract universal and [follows] an everyday practice where the tale is existence, relation and attention" (Cavarero 2000, 54). In dialogue among women, the acknowledgment of the uniquely evolving occasion previously considered acquires particular significance:

Taken as a concept, uniqueness corresponds with the extreme form of the particular—or better, to the absolute 'one'; or rather, to a form of the particular that is free of any universality that tries to redeem it, or erase the miracle of finitude. (Cavarero 2000, 53)

Furthermore, Cavarero (2000, 53) suggests that

the mission of philosophy, seduced by the universal, originally decided to take it upon itself: to redeem, to save, to rescue the particular from its finitude, and uniqueness from its scandal. This task of redemption, however, logically transformed itself into an act of erasure . . . Rather than salvation, the accidental needs care. To tell the story that every existence leaves behind itself is perhaps the oldest act of such care.

Conventionally, a story is a local event, immediate to the lives that gave rise to it. It is separate in scale from the universally held concept of history. Cavarero, following Arendt, suggests that the telling of the story becomes political when it can happen in a scene where uniqueness constitutes itself "in relation" and in which the feminine custom of "self-narration" finds a "political scene," shared and interactive (Cavarero 2000, 61). In *Holds No Memory*, this happened within the context of dance theater, a context that in this writing I have aligned with a philosophical dialectical inheritance, whereas in "An(n)a Annotated" I proposed its politics. What I am now proposing is a reconciliation of the philosophical dialogue with female narration. In *Holds No Memory*, our method is dialogical, our politics in action through the desire to find, in and through dance, a mutual place for exposure, a *skène* for a narratable self.

In engaging with art and in the questioning of art, this project seeks to explore the relationship between the "microscopically personal and intimate, to the impossibly global and political, in order to address issues of performance politics and the politics of performance within contemporary choreographic practice. The life that spawns between them (of which this narrative is a dimension, not its totality) provides the experiential and empirical data that supports the thoughts articulated in this essay as a life-fact" (Sánchez-Colberg 2004, 194). Or in Efva's words: "I feel challenged by what I do not understand, and I attempt to uncover the images I have not yet seen. My body is to be made use of and new experiences created at the same time as what is familiar is revisited, gone over and over again . . . I keep wondering whether this life is my own or whether it possesses a universal applicability that makes it a social concern?" (Lilja 2004, 11).

In slightly different ways both Efva and I are concerned with the relationship between the local and the global: the localized, unique

Efva 1.
Photo: Håkan Larsson, extremeproduction.se

story within each dancing body (including our own) and notions of the global (here used as a substitute for universal), positioned here as an expositional, shareable dance. Through our dialogue, we are actively participating in a type of narration (movement) in which stories have become interwoven. I would propose that it is the interwoven quality of the unique stories, not their replication, that creates the tapestry that allows us to claim a direct link of cause and effect between the local and the global. It is the telling of each unique story that sets up a politics of action that is able to cut across scale. In our modern world of continual depoliticization and domination masquerading as technological and economic progress, this potential to open up a shared space of action seems all the more relevant and necessary.

This idea of *embrouillé*, of interweaving, is also applied here to the writing: Viewpoints shift from personal recollection to diary notes, theories about dance and dialogue, philosophy, self-parody, and humor. This comes from a desire to allow the very act of writing the stories of performance to reveal the complexity of their origin in relation to the work that engenders them.

Words and Dance, Words on Dance, Words That Dance

The genesis of the particular story of *Holds No Memory* goes back to a chance encounter in Helsinki during the Making a Difference in Dance conference sponsored by the dance department of the Helsinki Theatre Academy (Sánchez-Colberg 2004). I had been part of an international group of dance artists and scholars (coincidentally, all women) who over the course of two years explored ethical and political issues in dance from the perspective of education, sociology, philosophy, gender studies, and creative practice. The conference was the end of the project, at which the publication *The Same Difference* was launched.

A parenthetical note must be added here to give credit to the team of women who organized the conference and their desire to structure the event in a different way from conferences where the hierarchies and economies of the expert rule. Sessions were structured as dialogues, in rooms where audience and interlocutors were positioned in proximity, blurring the boundaries between speaker and audience. Equal time was given to discussion as to presentations. Arguments were possible, heated at times, yet all in the spirit of collaboration and cooperation. I had contributed the essay "An(n)a Annotated," which in many ways is a preamble to this writing. I also presented the two works discussed in the essay, *Inside Heiner's Mind* and *Mahler's Fifths,* as a way to keep the theory closely related to the practice that generated it. Efva had been invited to give one of the keynote presentations on December 11, 2004, in which she read sections from her new book *Dance: For Better, for Worse.* Written as an open letter, Efva began her tale:

> For you, I dreamed of filling up a book . . . of saturating a whole book with words of love. I woke up and all that came to me were a few well-used ones. We often exchange them, you and *I.* And yet writing them is so different. It is silent. . . . (Lilja 2004, 5).

From there, Efva begins to shape a worldview on dance based on this practical metaphor of a love for an other, the audience, the dancers, life, of trying to define the unique experience with already-used words, to live a unique life through movement inherited and innate. As I listened, I began to trace similarities between Efva's dance-view to the thoughts expressed in "An(n)a Annotated," presented earlier in the conference. In the essay, I discussed Arendt's existential phenomenology as a way to understand my dance. My thinking as to the why and wherefore of dance was aligned to Arendt's proposal that identity is "expositive and relational in character" in which to become is to "appear to an other" (Arendt, in

Cavareto 2000, 111). I established a parallel to the act of choreography, proposing it as an actuality held, and holding, others and me. This giving to another inhabited the same artistic world as Efva's words on dance, life, and love: "What I do know is that life does not create itself. We all participate in its coming into being . . . loving is part of that coming into being, of becoming real. Dance is that, too, for me" (Lilja 2004, 11).

Central to Efva's narration was the notion of memory and inheritance:

> Forgetting what wants to be forgotten, annihilating memories images that do not want to be remembered, is something fairly easily done. We forget. We remember what we want to remember and forget the rest. Forgetting has its own terrain: wild, impenetrable and usually surprising and striking the times we stumble upon it . . . What I do, I do against the background of what I have previously done, whether I am aware of it or not. In this way, what I am doing now will affect what I will subsequently do. It is all woven together. Like here and there, for example. . . . (Lilja 2004, 10).

Similarly, in "An(n)a Annotated" I spoke of my work as a journey that

> weaves together the thoughts and lives of hundreds of individuals artists, friends, parents, siblings, loved-ones, students, peers and progeny—those met and also those who have more or less indirectly shaped either the thinking or the actuality of a context that, desirably or not, continues to mould the topography of this trajectory. (Sánchez-Colberg 2004, 193)

The occurrence of weaving together our statements made me reflect back on Cavarero's proposals. At the end of that day, I decided that an unfolding needed to take place, but that as dance artists, our tapestry must be woven in time and space, in a studio. Our narration is in movement, and any words that would be formulated would be inextricably bound to that process of time (life) through space (flesh). This might necessitate new words, new syntax, new references, and new pages. On my arrival to London, I wrote the following letter to Efva:

> Only this once, may I give you an introduction to the thoughts behind this she/body who dances . . . and the reasons that she who dances had in her intuitive desire to work with you . . . . Like you, my work—intentionally or intuitively, I am not quite sure—seems to always revert to the relationship between memory and knowledge of self, and action. I will not repeat what I think I say better in the essay in the Helsinki anthology, but lately this seems to be a very

strong drive. I believe that memory is entrenched in muscle tissue and that memory is both of events in our lifetime as well as those imprinted in the collective physical memory within the millenarian patterns of our physiognomy contained in the DNA. At times they feel like irrevocable patterns of being and living and therefore, feeling—sometimes for better, sometimes for worse. I am not thinking about esoteric karmic philosophies. What I am considering is more like a memorial physical inheritance which is part of my kinesthetics, evident now that I see myself becoming my mother—physically as much as emotionally—as I myself have become a mother, and see extraordinary identical traces of behavioral patterns in my daughter as I used to have when I was her age. These are memorial, not learned, evidenced when I witness her in action as if a memory of my younger self was momentarily replayed in front of me—she is, as me, terrified of silence and darkness, the sight of a dying butterfly can make her weep, she also loves spinning and skipping rope and running . . . I see more than a psychological inheritance, there is a physical inheritance of action as well as of form. A memory determinant.

These memory determinants are, to quote poet Adrienne Rich, "my angels and my polarities." I am humbled and in awe by the weight of this millenarian inheritance when it leads to the beauty of my family, my daughter, my ageing, my parents ageing, our eventual death . . . I am troubled by this when it constricts through an unquestionable expectation and acceptance of "how things should be" and "this is how things are" and we hide behind fear, cowardice, and we stop searching for a new truth of ourselves and of others, we fail to be the ones to create new patterns, easily giving into those received. . . . This brings me to now. . . .

Sometime in December I found myself thinking long and hard about this desire to inscribe new patterns of memory. That long night of thinking coincidentally took place the night before I then heard you read from your book. And what you chose to read to the group could have been direct response to some of my doubts . . . and that's what made me think that there was a dialogue to take place about art, in art, through art. In my thinking there are some oblique coincidences between this question and your recent concern with ageing and the future (and relevance) of those now older. True, we are inscribed and there is a rich history engraved in our bodies and therefore a richness to be unearthed from that place . . . but is who we are when we are old (getting older) just a repetition of that identity (what did you call it, isolated storage) . . . how is that memory richness given a place to affect the not-yet-known . . . let the old be allowed to make new not just make anew . . . in order for that to happen, must we know that we must forget? In a place of darkness and frustration . . . I came out with this idea of holding no memory . . . which does not mean one has no memory, but how we hold it in relation to our history, and in determining our history, is questioned . . . This is how I can best present you were I/she is now. . . and what the body is attempting to do, and what the art is seeking to deal with. (personal communication, May 5, 2005)

We arrived at a focus for the research, described in a news release as follows:

A dialogue in art through art has started as they found strong coincidences in recent creative focus: the role of memory inscribed in the body and the effect of that inscription on how movement develops into a kinesthetic language of performance. These issues include also the artist's attitude toward her memory and body, how that shapes identity, as well as the socio-cultural parameters that circumscribes age/movement/expression within society generally and dance culture specifically. The title *Holds No Memory* is articulated as a negative, in an effort to reevaluate the act of reinscription, examining memory as something that shapes a future potential as opposed to rearticulating past. Central to the project is the fact that two artists in very different stages of their careers are coming together. This difference marks two different perspectives, two differently inscribed bodies, and two different kinesthetics embedded in the work itself as it generates its particular kinaestheticsat the moment of performance

The Local Story: Memory and the Kinaesthetic, Choreodrome, London, August 2005

The dialogue with Efva began as a series of questions. Some were exchanged in brief electronic communication before August. Other questions were jointly discovered during research in the studio. As previously mentioned, two key questions drove us: first, an inquiry into the role of memory in defining a kinaesthetics and second, a rearticulation of the relationship between the particular memory of a single dancing body to a memorial collective. If Cavarero proposes a definition of identity within the literary narration of a story, we endeavored to explore the implications of that within the realm of action, in the possibility of a narratable self manifested within dance.

Our reciprocal narration begins in London. Similar to a Platonic dialogue, our creative process was intended, framed. The research and development was housed within Choreodrome 2005, The Place Theatre's biennial summer research project. Choreodrome provides free space and support for choreographers, dance filmmakers, and dance artists to develop their ideas without the pressure of delivering an end product. We were 2 of 37 contemporary dance artists chosen to take part in 2005. It was understood that from the hidden, personal, arguably domestic world of our two weeks of Choreodrome, a new work that was public, share-able, and revelatory would be created. This would in turn be an attempt to make explicit the links across scale previously discussed, between the personal and the public, the microscopic and the macroscopic, the local and the global.

In reflecting on this first stage of the project as the local story, I am purposely acknowledging the microscopically personal dimension of

Efva 2.
Photo: Håkan Larsson, extremeproduction.se

the genesis of the project. Efva's question of universal applicability of one's life—and dance—that makes it a social concern comes back to the foreground. In the encapsulated question of *Holds No Memory,* I am identifying a main concern with the nature of choreographic practice, extending the questions raised in the previous three works with regard to this applicability of the theatrical to the extratheatrical. If *Inside Heiner's Mind* was a confrontation between the performing self and the spectator, and *Mahler's Fifths* a confrontation between the comakers–performers in front of the audience (as well as new ways of collaborating with the composers–musicians who were part of the work), the work with Efva marked a logical next stage of development.

In this stage, I placed myself as maker–performer under scrutiny with Efva. The challenge was to find new forms of movement, new definitions for performance and therefore of choreographic structure, and new practical metaphors from which to move forward the understanding of the act of performance. This necessitated putting my work and all its dimensions under scrutiny, through a dialogic questioning, from which a potential narration would emerge. It was therefore a process of research and exploration that sought to understand how the microscopic aspects of movement detail in the studio related to the macroscopic landscape of public performance and all its interrelated strands. It marks a first attempt to link the politics of female appearance through narration generally and to the process of narration and appearance on stage specifically.

The day before Efva's arrival, an image came to mind that began to materialize a possible way forward. In my journal I describe an imagined theatrical moment, a theatrical metaphor to an unknown audience.[1]

Darkness—step back. I have been there before. When light finally comes, what do you see? What do you see when you see me? How do you see me? After years in darkness, I no longer have a memory of who I was—I only know this here, this now. I ask you again. What do you see when you see me? To be able to continue, to be able to step out of that darkness [empty space where once was she who is no more and does not want to be]. I must know. How can denial exist in movement? Or how can movement come out of denial? My first question to Efva.

29th-30th July 2005. Efva arrives. I pick her up at the airport. We drive to Blackheath, dinner. I am surprised at how easy it all seems, so possible, considering we barely know each other. At dinner she is attentive to everything I say and do. She says, "I am sorry if I lose track of what you are saying, I am just focusing on how you move . . . the you coming through the movement." She says that is where the dance is. All I remember is that I have not stopped talking for hours, explosion of the ideas and thoughts that bring us to today. Then again, that was part of the project, to confront head-on this gap between the world of words and this world in a body, silenced and hidden (without which the words and ideas that so many want and expect from me would not be possible). My biggest contradiction. It exists in my body, it exists in my dancing. This is the starting point, to change the pattern that acknowledges the words, but not the body, the practice.

We begin with the "Holding no . . ." Little is said. The first explorations into movement focus on letting go, of the carriage, the skeleton. Efva asked me to walk the room, paying attention to the emergent rhythm of the walk, my breadth, to become aware of my stance, to sing if it feels appropriate. For the first time ever, the gaze of movement observation—with which I engage with others while teaching and choreographing—is turned upon myself. I discovered what I always knew in the flesh but time and space did not allow to address—"Healer, heal thyself." I hold myself with attention to space, both direct and indirect, with strong weight and bound flow, but little attention to time. *Looking and looking again.* I became painfully aware of my posture; the contradiction within my kinesphere: Arms and hands project in nonstop gestures as I speak words that fill up the transversal and the periphery. The center is held back, hunched, protected, chin jutting out in defiance, heart hidden; the *she* in *Inside Heiner's Mind* lives here. I do not pay attention to energy through time; I am my worst enemy, *too much force,* making the movement more difficult that it needs be, focus is projected outward, to those looking. *Learn to contain.* That may need me not to give as much, so much. I find that hard. To find silence, inside.

1st-5th August 2005. We begin to try physical images. I noticed an interesting difference in the way we arrived at the material. *Efva asks me to try something, a movement that comes from her, she is giving me a form. But the form comes from her observations of me. It is not a fully improvised situation where I produce from latent embodied and technical knowledge, nor is she simply putting material in me. As a dancer I am listening and observing from a different perspective. I am listening/looking for/at this Efva/Other offering a mirror of this me that also reveals her. The other, in which she also mediates herself in and through me, mediates me. In that mirrored reciprocity the image offered is both familiar and alienated. I think I begin to understand the possibility and the actuality (in theater terms) of the idea of a dialogue—of questions—leading to reciprocal narration.*

The listening and observing that I am undergoing with Efva converts into felt experience—motivation, a need to, a desire to and for—that then underpins the movement-action. Affect becoming effect. In this case, movement as a process of representation into semiosis (or at its other end, pure abstraction) is just not relevant. The process shared so far brings us back to the tacit agreement between us, to that first question, What do you see when you see me? She doesn't tell, she shows, through me, and in doing so makes me reexperience myself, question myself.

Ana Sánchez 2.
Photo: Håkan Larsson, extremeproduction.se

The first image is difficult, yet it encapsulates the first ideas: a launch forward—full force, full weight—onto my left leg, reaching forward as if pulled, three times, focus to the floor. Then immediately there is a push back to return to a neutral point, as if there had never been a fall, only to fall again. I am frustrated; this is a too familiar place, a place that I no longer want to be in. I have made a career of being the ugly duckling on stage. No more, I wanted to say to her, but I didn't, so my back spasmed, which meant we couldn't rehearse, so we had the conversation anyway. Efva said that the process needed me to stay in that place until I could transform it. She reminded me that to simply jump over this issue would be an exercise in pure aesthetics, not the point of all this, of why we had gathered. She challenged me to stay constant and consistent to my own proposal. My back eased. We went back to the studio to rehearse the first image over and over again, right into that place.

I wanted to find the other *she* of *Inside Heiner's Mind* and *Mahler's Fifths*, not forward, not back, but in place. Efva began to take me away from a denial to a place to make open, available, that can set the conditions for things to happen, for those new memories that I was searching for. *Five very intensive days. The processing seems to be happening physically for the first time in a long while.* Knowing *is happening beyond words, yet it is still very tangible. A new understanding normally measured in my ability to say something has been shifted to an ability to do something (movement as an act, not as a form, and all the aesthetic and political implications of that).* A new place in myself, silent, embodied in the simple task of learning to breathe from a position that looks like a cambrée back, but is not quite, a head-back-looking-at-the-sky-chest-open-long-quiet state that is forcing me to relearn a balance actual and metaphoric. It reestablishes my propioceptive knowledge.

8th August 2005. During coffee at Jerwood Space, the issue about dance as a language sprang. Although we both use the word linguistics, *we are referring more to the abstract symbology akin to mathematics and astronomy than that of verbal language. Efva retells the story of working with an astronomer. In astronomy a whole series of astronomical events (back to actions not form, actual finite experience in time and space) can be expressed (not the same as represented) with algebraic formulas. The two-dimensional symbol acts as a window to a three-dimensional time-space.* In Greek, *"symballein* means to throw together: two separate objects become inseparable" (Armstrong 2005, 16). You observe the mathematical earthly numbers in order to see into a tangible reality in the cosmos; a bridge, a link from one reality to another, from one scale to another. This we propose has compatibility to the notion of dance as a linguistic phenomenon, a symbology of movement that results from systems of operations of and from a body. The very concept of movement—as an action in the Arendtian sense—is returned to its link to bios, the narratable self. We are reminded of the complexity of our medium. We therefore propose that we have radically shifted from the too easily repeated, but so little investigated, conventional view of theatre as absence or death—of Derrida's nihilistic ever-deferred sense, of Barthes' death of self for the life of texts—to the notion of symbol as a positive valence in presence and actuality, two elements superseding the sum of their parts.

9th-12th August 2005. We work on finding, the pleasure, of the moment of movement, away from the focus on result of execution, finding the feeling inside the form. Efva asked me to focus on sensing, not shape. In another fragment I lie on the floor facedown, collect the space around me into a funnel, I speak the word hello, *and listen, ear to hand, to the sound of my echo.* In a critique of postmodern theory, Cavarero suggests that

> making every language into a text, also turns every real existent into something definable as "extra-textual" or "extra discursive" . . . by swallowing life, the text also risks swallowing the unrepeatable uniqueness of each existent. Omnivorous texts hungry for life and ready to offer themselves as the more dignified replacements of an all too human corporeality—this is how the more refined post modern theory seems to be. . . . (42)

We never speak of the meaning of this or that moment. We concentrate on its momentary sensation, gone the moment another sensation comes to the foreground. In another instance I gather into all fours and crawl, focusing on the touch of my hand on the floor, dusty. I lick my hand and make a handprint, in front. I crawl forward, then sit, and put my hand back, behind me, into the place where the spit print is beginning to evaporate. The taste of dust remains in my mouth. This is not merely unsymbolized flesh, as Lacan would have it, not yet a self. This is identity found in the practicosensorial model of Lefebvre in which I find "the everyday certainty of the self, which comes from sensing oneself to be this and not another" (Cavarero 2000, 43). I think back to Efva's words, I do not need discourse to comprehend physically, *here* not *there*, *me* not *other*. I recapitulate to the ephemerality of the moment, at peace with the ephemerality of myself. We have shifted away from the death principle, paradoxically embodied in the attempt to achieve universal perdurability, to a birthing one in which, again paradoxically, a moment of life is superseded by another moment in and of life. *At the end of these days having agreed and rehearsed and rehearsed and rehearsed content for the sharings, she smiled and said, "It is yours . . ." A good day.*

Everything seems totally connected. Everything feels totally discreet, exact, and independent.

12th August 2005. Driving to and from the rehearsals we engage in the exchange of fragments of life history: of the 25,000 things we have done to survive in art, of sacrifices, of giving away the work. Efva speaks of her desire to not just to do, but to stubbornly do differently. I reply, ironically, that I always thought we called that Art. *Yet it does not matter how much we try to do differently, we cannot become other, we can only transform self. Is this the voice of the now mature artists? Is that the primary difference, a shift in how things are possible, not that they have to become less possible?* Final day, a public sharing. *Our project has had interesting dynamics with inside and outside. In our case these two weeks have sustained a whole serendipity of moments, not just the time in the studio; there is actually no in or out. Efva and I, as artists and persons, are dwelling on that thought for a while.*

Conclusion

More than a year has passed. I am writing this from Stockholm, a city that has now become strangely familiar. Throughout autumn 2005 and spring 2006, Efva and I continued our dialogue across two cities, meeting to continue the research in both London and Stockholm. In this way the local, domestic world of Choreodrome expanded into the public, global domain as our questions became shared though a performance that took place in May 2006 as well as through my visits to Stockholm as guest professor at the University College of Dance, where Efva is now rector.

The thoughts in this essay are not proven right, so to speak; that would be against the principles discussed. However, the thoughts and intentions are reaffirmed and confirmed. The dialogue is now framed by another creative process that has organically grown from this. *We: Implicated and Complicated* is a work that has brought together the team of artists that have worked with me in London over the past year with the students and staff at the college. The dialogue has resulted in two parallel streams emerging from a common source. One is an exploration through a dance theater duet into the nature of *we* in relation to self and other. This material is still in process and is the first stage of propositions toward a larger group project involving mature dancers and artists.

The second exploration involving the New Circus students at the school addresses the complexities of the individual within a collective and the landscapes—concrete and virtual—that forge and determine such interactions. The works shift through layers of *we:* intimate, theatrical, and social layers, where the act of witnessing implicates and complicates all present. In the piece, the focus shifts fully to the conditioned world of Arendt as an actual terrain from which the inherent drama between being and becoming emerges. In *We: Implicated and Complicated,* the spaces created and inhabited—including the body of the others possessed and reimagined—result in a powerful economy of conflicting desires, out of which the work is coming to surface. This has allowed for a complete interrogation of Arendt's political arena in which narratable selves have given life to the stories that have become intertwined within that space. The piece, which premieres tonight, opens with a single female performer speaking words from my journal (written January 18, 2007):

On beginnings:

The architect begins with a point in the empty space, the horizon point, imagination becoming real. The point will lead to a line, many lines will intersect to create a map, a map contains a journey, a journey betrays a story—stories of origins, stories of beginnings, stories of departure. Stories and drawings share a common principle, a common origin. Stories and drawings begin with a point. Stories have a point of departure, the once upon a time, in a land far, far away, in another galaxy, a point being a place. Drawings begin with a point, the first touch of pencil or brush on the empty canvas that forms that primal point-blot, that disperses ink in time and space, opens a space, empties time. . . .

REFLECTIONS

Creating dialogue across borders has historically been part of the construction of dance in both formal and informal forms. Placing this process at the center of inquiry, though, has been rare. Here, Ana Sánchez-Colberg shares her work with Efva Lilja as they pursued the meaning of knowledge as it is constituted and embodied within movement, intuition, and experience. Their work took them across countries and cultural boundaries. Ana reminds us that raising questions concerning factual or empirical evidence as it relates to research in the arts is antithetical to the subjective nature of this human activity. The essence of art is not to be found in theories of truth or empirical propositions but in the questions it poses about the mysteries of human existence.

Focusing on the intuitive, Ana brings our attention back to the observer's responsibility as the observer engages in a dialogue with the dance. Ana suggests to us that we must to go beyond the Socratic, where one simply asks questions in order to find the so-called truth. Instead, she argues, we must engage in the process of making meaning ourselves. The audience must actively participate in that reflexive and interpretive process through which we can come to learn about not only ourselves but the way we come to see the world.

Central to Ana's process of dance making is Hannah Arendt's concept of vita activa in which human beings come together to enhance their powers of self-understanding through dialogue and engagement with one another in a public space. No longer do we see dance as a product meant to represent a thing in itself; instead, what is to be created, displayed, and observed is the act in which people create both themselves and other. This act of attending to the creative interactions between human beings can help us understand our shared humanity as something that is constituted by both local and global influences. Indeed, current understanding helps us to understand that the boundary between the local and global is far less sharply drawn than we once thought; identities represent a fusion of multiple human influences. Our coming into being can be understood as a relational process that requires the presence of others. The reciprocity of bringing each other into existence also brings with it a responsibility to each other.

Memory, history, and intuition interact as they shape how we feel, think, interpret, and take action. We are inscribed by all that we have known, felt, touched, witnessed, or experienced. This embodiment of cultural experience both creates and hinders movement, whether in dance or elsewhere in the cognitive and physical life of human beings. As Ana and Efva experienced, our ability to hold no memory, that is, to exist as some sort of blank, is simply not possible. We cannot become other, but we can become more open, more aware, more sensitive, and more attentive and do more listening and less speaking. We can act in a more conscious and less programmed manner. We can be less right and more humble, less sure and more curious, less *me* and more *we*. Ana Sánchez-Colberg points the way to understanding an aesthetic process in which meanings are constructed both by those who dance and those who observe the dance. In each case, these meanings reflect the deep cultural assumptions that structure our lives.

Note

1. I have italicized the writing that quotes material extracted from my personal journal, *thoughts started in Helsinki,* ongoing since December 2004.

twelve

Dance in a World of Change: A Vision for Global Aesthetics and Universal Ethics

Sherry B. Shapiro
Professor of dance and director of women's studies
Meredith College
Raleigh, North Carolina

The body knows and re-members even in the silences of our lives. In dance the familiar can become strange . . . more than movement it is the act of transformational possibility.

Globalization is not a new topic for discussion. Many of us are aware of the changes in our societies and across the world that have come as direct or indirect responses to globalization. Current themes, whether concerning the economy, culture, transnational families, or the environment, have become part of our global discussions. We can not ignore the effects of globalization and how it challenges our notion of stable identities, unchanging traditions, or the processes that affect these changes. Fluidity and flux have become significant metaphors for the way we define our cultures and our world.

Because the arts, dance in particular, are a product of culture, we tend to not see the forest for the trees. I'm referring here to the assumptions that we have about dance and its ability to speak across cultures using movement as a common language. Housed in this assumption is the notion that when dance is experienced as a cross-cultural event we have created some form of positive partnership between differing peoples. This is a nice romantic idea and one which I myself have shared. As I have had the opportunity to observe children from different countries and cultures, socioeconomic backgrounds, races, ethnicities, genders, and physical abilities sharing dance experiences, I too can sometimes envision all becoming equal as they transcend the barriers of difference. In these kinds of cross-cultural experiences, dance provides a common language, as if this somehow transcends and obliterates all other differences. I do not wish to posit that this experience isn't significant and valuable for children in and of itself; rather, I wish to suggest that we can ask more of the arts and dance than this. What I am encouraging here is an examination of what dance can offer a global society. Perhaps we might go beyond sharing our cultural diversities in a communal space, learning each others' dances, and adding world or African dance to our curriculum and consider how dance is being shaped through globalization. Even more importantly, how might we shape the effects of globalization through dance?

Dance, it is well understood, offers a unique and powerful form of human expression. It allows us to speak in a language that is visceral and far less mediated by our thoughts and abstract conceptualizations. It provides, at times, a raw, embodied way of capturing human experience. It allows free reign to the sensual and the sentient—things that elsewhere are often circumscribed by custom and convention. It also manifests that form of playfulness that is so delightfully found in young children and so often erased from adult life. Dance, like other forms of art, provides a space in which we can touch the transcendent and experience new possibilities that are outside of the life practices we take for granted; it is a space that encourages and nurtures the ability to imagine different ways of feeling and being in the world. And it is the human body that makes dance concrete. To think of dance in a way that makes the global leap without an appropriation of others' experiences, assuming a hierarchical stance of cultural superiority or arrogance, calls for a sense of *global aesthetics.* Now, the question is: What is meant by *global aesthetics?*

In developing some thoughts on globalization and dance, I draw on my considerable experience as an educator who has focused on art, the aesthetic, and the body as a medium for self-change and social change. I also draw on the work of postmodern and feminist scholars who have written on globalization as a way to reconceptualize what it means for the arts to engage in human change and, particularly, how the body, grounded in memory and experience, provides a powerful resource for change. And, finally, I discuss how the coexisting forces of self and other constitute the universal relationship in which the body becomes the concrete place where questions of human compassion *and* human barbarism are simultaneously engendered.

Writing from the global North[1] and as a White, female, middle-class dance educator from the United States, I cannot dismiss the context of my perspectives and my privileged position. Acknowledging this position with sensitivity leads me to recognize my own limitations and perspectives. I seek only to be part of the larger discussion, recognizing my voice as important but not the only voice of Truth.

Dominating Aesthetics

A global view of aesthetics recognizes diversity and acknowledges that there are multiple meanings of what dance is or what good dance is. The different meanings are responsive to the needs of different cultures in different social contexts, regions, societies, and nations. Despite our best intentions, we often fail to see the forest for the trees. It is important to recognize the ways in which we have acted that are exactly the opposite of what is needed to create a sense of global aesthetics. Though we have begun to acknowledge the rich presence of diversity, to respect a more multicultural approach to dance, and to develop our sense of honoring the "particular," we must also examine the underlying assumptions and dispositions we continue to hold as part of our embodied ideology of the aesthetic. What I mean by this is the way in which we continue to see particular dance forms as superior while giving other forms less value. This is a vital first step as we seek to seriously encounter the meaning of the arts within the context of a global society.

The western European dance forms have typically been identified as the superior forms, which are historically situated within a structure dominated by men or a masculine paradigm. Though this is a reductionist view of a complicated system, what I want to problematize is the way in which dance has capitalized on the power of the global North to devalue and subsume the global South.[2] While, with our increased multicultural sensitivity, we in the global North have given, to a certain extent, more space, time, and effort in our classrooms and studios to the dances of the global South, this effort has been overshadowed by the powerful ability of the global market to erase differences and impose a homogenous cultural space. While we are encouraging classroom learning about dance, food, dress, and music of other cultures, mass media such as music videos, MTV, and movies are continuously pumping out dance, dress, and music to places around the globe. Whether it is hip hop, Starbucks, or McDonald's, the culture of the global North has become the desired forms of expression and pleasure.

In a parallel way, Western forms of dance are portrayed as the epitome of artistic expression. Recognizing this, I want to add my voice to the suspicion of any form of dance, such as ballet, that has universal pretensions or assumptions. There must be a balance between respecting cultural diversity and priviledging any particular culture or dance form over another. without allowing the privileged value of a particular culture or dance form to make claims over another. This proves to be no simple task. Respecting diversity while children across the globe seek to imitate the fashion, music, and dance of the West seems of little consequence. The global media have far more control of what youths are exposed to in terms of dance than the "official" dance world has.

Recognizing the power of the global media and market, we must also recognize that there is a struggle against globalization as a force that homogenizes culture and erases the particular, the local, and the indigenous. It is only in our recent history that we have begun to attempt to respect cultural diversity and sought to avoid ethnocentrism. Burn (2005, 8) talks about the need to both celebrate differences and emphasize commonalities in reference to a cross-cultural study of women:

> The goal of this sort of multiculturalism, or interculturalism, is in ". . . helping people to understand, accept, and value cultural differences between groups, with the ultimate goal of reaping the benefits of diversity" (Ferdman 1995). The goal is to both celebrate differences and emphasize the dimensions of commonality or inclusion that supersede these differences (Devine 1996).

A multicultural approach goes against what some regard as our natural human tendency to reject people and cultures that are different from our own. We like to believe that our way of doing things is the right way. Our discomfort with those who are different from us provides a challenge to dance within the complexity of achieving diversity within unity. The task is in finding ways that accept the particular and at the same time transcend the differences. What isn't answered is, Why is this important to dance? What is the goal?

Erasure at a Price

Critics of globalization have given much attention to the erasure of local traditions under the effects of transnational capitalism. They have made us far more mindful of the terrible losses that come with the erasure of these local traditions. Local customs, dialects, religious practices, crafts, artistic expressions, foods, and, of course, dances are the accumulation of human wisdom, ingenuity, and sensibility over the course of countless generations. Their mere existence enriches the cultural treasure of life on earth. They provide evidence of the almost infinite number of ways in which human beings have learned to adapt and negotiate their existence within their natural and social habitats. The loss of local traditions, occurring within one generation, is equivalent to the eradication of books, which are the record of human intelligence and imagination, in bonfires built by dictators. The homogenization of culture means the loss of the record of human struggle against natural adversity, exploitation, and oppression. It means the erasure of the magnificent record of human accomplishments in all of their myriad forms and expressions. Sadly, a local dialect, dance tradition, or other social artifact born within a local community can rarely be recreated once gone. The loss is not just a loss of a specific community but a depletion of the totality of the universal human culture.

The study of dance has included the understanding that cultural traditions have been passed down through dance. We have learned to read dance as a text and to value how this reading can provide insights into the values, attitudes, and beliefs of other cultures. Whether we are looking at issues of gender, patriarchy, sexual orientation, relationships, or other representations of human identity, dance has provided us with an avenue for making sense of the global culture and making us knowledgable of our differences and similiarities. Understanding the power of dance to document this kind of historical, geographic, and specific information about culture must lead us to think carefully about the erasure, homogenization, or commodification of such forms of knowledge. Thinking about dance as we do writing might help to make this issue clearer. If we were to suggest the rewriting of some of our most cherished books, there would be an outcry to save what has been written. Who would dare to rewrite the works of Walt Whitman, Gabriel Marquez, Virginia Wolff, or any of the many authors throughout our world who have captured in their writing the particular and the universal, the historical and the imagined, the poetic and the prosaic, the longings and the transformations? Why then is there no outcry to preserve dance? Should we not closely attend to the possible loss of a rich dance tradition through the processes of globalization?

Conflicting Identities

Another threat to indigenous traditions exists. Not only do we have the migratory influence of the global North on the global South, we also have what is termed *glocalizaton* (see chapter 1). Glocalization is a process in which the local affects the global and the global influences the local. An example of this is *Riverdance*, which was developed explicitly as a hybrid Irish national dance reflecting some of the Irish dance traditions as well as some of the more global styles emphasizing sensual energy, pulsating rhythms, and romanticized imagery. *Riverdance* was created to appeal to an international audience and to inject Ireland into the global scene. Venable (2001) states that in the post-*Riverdance* era there has been a global growth of Irish dance that continues to invent tradition. Indeed, she says (286), "One of the most ironic aspects of Irish dance is the continual redefinition of the word 'traditional,' especially where movement is concerned. . . ." Wee girls with their long curly wigs, tiaras, bejeweled costumes, and laced shoes take their turn performing steps learned directly from the videos of *Riverdance*. They dance in the pubs for their family and friends, dreaming of unsurpassed beauty and becoming the chosen partner of one like Michael Flatley.

What is the "real" dance becomes a common question in dance practices that are borrowed, infused, or considered a hybrid form of traditional dance. Of course, borrowing is not new in dance. Dance has always taken from other cultures and expressive forms. What is different is the speed and ease of which the dance traditions are being changed, often without acknowledgement or choice.

Rehearsal of dance "...and Sarah Laughed"—exploring difference
Photo courtesy of Sherry Shapiro.

In the global market, we not only question whether a dance is real because it has changed its steps or form but also question if a dance is authentic if it is taught outside of its culture. In a conversation with an African dance teacher at the University of Cape Town, I asked, "Is it still considered African dance if it is taught by someone who is not African?" Of course, we must recognize that there is no single African dance and that insinuated in my question is also the question, "What makes it African dance?" The teacher's answer did not surprise me. He said, "African dance is about a people's history, their stories, their life; one cannot simply take the steps and then be dancing African dance." Though others may not agree with his definition, his point cannot be dismissed. African dance, he argues, is a story of a people. It is not a series of steps to be learned as a dance style. Like other traditional dance forms, it has specific movements or gestures that represent particular ideas, expressions, or emotions, but it is not the dance vocabulary that is important. What is significant is the story of the people. Teaching African dance steps out of context is like taking the dictionary and learning some of the words of a culture rather than reading a story of the culture. Teaching African dance out of context as a mixture of steps or movements is more of a co-option of a tradition rather than a respect for diversity. Of course, this is only one way of thinking about African dance. Other people may argue that as we engage in dancing the particular movements of a culture, we also engage in a somatic understanding of that culture. What might be helpful here is to switch directions. Rather than moving from the global North to the global South, we may ask instead, "What do South Africans learn about the United States as they learn hip-hop?"

Looking in my own backyard of dance in the United States, we find that seeking diversity within unity has not been easy. We have not found simple solutions. A good example of this can be found in Carol Paris' article "Defining the African American Presence in Postmodern Dance from the Judson Church Era to the 1990s." In this article Paris lays out some of the difficult choices African American choreographers had to make during the early postmodern dance movement. The aesthetic changes of the avant-garde artists, who "saw the body merely as the material for a movement for movement-sake approach; not the interpreter of emotions, linear narratives, musical melodies, or explosive rhythmic structures" (Paris 2001, 235), presented a conflict to African American choreographers. This change of aesthetics in dance in the United States happened during the time of the civil rights movement, antiwar protests, and political assassinations. It was a historic time in which some African American choreographers wanted to continue to use the body and dance as a way of examining the social and political world and not use it simply as an exploration of dance or the process of making dance itself. During the 1950s and 60s in the United States, the Black body could not be severed from its cultural identity, and many of the African American choreographers of the time did not want to strip this representative Black body of its power to evoke the passionate narrative of oppression and the desire for freedom. To give up this particular form of embodied expression also meant to silence a country's history, a people's story, and the chance to learn from the past.

Universalism as an Ideal

Yet, in the struggle against the erasure of identities and the fight against homogenization, I do not believe we should rid ourselves of universality. Indeed, my argument is more nuanced in regard to universal claims. My assertion is that there is a universality that must be attended to along with the particular. The danger is in saying that we are all the same, when we are not, or in saying that one culture's forms and ideas are better than another's. Because dance and the body are one and the same (dance does not exist without the body), dance has a unique possibility to advance what Burns (2005, 313) defines as "universalism—the idea that all humans share the same inalienable rights." To make such a giant leap from globalization to dance, to the body, and to a universal human ideal creates a definite challenge for our cultural and ethical imaginations.

Taking care not to diminish the importance of difference (as we still have much to do to adequately recognize and value all of our diverse experiences, cultures, and traditions), I nonetheless want to draw attention to how we might understand human existence through our commonalities. Perhaps it is seeing the fear, suspicion, and hate that are so rampant in the world today that makes me want to search for, and affirm, our common human attributes. It is the commonalities of our bodies that offer ways of valuing the shared biological, emotional, and expressive human characteristics necessary for a more humane world. To address the importance of a common humanity is to understand that the struggle for *human* rights and *human* liberation is indispensable in a globalized world. So many of the threats we face today are threats to human beings as a whole—dangers to our very existence as a species. Together we face the possible extinction of life on our planet because of global climate change; lethal, transnational pandemics; and possible nuclear warfare that might make areas of our planet uninhabitable. There is a compelling need to see the commonalities of human life—the shared and universal qualities of human life (indeed, of *all* life)—as central to our quest for purpose and meaning. I believe that the body—*our bodies*—more than anything else is what grounds our commonalities. To address the importance of a common humanity grounded in universality is to understand that the struggle for human rights and liberation is necessary even while recognizing that the term *human* is dangerous as a vehicle for imposing a particular concept of who we are. It is hard to see how we can make the case for greater freedom, justice, peace, or human rights without making an appeal to the notion of a common humanity.

The universal is not an abstract idea or ideal; rather, it is acknowledging someone as a subject, granting that person the same status as oneself, and recognizing that person's sacred otherness. Ethical practices occur in specific situations. Practices in and of themselves may or may not be ethical. Rather, the rightness of the action, as it affects the lives and experiences of those it is directed toward, determines ethical behavior. The rightness of an action is not reducible to a response to the other. It includes a responsiveness to the other's values, beliefs, principles, and aesthetic and religious sensibilities—to the values and meanings of the other's world (Farley 1985). This is what we might call *compassion* or the ability to *suffer with others*.

At the core of the universal claim is that of corporeality—the body. Here, the body is not simply a physical body. Carved by the social order and designated as a representation of one's culture, the body has come to be understood as the aesthetic realm where meaning is made, life is experienced, and truth is understood as partial and relational. The body here is understood as the concrete material inscribed by cultural values, attitudes, and beliefs *and* as the vehicle for transcending our limited social identities. The body is a conduit for the particular and the universal, the material and the transcendent. When we accept the body as the aesthetic realm, the aesthetic realm necessarily becomes concerned with issues of power, justice, and the ethics of relationships. "The human drama," writes Morris Berman, "is first and foremost a somatic one" (1989, 108). As Emily Martin (1989, 15) might suggest for the understanding of human history, we must dwell "at the level of the social whole, at the level of 'person,' and at the level of body."

Transcending Limitations and Boundaries

Today we live in a global society in which cultural globalization, or the transnational migration of people, information, and consumer culture, is prevalent. The creation of dance in this context is no longer limited by space or time. Our ability to experience a virtual world as we remain physically in one place has changed our sense of boundaries, location, and even time. Recognizing the imaginary or constructed nature of our boundaries—the narratives of country, race, ethnicity, or gender—has spurred us to deconstruct what we referred to earlier as *real* or *traditional*. Within this context we must understand that it is not dance that creates us, but we who create dance. Dance always mediates who we are and how we live within time and culture. In this sense dance is nothing more than a book written by the body signifying how we experience and give meaning to our world. It is through these words written by the human body that we can begin to recognize and transcend the limitations and boundaries that up to now have closed off new possibilities. We can discover new ways to live, expand our sense of being, and establish new relationships with those who share our world (Shapiro and Shapiro 2002). The process calls us toward another kind of aesthetic, or meaning-making, process.

Meaning making as an aesthetic act that looks toward the rational *and* the sensual, the mind and the body, the individual and the society, the particular and the shared. It is an aesthetic "born of the recognition that the world of perception and experience cannot simply be derived from abstract universal laws, but demands its own appropriate discourse and displays its own inner, if inferior, logic" (Eagleton 1990, 16). Or, put more succinctly, "the aesthetic, then, is simply the name given to that hybrid form of cognition which can clarify the raw stuff of perception and historical practice, disclosing the inner structure of the concrete" (Eagleton 1990, 16). A global aesthetic, then, moves beyond the individual or the self to connect to the other, recognizing the concreteness of an ethical existence in a shared world.

A language that emerges from our bodily living speaks to a kind of rationality distinct from one that is rooted only in the intellectual. It speaks to the specificity of individual experiences and testifies against any simple abstraction of any category or label. The social worlds in which we form our identity are visceral—they are in our bones and our musculature. Our views of ourselves and others, our ethics, our values, and our manners of being and relating are instilled in our bodies—a place where our thoughts and actions are instantiated. The body is the ultimate destination of cultural forming, both local and global. This point of cultural ingestion occurs where both projections and formations mingle in creating a double-edged process. The body of the postmodern subject, as Terry Eagleton (1996, 69) states, "is integral to its identity." In modernity the body was where there was something to be done; it was a place for betterment. In postmodernity, it is a place where something—gazing, imprinting, regulating—is done to you. For the global body, imprinting by the concentrated power of the Western media is intensified and a sense of a local self is less important. But what is special about the human body is its capacity to transform itself in the process of transforming the material bodies around it.

What kind of world have we created? And, therefore, what role does the body play? We need not look far to find the answers. Hunger, homelessness, domestic violence, rape, loss of limbs from land mines, improvised explosive devices (IEDs), and torture all exemplify ways in which the human body is vulnerable—ways in which it can be harmed, mutilated, and destroyed. Human suffering extends *through and beyond* the boundaries of nationality, race, ethnicity, gender, social class, sexual orientation, or religious preference; it extends through and beyond all the ways we have of marking ourselves separate from others. Here, in our shared physical suffering, in the commonality of the body, is a place of deeper and mutual understanding and thus of transcendent possibility.

The Suffering Body Questions the Integrity of Globalization

Media images transmitted globally, albeit used to support particular political interests, have already proven their power of evoking an empathetic understanding of and compassion for the other. Etched into our memories are images of Iraqi children who have been victims of IEDs, child soldiers forced into acts of brutality, women trying to escape from possible rape or disfigurement, faces of people to be executed, people subjected to the fear and shame of interrogation and torture, thousands of tent cities in Darfur where emaciated refugees have been forced to flee from acts of genocide, and children of famine lying listlessly at their mother's dry breast. We experience these global images not as abstractions but as the way we come face to face with our own humanity. The suffering body transcends the particularity of human existence and becomes a potent means of generating a sense of shared humanity. Ana Maria Araujo Freire (1994) wrote passionately about the effect of denying or prohibiting the body in her epilogue to Paulo Freire's book, *Pedagogy of Hope*:

> I am fed up with bans and prohibitions: bans on the body, which produce, generation after generation, not only Brazilian illiteracy (according to the thesis I maintain), but an *ideology* of ban on the body, which gives us our "street children," our misery and hunger, our unemployment and prostitution, and, under military dictatorship, the exile and death of countless Brazilians. (Freire 1994, 204)

To blind ourselves to what the body experiences, to what it feels, and to what we might experience through our empathy toward shared pain is dangerous because it keeps us in the rational world where a person can explain, without any necessary compassion or ethical sensibility, the problems of our world. But the body refuses to be understood as an abstract object. It is not other. It is real. It is the presence of all that we know, albeit housed in narratives of meaning.

To engage in global aesthetics with a universal ethics as the goal requires from us a different kind of dance education. Pedagogically we begin with the body—the body that we understand as the concrete material inscribed by cultural values, both local and global, and the vehicle for transcending our limited social identities. A pedagogy of the body may direct us toward the recognition of a universal humanity, the still-radical idea that all humans share the same inalienable rights.

Pedagogic practices that draw upon the body and aesthetic processes that provide ways of understanding the world and ourselves intellectually, sensually, mentally, and emotionally are all but nonexistent in traditional educational textbooks, teacher education programs, classroom practices,

Rehearsal of dance ". . . And Sarah Laughed"—silencing other
Photo courtesy of Sherry Shapiro.

and dance studios. This absence is troubling at a time when the body has become so central to theory and cultural practice—troubling because it is the body where the global influences of the West shapes our images of physical beauty, success, and desire. Laurie McDade (1987) writes that knowing in the mind does not lie dormant, separate from the knowing of the heart and of the body.

Everyday moments of teaching at school in communities, then, are personal, pedagogical, and political acts that incorporate the minds and bodies of the subjects as knowers and as learners. When we are at our best as teachers we are capable of speaking to each of these ways of knowing ourselves and our students. And we may override precedents in the educational project that value the knowing of the mind and deny the knowing of the heart and body. Students, the partners in this enterprise of knowing, are whole people with ideas, emotions, with sensations. If we as teachers are to arouse passions now and then (Greene 1986, 441), the educational project must not be confined to a knowing of only the mind. It must also address and interrogate what we think we know of the heart and of the body (58-59).

Some of the reasons for the dismal construction of pedagogic practices that exclude embodied knowledge and aesthetic processes include the lack of previous educational experiences of teachers, the lack of understanding of how body knowledge can contribute to a broader social critique, the inability to turn body knowledge into an end-of-grade test, and the need to be able to order and control knowledge, which is impossible in a curriculum in which students genuinely seek their own meaning.

In the following I want to share an example of how a person might draw upon embodied knowledge and connect it to social and ethical critique. This act of educating for a kind of global aesthetics cuts across cultures and unites the arts in the struggle for connection, healing (that is, overcoming fragmentation and making whole), and compassion. Each of these speaks to the need for us to see ourselves, and experience ourselves, as part of a larger community in which the quality of our lives is inextricably connected to the well-being of others. Though I describe a process I have created for dance, it is by no means only for dance or only for the arts.

By the Virtue of Being Human

Twyla Tharp said, "Modern dance is more, not less." I would add, "Teaching dance is more, not less." Only those who haven't been teachers hold the old adage, "Those who can't dance teach." What we as educators understand is that teaching demands us to know something about what is and what is possible of our students and of our discipline. Some important questions that confront us as dance educators are, "What should we teach?" "How should we teach?" "Who should we teach?" "What is the role of the teacher?" And, most importantly, "For what are we teaching?"

Asking *what is* brings us to question dance. Is it a discipline? Is it an art form? Is it a way of learning about other disciplines? Is it something to learn in itself? Can it tell us something about our cultures and ourselves? Is it a way of knowing the world, or is it something to know? Can it tell us about the human condition? These are questions about visions that compel us to examine dance in the broader context of education. They ask us to name what we care about, what concerns us, and, further, our vision for humanity and how education gives shape to this articulated vision. I am reminded of the time I interviewed with one of the faculty from my doctoral program. He asked me, "What would your world be like if there was no such thing as dance?" His question brought me to reflect seriously on the significance of dance in my life. Since that day I have found many answers to that question, but it is the question that remains as part of my thinking about dance and about dance education. James MacDonald (2005) asked two specific and related questions that I later encountered in my studies: "What does it mean to be human?" and "How shall we live together in the world?" These questions take us beyond dance by recognizing the moral and political connections that accompany any act of education. It is an act of transcendence that reminds us that education, any education, must engage our students in all of their different narratives—narratives that are shaped by ethnicity, harnessed by social class, and textured by culture. To know ourselves is to understand the way in which our thoughts, ideas, and desires are always bound up with the way of being that comes from the lives that emerge out of both our local situations and global influences.

With all of this in mind I must say I have come to feel, like bell hooks, that any education worth its name must illicit the passion, the intellectual curiosity, the moral conviction, and the spiritual sensitivity of students. Giroux and Simon (1988) summarize the concerns of this kind of education:

> This means that teaching and learning must be linked to the goals of educating students: to understand why things are the way they are and how they got to be that way; to make the familiar strange and the strange familiar; to take risks and struggle with ongoing relations of power from within a life-affirming moral culture; and to envisage a world which is "not yet" in order to enhance the condi-

tions for improving the grounds upon which life is lived. (Giroux and Simon 1988, 13)

Such a pedagogy engaged in ideological critique inevitably raises moral concerns. It exposes questions of social injustice, inequality, asymmetrical power, and the lack of human rights or dignity. This educational discourse is meant to provide a theory and a process for critiquing everything that privileges some rather than all, separating us into categories of those who deserve to live well and those who do not. Critical inquiry here means to learn to question what we take for granted about who we are and how the world functions. It does not mean the kind of critical thinking, or problem solving, that is often used in education for solving abstract problems such as the following: There are four one-gallon (four-liter) buckets of water and 12 people. How much water does each person get if one person gets one-half of all the water and the other 11 divide what remains? Instead, central to critical pedagogy is a kind of understanding in which students make sense of their lives as they become aware of the dialectical relationship between their subjectivity and the dominant values that shape their lives. These values may be ones that are fixed locally in early life, although these days they are more likely to result, at least in part, from the influence of a global ideology. It is helping students learn how to examine, to reflect, to ask questions, to look for relationships, and to seek understanding of themselves and their world.

Over the past 15 years I have worked in the field of dance education, teaching at a small liberal arts college for women in the southern United States. In this position I have had the opportunity to evolve in my own thinking about dance education. I started from the most primitive way of teaching—having students reproduce the steps they had been given—and then progressed to creative movement—having students learn to create from a movement vocabulary—and then finally arrived at a philosophy for education, arts, and dance—a philosophy that focuses on developing a critical global aesthetic process that takes students through questions of identity and otherness and toward compassionate and ethically responsible behavior. I share one example of my pedagogic philosophy in my choreographic work. It is this philosophy, or vision, through which all the courses I teach are filtered.

This particular choreographic example centers on the biblical story of the relationship between Hagar and Sarah. I selected this story because it lends itself to raising issues of power, jealousy, domination of the stranger, compassion, and the value of women in society (the value of women as determined by their ability to bear children). Since it is being taught in a women's college in North Carolina (in the Bible Belt of the

Rehearsal of dance ". . . And Sarah Laughed"—crossing borders
Photo courtesy of Sherry Shapiro.

United States), this narrative takes on special significance. Christianity has played an important role in the students' development as ethical human beings and in providing meaning to their lives. This story offered them a powerful and resonant narrative from which they could critically examine issues in their own lives. I read parts of the chapters in Genesis, asking the students to discuss their interpretations of this story. Specifically, I asked them to write a reflection about an experience they had in their own lives that made them feel as the other. The students hesitated very little in naming such experiences. I then asked them to reflect upon their memories and to return to their felt experiences. They shared with each other the times they had been shunned, the times they had been unable to become part of groups they so desperately wanted to be in, the times their families had separated, and the times they didn't possess the right characteristics to be socially acceptable. From their embodied memories they created movements that expressed their life stories and reflected their pain, humiliation, and sorrow.

Next, I asked them to reflect upon the times they had made another person to feel as the stranger. At first they didn't remember any times that they had done this. Blocked by their inability to accept their own behavior, which might have been experienced as hurtful or cruel by others, they were saved from, or avoided, a sense of responsibility. Also, sometimes their level of understanding did not allow them to see the larger structures in which they participated that might be hurtful to others—whether their religious beliefs, choice of roommates, fear of Black men, and, more significantly, place of privilege as White middle-class women. Yet, they did remember. They had to acknowledge their own participation, whether it was through action or nonaction; they acknowledged experiences that they had ignored, distanced themselves from, or lied to themselves about. For example, some allowed themselves to believe that the plight of the less fortunate is a result of laziness, indifference, or failure to make the effort. As one student noted, "They [the poor] don't deserve what I have or they would have it." Some of these same women described themselves as being Christians, concerned, caring, compassionate, or generous—as women who have "big hearts." Again, after writing their own stories, sharing with others, and discussing their experiences within the larger questions about who deserves what, they recreated their stories through movement.

To have the students enter into their feelings is to do more than talk about these feelings. I use movement and the body as both the critical and the creative tool to form the connections between what they know and what they have yet to name. *Talking is not enough to address peoples' feelings.* Here the arts can offer a powerful pedagogy. Too often the arts are thought about only in ways that relate to performance, technical virtuosity, or beauty in the traditional sense of the aesthetic. Using movement as a pedagogic method, as I do, allows students to focus on their bodies, not as objects to be trained, but as subjects of their world. They come to know their bodies as possible actors in history as well as repositories of history. Indeed, without this sense of agency, there can be no talk of emancipation and possibility. Education, for the most part, continues to disavow the aesthetic process as something that can tell us what is and what might be in life. For aesthetic processes, the expectation is that students will gain skills in perceiving, interpreting, selecting, shaping, and synthesizing meaning so that they can create coherence and clarity in how they see the world. They learn to attend to their existential projects, their feelings and their beliefs, thinking creatively and imaginatively. Most significantly, they learn how to name the world as they experience it. To move into global aesthetics means to transcend art itself and connect the meaning-making process to self and world. In transferring these aesthetic ways of knowing and directing them toward critical, ethical, and embodied social analysis, students begin to engage in a radical pedagogy and possibly gain a sense of universal connections and responsibilities. While engaged in such pedagogy, they come to understand the relational and therefore moral aspect of life. As Zygmunt Bauman suggests, they can reach a place where they may "grasp hold of the self and to awaken it as an active moral agent disposed to care for the other; a self that experiences a sense of obligation even before it grasps the Other's existence" (Smith 1999, 181).

The final question I asked the students referred them back to a time in the story when Sarah hears God speaking to Abraham about her forthcoming pregnancy. I asked them to reflect upon a time that something happened to them, as it did to Sarah—a time when they were surprised by something that they thought could not happen. My expectation was that they would name joyous memories. Instead, each and every one told stories of pain and sorrow: a father's suicide, a mother's mental illness and family breakdown, a rape by a teacher, an affair that led to the end of a marriage and the beginning of another. They cried, they mourned, and they told things that shamed them. They did what they are not allowed to do in schools. They shared the things that make them most human, their erotic selves. They integrated themselves into the world of feeling, and of common humanity, capturing the transformative possibility of education. As I mentioned earlier, what is of concern here is not so much the methodology but the vision and philosophy. Guided by a purpose of education concerned with social justice and moral agency, the methodology must elicit possibilities for students to examine the social construction of their reality, reflect upon and experience themselves as rational and sensual beings, and question the significance and meaning of their own lives. I use a pedagogic form of movement, as well as reflective writing, discussion, poetry, reading, video viewing, eating together, and performing together, to connect the personal and the political, self and others, and each pedagogic process to a sense of responsible choices. It is to this place that any education concerned with an ethical humanity must be brought. This is not an approach that should be viewed as affective *or* cognitive *or* moral. It transcends those differences, remembering that, as Martin Heidegger argued, "reason is the perception of what is, which always means also what can be and ought to be" (1968, 41). It is this understanding of reason that concerns itself with possibility grounded in sensate-lived experience and that is made sense of through critical understanding and global ethical responsibility. Through this process of sensual reasoning, a person can become actively engaged in re-fusing the mind and the body, the particular and the universal, the self and the stranger (Shapiro 1999).

The dance, which results from this process of reflection and connection, takes form, imaging the joys and struggles of the dancers' lives. It speaks a language of common humanity to the audience as it presents memories of self and other. Through this critical and aesthetic process, the students have named their own oppressions and the ways in which they have oppressed others. They have recognized that their bodies hold knowledge of their world, and they have learned the meaning of their bodies as the materiality of existence. Coming to know themselves as body and subjects, they explored, examined, and created connections between inner sensibilities (local) and outer contexts (global). The body memories that are central to my pedagogy are, at least in part, records of the *felt world* of self and other in all of its sensuous and relational qualities. It is surely the latter that grounds the desire for a different kind of world, one of compassion, love, and justice. Remembering in this sense becomes the act of identifying the self in all of its creative, critical, and ethical dimensions; it becomes the process of finding a home in this torn and afflicted world (Shapiro 1999).

No longer can we suggest that the ability to rationally apprehend a situation is enough. Recognizing wrongs requires recognizing the humanity of our victims. The overstressed focus on the cognitive in education has left us with people who can build smart bombs and provide means of efficient interrogation and has supplied us with obedient soldiers. But let us not forget the moral challenge posed by the solitary individual when confronted by the stranger: What responsibility do I feel for the other? As Bauman argues, this feeling, this moral urge, is inherent in the human context. It is rooted in the autonomy of the I and its need for relationship. When moral rules have disintegrated with the postmodern, there remain only moral standards— standards that demand interpretation and choice. Our challenge as educators is to transcend the traditional ways of educating the mind and envelop the wisdom of the body. It is in that wisdom that we can find glimmers of compassionate connection, the discernment of concrete existence, and the desire to live in a humane world.

Conclusion

Like nothing else in the education of our children, art offers ways to transcend a consciousness that fixes our world as if it is something that is unchangeable. Art allows us to see what is in our world and to imagine what might be. As it nurtures the imagination of children and attends to their perception, it helps them to develop the ability to reimagine and reshape their world. Here is where art lays the groundwork for addressing the challenges of globalization. This includes challenging the limited ways of thinking about our national capabilities and powers to acquiring a transnational consciouness thereby, gaining the possibility for imaging change. "The results," as Falk states concerning the consequences of not seeing the global nature of our world (2003, 188), "have not been pretty: frequent warfare, many incidents of ethnic cleansing and genocide, catastrophic risks of environmental collapse, massive poverty, a disregard for future generations." We can begin to understand the critical responsibility of art in a world that teaches children to accept and conform to what is and not to question what they are taught or the nature of their own experience. Though art is not, and should not be, a direct mirror of life, it tells us about life in ways that, as Maxine Greene (1988) says, makes the familiar strange and the strange familiar. In other words, art should help us to see what was obscured before and help us to imagine that which was unimaginable. Arts education, then, becomes revolutionary in showing us reality in ways that heighten our perceptions and in presenting images of what might be possible or preferable.

As dance educators, we can help children learn how to give voice to their life stories through dance. Moving their own stories as giving voice to their own life experiences is pedagogically valuable, as seen in the previous example, as a way to deepen their understanding of who they are. In addition, moving for others provides a place for students to share their stories. In voicing their stories, they can begin a dialogue. In learning how to represent the world as they experience it, they become better able to see themselves in others and to develop the empathy—empathy for the life of another—that global aesthetics and universalism demand.

As I come to understand the power of dance education as a transformative experience—one that is badly needed to overcome the limitations of our differences and to recognize our commonalities—I become more convinced that dance educators have been given a unique gift. We have the opportunity to work with children and young people in ways that affirm their identities, challenge their taken-for-granted assumptions, and impart a way of being in the world that is compassionate, critical, creative, and bound up with a vision for a more just global community.

Such a community, unlike our present fragmented and competitive world, would be a place that we could count on and be secure in, where we could understand each other, where we would never be an outcast or a stranger, where we could trust each other, and where we would be safe and assured well-being. While such a community is the kind of world that is not yet available to us, it is, I believe, the loving and just world that our children need and deserve. And it is one that we as educators must struggle to make possible.

REFLECTIONS

When rereading my own work, I am almost overpowered by my expectations for dance and dance education. Why can't we just dance, have fun, and enjoy moving? Isn't that valuable enough? Many of my students tell me that they dance because it makes them feel good and that the dance studio is a place where they can simply focus on themselves. Do I really want to insist that this is frivolous as compared with changing the world? I laugh as I write this. But the laughter is not decisive. I do not want to argue about the value of these dance experiences or about the many significant things that each of us could say we have gained from dance. For all of those things I am grateful. Yet I cannot deny that I hope for more. As a dancer, an educator, and an artist, I have learned how to observe, explore, reflect, interpret, imagine, and create. It was with these tools that I came to examine why dance is important to my life. Being able to understand that what we know is an embodied knowing has allowed me to better understand that dance offers us another modality for knowing ourselves and our world. It was with this knowledge that I was able to draw a framework in dance that connects self and other, passion and compassion, sensitivity and imagination to ethical commitment. Maybe there is room in dance for both: for enjoying the freedom of our bodies while respecting the knowledge that they possess. The idea for a global aesthetics, in which language and insight emerge from our bodily experiences, and the commonality of the human body provide us with a site for mutual understanding. I believe that this is a good place to begin when seeking a universal ethics. As Laurie McDade (1987) reminded us, the mind does not lie dormant, separate from the knowing of the heart and of the body. To deeply understand the human condition requires us to transcend the limitations of dualistic thinking, which for so long (in the West, at least) has separated and subordinated our sensuous knowing for rationality. Martha Graham (Schrader 2005) offered us this wisdom: "The body never lies." Graham understood that the body offers us a vehicle that can speak truth to deceit, banality, and ill-used power. Clearly it depends upon us who are involved in dance to articulate for others what role dance may play in an increasingly globalized world that calls out for a new vision of human community, for social justice, and for the sacredness of the earth itself.

Notes

1. *Global North* is a term for richer and developed countries such as those in Europe and the United States that are usually found in the northern hemisphere.

2. *Global South* is a term for the poorer countries such as those in Africa, Asia, and Latin America that are mostly located in the southern hemisphere. *Global South* is a preferred term for *third world* or *developing countries*.

PART IV REFLECTIVE QUESTIONS

- What does it mean to talk about embodied knowing?
- What memories of your own life and experience does your body hold?
- How would it transform education if we viewed knowledge in a more holistic manner and if we incorporated mind and body?
- In what sense does the human body provide a means for recognizing our common humanity?
- How have the readings in this book transformed your view of the purpose and value of dance?
- How does aesthetic experience improve the quality of human life?

references

preface

Bauman, Zygmunt. (1998). Globization. Oxford: Blackwell Publishers.

chapter 1

An Chomhairle Ealaíon. 1994. *Arts plan 1995-1997*. Dublin: Author.

Bourdieu, P. 1993. *The field of cultural production*. New York: Columbia University Press.

Brinson, P. 1986. *The dancer and the dance*. Dublin: An Chomhairle Ealaíon.

Celtic Tiger Live. n.d. www.celtictigerlive.com/show.php.

Cunningham, G. January 24, 2000. Harris stokes up attack on "Ashes." *Irish Independent*.

Foley, C. 2001. Perceptions of Irish step dance: National, global and local. *Dance Research Journal* 33(1): 34-45.

Gardiner, K. 1994. The Irish Economy: a Celtic Tiger? *Ireland: Challenging for Promotion*, Morgan Stanley Euroletter (1 August).

Keynes, J.M. 2004. *The economic consequences of the peace 1919*. New York: Dover.

Kirby, P. 2002. *The Celtic tiger in distress*. Hampshire: Palgrave.

Krugman, P. March 1998. The trouble with history. *Washington Monthly*.

Martin, R. 1998. *Critical moves: Dance studies in theory and politics*. Durham, NC: Duke University Press.

McManis, S. October 16, 2005. Raising his Eire: Michael Flatley has an Irish tiger by the tail. *Sacramento Bee*.

Mulrooney, D. 2006. *Irish moves: An illustrated history of dance and physical theatre in Ireland*. Dublin: Liffey Press.

OECD. 1994. *Economic outlook (December)*. Paris: OECD.

O'Sullivan, M.J. 2006. *Ireland and the global question*. Cork: Cork University Press.

O'Reilly, G. 2004. Economic globalization: Ireland in the EU 1973-2003. *Acta Geographica Slovenica* (Volume 44 No.1).

O'Toole, F. 1997. *Ex-isle of Erin: Images of a global Ireland.* Dublin: New Island Books.

O'Toole, F. March 12, 2005. More Broadway than Bunratty. *The Irish Times.*

Seaver, M. June 17, 2005. The Irish step beyond "Riverdance." *Christian Science Monitor.* www.csmonitor.com/2005/0617/p11s02-almp.html

Taylor, C. May 21, 2006. Michael Flatley. *Sunday Times.* http://entertainment.timesonline.co.uk/tol/arts_and_entertainment/article720675.ece.

The Irish Times, September 25, 1928. Dancing at the Abbey.

Watkins, K. 2005. *2005 Human Development Report,* New York: United Nations Development Programme.

chapter 2

Blom, L.A., and L.T. Chaplin. 1994. *The intimate act of choreography.* Pittsburgh: University of Pittsburgh Press.

Dalcroze, E.J. 1919/1988. Euritmika i pokretna plastika. [Eurythmics and the moving plastics.] In *Glazba i plesač.* [*Music and the dancer.*], ed. Miroslav Mićanović, 19-35. Zagreb: Naklada MD. London: Dalcroze Society.

Desmond, J.C. 1997. Embodying difference: Issues in dance and cultural studies. In *Meaning in motion: New cultural studies of dance,* ed. J.C. Desmond, 179-205. Durham: Duke University Press.

Desmond, J.C. 1997. Utjelovljenje razlike: ples i kulturalni studiji. [Embodying difference: Issues in dance and cultural studies.] In *Meaning in motion: New cultural studies of dance,* ed. J.C. Desmond, 179-205. Durham: Duke University Press. In Govedić, N., ed. 2003. *Korpografije: 20 godina tjedna suvremenog plesa.* [*Corpographies: 20th anniversary of the contemporary dance week.*] Zagreb: Hrvatski institut za pokret i ples.

Đurinović, M. 2003. Dancing in Croatia. In *Guide to Croatian dance,* editorial board M. Đurinović, N. Dogan, I.N. Sibila, K. Šimunić, Ž. Turćinović, L. Zoldoš, 58-64. Zagreb: Hrvatski centar ITI Unesco.

———. 2000. *Mercedes Goritz-Pavelić.* Zagreb: Naklada MD.

Đurinović, M., and Z. Podkovac. 2004. *Mia Čorak Slavenska.* Zagreb: Naklada MD.

Fortin, S. 1998. Somatics: A tool for empowering modern dance teachers. In *Dance, power, and difference: Critical and feminist perspectives on dance education*, ed. S.B. Shapiro, 49-71. Champaign, IL: Human Kinetics.

Govedić, N. 2002. Izvedbeni i rodni izbori. [Gender and performance as a matter of choice.] In *Izbor uloge, pomak granice: književne, kazališne i filmske studije.* [*Choice of role, shift of boundaries: Literary, theatrical and film studies.*] Zagreb: Centar za ženske studije.

Horst, L., and C. Russel. 1961. *Modern dance form in relation to the other modern arts.* San Francisco: Impulse Publications.

Huxley, M. 1994. European early modern dance. In *Dance history: An introduction,* ed. J. Adshead-Lansdale and J. Layson. London and New York: Routledge.

Janković, I. 2004. Laban u praksi. [Laban in practice.] *Kretanja* [*Movements*] 02:104. Zagreb: Hrvatski centar ITI UNESCO.

Maletić, A. 1983. *Pokret i ples.* [*Movement and dance*] Zagreb: Hrvatski sabor kulture.

Maletić, A. 2003. Notes on the author. In *Povijest plesa starih civilizacija: Azijske plesne tradicije, drugi dio* [*The history of the dances of old civilizations: Asian dance traditions, part two*], Zagreb: Matica Hrvatska.

———. 2003. *Povijest plesa starih civilizacija: Azijske plesne tradicije, drugi dio.* [*The history of dance of old civilizations: Asian dance traditions, part two.*] Zagreb: Matica Hrvatska.

Maletic, V. 1987. *Body-space-expression: The development of Rudolf Laban's movement and dance concepts.* Berlin: Mouton de Gruyter.

———. 2005. *Dance dynamics: Effort & phrasing.* Workbook and DVD companion. Columbus, OH: Grade A Notes.

Marques, I.A. 1998. Dance education in/and the postmodern. In *Dance, power, and difference: Critical and feminist perspectives on dance education,* ed. S.B. Shapiro, 171-185. Champaign, IL: Human Kinetics.

Sanchez-Colberg, A. 1998. Space is the place: A reconsideration of Laban's principles of space for contemporary choreographic education and choreographic practice. In *Continents in movement: Proceedings of the International Conference New Trends in Dance Teaching,* ed. A. Macara, 230-235. Oeiras: Portugal.

Shapiro, S.B., ed. 1998. *Dance, power, and difference: Critical and feminist perspectives on dance education.* Champaign, IL: Human Kinetics.

Slunjski, I. 2005. Komu treba hrvatski ples? [Who needs Croatian dance?] *Kretanja* [*Movements*] 3/4:120-7. Zagreb: Hrvatski centar ITI Unesco.

Sorell, W. 1967. *The dance through the ages.* London: Thames and Hudson.

chapter 3

Abrahams, R.D., and J. Szwed, eds. 1983. *After Africa: Extracts from British travel accounts and journals of the seventeenth, eighteenth, and nineteenth centuries concerning the slaves, their manners, and customs in the British West Indies.* New Haven, CT: Yale University Press.

Barnet, S. 1977. Jonkonnu and the Creolisation process in Jamaica: A study in cultural dynamics. Master's thesis, Antioch International.

Beckford, W. 1790. A descriptive account of the island of Jamaica. Vol. 2. Printed for T. and J. Egerton, London.

Bettelheim, J. 1976. The Jonkonnu Festival: Its relation to Caribbean and African Masquerades. *Jamaica Journal* 10(2): 21-7.

Bettelheim, J., J. Nunley, and B. Bridges. 1988. *Caribbean festival arts.* Seattle: University of Washington Press.

Bogle. 2007. The uncrowned king of the dancehall. Interview by Montana. www.chicagoreggae.com/bogle.htm.

Bogle. December 1997. Interview by Merton "Scrapy D" McKenzie. www.dancehallreggae.com/bogle.html.

Burton, R.D.E. 1997. *Afro Creole: Power opposition and play in the Caribbean.* New York: Cornell University Press.

Characteristic traits of the Creolian and African Negroes in Jamaica. April-October 1797. 1976. *Columbiam* Magazine. Repr., ed. Barry Higman. Mona, Jamaica: Caldwell Press.

De La Beche, H.T. 1825. *Notes on the present conditions of the Negroes in Jamaica.* Printed for T. Cadell, in the Strand, London.

Ebanks, Neila. February 21, 2007. Interview by Christopher A. Walker.

Lekis, L. 1960. *Dancing gods.* New York: Scarecrow Press.

Long E. 1774. *The history of Jamaica.* Vol. 2. London: T. Lowndes.

Moncrieffe, Frederick "Tippa." November 17, 2006. Interview by Christopher A. Walker.

———. January 29, 2007. Interview by Christopher A. Walker.

———. February 12, 2007. Interview by Christopher A. Walker.

Nettleford, R.M. 1985. *Dance Jamaica: Cultural definition and artistic discovery.* New York: Grove Press.

Pinckard, G. 1806. *Notes on the West Indies.* Vol. 1. Baldwin, Craddock and Joy etc., London.

Pottinger, Diane. June 20, 2006. Interview by Christopher A. Walker.

Ryman, C. 1980. The Jamaican heritage in dance. *Jamaica Journal* 44: 2-14.

———. 1984a. Jonkonnu: A neo-African form Pt. I. *Jamaica Journal* 12(1): 13-23.

———. 1984b. Jonkonnu: A neo-African form Pt. II. *Jamaica Journal* 17(2): 50-61.

Sloane, H. 1707. *A voyage to the islands of Madera, Barbados, Nieves, S. Christophers and Jamaica.* 2 vols. London: Printed by B.M. for the author.

Stewart, J. 1823. *A view of the past and present state of the island of Jamaica.* Edinburgh: Oliver and Boyd.

Stolzoff, N.C. 2000. *Wake the town and tell the people.* London: Duke University Press.

Walker, C.A. 2004. Jamaican dance theatre: Folk origins and contemporary aesthetics. Master's thesis, State University of New York.

Walker, C.A. 2007. From yard to stage and beyond. *NDTC Quarterly* 3(1): 12-18.

Walker, C.A., D. Bailey, and A. Bright-Holland. 2003. Minstrelsy: Then and now. Lecture at the Diversity Conference, State University of New York, New York.

chapter 4

Albright, A.C. 1997. *Choreographing difference.* Hanover and London: Wesleyan University Press.

Animated Magazine. 2002. Foundation for community dance.

Benjamin, A. 2002. *Making an entrance: Theory and practice for disabled and non-disabled dancers.* New York: Routledge.

Cunha e Silva, P. 1999. O corpo que dança: Uma abordagem bioestética do movimento. In *Continents in movement,* ed. Daniel Tércio, 23-6. Cruz Quebrada, Portugal: Faculdade de Motricidade Humana.

Crepúsculo Manifest. 2002. *Belo Horizonte.pamphlet.*

Deleuze, G. 1988. *Diferença e repetição.* Rio de Janeiro: Graal.

Frank, A. 1993. For a sociology of the body: an analytical review. In 1997. *The body: social process cultural theory.* Feartherstone, M. M. Hepworth, and B. Turner, eds.. London: Sage, Quoted in Villaça, N., and F. Góes. 1998. *Em nome do corpo.* Rio de Janeiro: Rocco.

Foster, S. 1996. *Corporealities.* New York: Routledge.

Foulcault, M. 1987. *Vigiar e punir: Nascimento da prisão.* Petrópolis, RJ Rio de Janeiro: Vozes.

Freire, P. 1996. *Pedagogia do oprimido.* São Paulo: Paz e Terra.

Brazil Fundação Nacional das Artes Funarte. 2004. Art Without Barriers Program. www.cultura.gov.br.

Green, J., and S. Stinson. 1999. Postpositivist research in dance. In *Researching dance: Modes of inquiry,* ed. S. Fraleigh and P. Hanstein, 91-123. Pittsburgh: Pittsburgh Press.

Greiner, C. 2005. *O corpo: Pistas para estudos indisciplinares.* São Paulo: Annablume.

Greiner, C. 1999. A cultura e as novas dramaturgias do corpo que dança. *Cadernos do GIPE-CIT: Grupo Interdisciplinar de Pesquisa e Extensão em Contemporaneidade, Imaginário e Teatralidade* 8(December): 65-70.

Greiner, C., and C. Amorim. 2003. *Leituras do corpo.* São Paulo: Annablume.

Hall, S. 1997. *A identidade cultural na pós-modernidade.* Rio de Janeiro: DP&A.

Iannitelli, L. 2004. Técnica da dança: Redimensionamentos metodológicos. *Revista Repertório* 7:30-7. Salvador, Bahia: UFBA.

Lyotard, J F. 1993. *O Pós-moderno explicado às crianças.* Lisbon: Dom Quixote.

Maffesoli, M. 2000. *O tempo das tribos.* São Paulo: Forense.

Manifesto Crepúsculo. 2002. Pamphlet.

Matos, L. 2006. Mapping multiple dancing bodies: The construction of new corporal territories and aesthetics in contemporary dance in Brazil. PhD dissertation Scenic Arts Program. Federal University of Bahia, Salvador.

Matos, L. 2002. Corpos que dançam: Diferença e deficiência. *Revista Diálogos Possíveis* 1:177-85.

―――. 2000. Múltiplos corpos dançantes: Diferença e deficiência. In *Temas em contemporaneidade, imaginário e teatralidade,* ed. Armindo Bião et al. Armindo Bião, Antonia Pereira, Luiz Cajaiba and Renata Pitombo, 213-28. São Paulo: Annablume.

―――. 1998. Multiple views of the deafbody: The corporeity of the deaf adolescent in dance teaching. Master's thesis, School of Education. Federal University of Bahia, Salvador.

Pealbart, P.P. 2004. Um mundo no qual acreditar. http://geocities.yahoo.com.br/guaikuru0003/ deleuze_doss.html.

Pick, J. 1992. Why have there been no great disabled artists? *DAM, Disability Arts Magazine* 4 (Winter): 19-23.

Rubidge, S. 1998. Change and identity. In *Continents in movement: New trends in dance teaching,* ed. Ana Macara, 93-98. Oeiras, Portugal: Universidade Técnica de Lisboa, Faculdade de Motricidade Humana, Departamento de Dança.

Shakespeare, T. 1996. Disability, identity and difference. www.leeds.ac.uk/disability-studies/ archiveuk/Shakespeare/Chap6.pdf.

Shapiro, S. 2002. The body: The site of common humanity. In *Body movements: Pedagogy, politics and social change,* ed. S. Shapiro and S. Shapiro, 337-352. New Jersey: Hampton Press.

Schlicher, S. 2001. O corpo conceitual: Tendências performáticas na dança contemporânea. Tradução Ciane Fernandez. *Repertório: Teatro & Dança* 5:30-6.

Schöpke, R. 2004. *Por uma filosofia da diferença: Gilles Deleuze, o pensador nômade.* Rio de Janeiro: Contraponto.

Sodré, M., and R. Paiva. 2002. *O império do grotesco.* Rio de Janeiro: Mauad.

Tucherman, I. 1999. *Breve história do corpo e de seus monstros.* Lisboa: Vega Passagens.

Villaça, N., and F. Góes. 1998. *Em nome do corpo.* Rio de Janeiro: Rocco.

chapter 5

Adair, C. 1992. *Women and dance: Sylphs and sirens.* New York: New York University Press.

Akindele, S., T. Gidado, and O. Olaopo. 2002. Globalisation: Its implications and consequences for Africa. *Globalization* 2(Winter): 37-48.

Anderson, D. 1995. Lesbian and gay adolescents: Social and developmental considerations. In *The gay teen,* ed. G. Unks, 17-30. New York: Routledge.

Arkin, L. 1994. Dancing the body: Women and dance performance. *Journal of Physical Education, Recreation and Dance* 65(2): 36-8, 43.

Bailey, J., and M. Oberschneider. 1997. Sexual orientation and professional dance. *Archives of Sexual Behavior* 26:433-44.

Battles, K., and W. Hilton-Morrow. 2002. Gay characters in conventional spaces: *Will and Grace* and the situation comedy genre. *Critical Studies in Media Communication* 19:87-105.

Baumgarten, S. 2003. Boys dancing? You bet! *Teaching Elementary Physical Education* 14(5): 12-13.

Besner, F., and C. Spungin. 1995. *Gay and lesbian students: Understanding their needs.* Philadelphia: Taylor & Francis.

Biersterker, T. 1998. Globalisation and the models of operation of major institutional actors. *Oxford Development Studies* 20:15-31.

Blume, L.B. 2003. Embodied [by] dance: Adolescent de/constructions of body, sex and gender in physical education. *Sex Education* 3(2): 95-103.

Bond, K. 1994. How "wild things" tamed gender distinctions. *Journal of Physical Education, Recreation and Dance* 65(2): 28-33.

Bryson, S. 1999. The decline of gay and lesbian culture. *Psychiatric Services* 50: 422-24.

Burt, R. 1995. *The male dancer: Bodies, spectacle, sexualities.* New York: Routledge.

Clark, D. 1994. Voices of women dance educators: Considering issues of hegemony and the education/performer identity. *Impulse* 2(2): 122-30.

———. 2004. Considering the issue of sexploitation of young women in dance: K-12 perspectives. *Journal of Dance Education* 4(1): 17-23.

Crawford, J. 1994. Encouraging male participation in dance. *Journal of Physical Education, Recreation and Dance* 65(2): 40-3.

Cushway, D. 1996. Changing the dance curriculum. *Women's Studies Quarterly* 24(3-4): 118-22.

Daly, A. 1994. Gender issues in dance history pedagogy. *Journal of Physical Education, Recreation and Dance* 65(2): 34-5, 39.

Dance Magazine College Guide 2004-2005. 2004. New York: McFadden Communications Group.

DeFrantz, T. 1996. Simmering passivity: The Black male body in concert dance. In *Moving words: Re-writing dance,* ed. G. Morris, 107-120. New York: Routledge.

Diagne, S., and B. Ossebi. 1996. The cultural question in Africa: Issues, politics and research prospects. *Dakar, Senegal: Codestria Working Paper Series* 3(98): n.p.

Dils, A. 2004. Sexuality and sexual identity: Critical possibilities for teaching dance appreciation and dance history. *Journal of Dance Education* 4(1): 10-16.

Doi, M.M. 2002. *Gesture, gender, nation: Dance and social change in Uzbekistan.* Westport, CT: Bergin and Garvey.

Ferdun, E. 1994. Facing gender issues across the curriculum. *Journal of Physical Education, Recreation and Dance* 65(2): 46-7.

Flintoff, A. 1991. Dance, masculinity and teacher education. *The British Journal of Physical Education* Winter: 31-5.

Garber, E., D. Risner, R. Sandell, and M. Stankiewicz. 2006. Gender equity in the visual arts and dance education. In *Handbook for achieving gender equity through education,* ed. S. Klein, 359-380. Mahwah, NJ: Erlbaum.

Gard, M. 2001. Dancing around the "problem" of boys and dance. *Discourse: Studies in the Cultural Politics of Education* 22:213-25.

Gard, M. 2003a. Being someone else: Using dance in anti-oppressive teaching. *Educational Review* 55(2): 211-23.

———. 2003b. Moving and belonging: Dance, sport and sexuality. *Sex Education* 3(2): 105-18.

Gilman, S. 1986. Jewish self-hatred: Anti-Semitism and the hidden language of the Jews. Baltimore: Johns Hopkins University Press.

Green, J. 2000. Emancipatory pedagogy? Women's bodies and the creative process in dance. *Frontiers* 21(3): 124-40.

———. 2001. Socially constructed bodies in American dance classrooms. *Research in Dance Education* 2(2): 155-73.

———. 2002-03. Foucault and the training of docile bodies in dance education. *Arts and Learning* 19(1): 99-126.

———. 2004. The politics and ethics of health in dance education in the United States. In *Ethics and politics embodied in dance,* ed. E. Anttila, S. Hamalainen, and L. Rouhianen, 65-76. Helsinki, Finland: Theatre Academy of Finland.

Hamilton, L. 1998. *Advice for dancers: Emotional counsel and practical strategies.* New York: Jossey-Bass.

Hamilton, L. 1999. Coming out in dance: Paths to understanding. *Dance Magazine* November: 72-5.

Hanna, J.L. 1988. *Dance, sex, and gender: Signs of identity, dominance, defiance, and desire.* Chicago: University of Chicago Press.

Harris, D. 1997. *The rise and fall of gay culture.* New York: Hyperion.

Hasbrook, C. 1993. Sociocultural aspects of physical activity. *Research Quarterly for Exercise and Sport* 64(1): 106-15.

Higher Education Arts Data Services, Dance Annual Summary 2002-2003. 2003. Reston, VA: National Association of Schools of Dance.

Horwitz, C. 1995. Challenging dominant gender ideology through dance: Contact improvisation. PhD dissertation, University of Iowa.

Katz, J., and J. Earp. 1999. *Tough guise: Violence, media & the crisis in masculinity*. VHS. Directed by Sut Jhally. North Hampton, MA: Media Education Foundation.

Kerr-Berry, J. 1994. Using the power of Western African dance to combat gender issues. *Journal of Physical Education, Recreation and Dance* 65(2): 44-5, 48.

Keyworth, S.A. 2001. Critical autobiography: 'Straightening' out dance education. *Research in Dance Education* 2(2): 117-37.

Kimmel, M. 2005. What about the boys? In *Critical social issues in American education: Democracy and meaning in a globalizing world*, ed. H.S Shapiro and D. Purpel, 219-225. Mahwah, NJ: Erlbaum.

Kimmel, M., and M. Messner, eds. 2001. *Men's lives*. Needham Heights, MA: Allyn & Bacon.

Kraus, R., S. Hilsendager, and B. Dixon. 1991. *History of the dance in art and education*. 3rd ed. Englewood Cliffs, NJ: Prentice Hall.

Lehikoinen, K. 2005. *Stepping queerly: Discourses in dance education for boys in late 20th century Finland*. Oxford: Peter Lang.

Lehne, G. 1976. Homophobia among men. In *The forty-nine percent majority: The male sex role*, ed. D. David and R. Brannon, 66-88. Reading, MA: Addison-Wesley.

Letts, W., and C. Nobles. 2003. Embodied [by] curriculum: A critical pedagogy of embodiment. *Sex Education* 3(2): 91-4.

Lodge, M. 2001. Dancing up the broken ladder: The rise of the female director/choreographer in the American musical theatre. PhD dissertation, Bowling Green State University.

Margolies, L., M. Becker, and K. Jackson-Brewer. 1987. Internalized homophobia in gay men. In *Homosexuality and psychotherapy: A practitioner's handbook of affirmative models*, ed. J. Gonsiorek, 59-69. New York: Haworth Press.

Marques, I. 1998. Dance education in/and the postmodern. In *Dance, power, and difference: Critical and feminist perspectives on dance education*, ed. S. Shapiro, 171-185 Champaign, IL: Human Kinetics.

McGuire, L. 1999. The year of the angry young men: Performing gender at championship tap dance events. Master's thesis, York University.

Ohiorhenuan, J. 1998. The South in an era of globalisation. *Cooperation South* 2:6-15.

Pollack, W. 1999. *Real boys: Rescuing our boys from the myths of boyhood*. New York: Random House.

Posey, E. 2002. Dance education in dance schools in the private sector: Meeting the demands of the marketplace. *Journal of Dance Education* 2(2): 43-9.

Risner, D. 2001. Blurring the boundaries: Hope and possibility in the presence of the necessary stranger in gay liberation. PhD dissertation, University of North Carolina at Greensboro.

———. 2002a. Male participation and sexual orientation in dance education: Revisiting the open secret. *Journal of Dance Education* 2(3): 84-92.

———. 2002b. Re-educating dance education to its homosexuality: An invitation for critical analysis and professional unification. *Research in Dance Education* 3(2): 181-7.

———. 2003a. What Matthew Shepard would tell us: Gay and lesbian issues in education. In *The institution of education,* ed. H. Shapiro, S. Harden, and A. Pennell, 209-219. Boston: Pearson.

———. 2003b. Rehearsing heterosexuality: Unspoken truths in dance education. *Dance Research Journal* 34(2): 63-81.

———. 2004a. Dance, sexuality, and education today: Observations for dance educators. *Journal of Dance Education* 4(1): 5-9.

———. 2004b. The politics of student-centered practices in dance in higher education: Challenges to the ethical treatment of undergraduate dance students in the US. Paper presented at the Ethics and Politics Embodied in Dance International Research Symposium, December 9-14, Helsinki, Finland.

———. 2005. Dance and sexuality: Opportunities for teaching and learning in dance education. *Journal of Dance Education* 5(2): 41-2.

———. 2006. Critical social issues in dance education. In *International handbook for research in arts education,* ed. L. Bresler, 965-982. New York: Kulwer.

Risner, D., H. Godfrey, and L. Simmons. 2004. The impact of sexuality in contemporary culture: An interpretive study of perceptions and choices in private sector dance education. *Journal of Dance Education* 4(1): 23-32.

Risner, D., and D. Prioleau. 2004. Leadership and administration in dance in higher education: Challenges and responsibilities of the department chair. In *Merging worlds: Dance, education, society and politics, Conference proceedings of the 6th Annual Meeting of the National Dance Education Organization,* ed. D. Risner and J. Anderson, 343-351. Bethesda, MD: National Dance Education Organization.

Risner, D., and S. Thompson. 2005. HIV/AIDS in dance education: A pilot study in higher education. *Journal of Dance Education* 5(2): 70-6.

Rofes, E. 1995. Making our schools safe for sissies. In *The gay teen*, ed. G. Unks, 79-84. New York: Routledge.

Samuels, S. March 2001. Study exposes dance gender gap. *Dance Magazine* 35-7.

Sanderson, P. 1996. Dance within the national curriculum for physical education of England and Wales. *European Physical Education Review* 2(1): 54-63.

———. 2001. Age and gender issues in adolescent attitudes to dance. *European Physical Education Review* 7(2): 117-36.

Schaffman, K. 2001. From the margins to the mainstream: Contact improvisation and the commodification of touch. PhD dissertation, University of California at Riverside.

Sedgwick, E. 1990. *Epistemology of the closet*. Berkeley, CA: University of California Press.

Shapiro, H., and D. Purpel, eds. 2005. *Critical social issues in American education: Democracy and meaning in a globalizing world*. 3rd ed. Mahwah, NJ: Erlbaum.

Shapiro, S. 1998. Toward transformative teachers: Critical and feminist perspectives in dance education. In *Dance, power, and difference: Critical and feminist perspectives on dance education*, ed. S. Shapiro, 7-21. Champaign, IL: Human Kinetics.

———. 2004. Recovering girlhood: A pedagogy of embodiment. *Journal of Dance Education* 4(1): 35-6.

Smith, C. 1998. On authoritarianism in the dance classroom. In *Dance, power, and difference: Critical and feminist perspectives on dance education*, ed. S. Shapiro, 123-146. Champaign, IL: Human Kinetics.

Spurgeon, D. 1999. The men's movement. Paper presented at Congress on Research in Dance, Pomona College, Claremont, CA.

Stinson, S. 1998a. Places where I've been: Reflections on issues of gender in dance education, research, and administration. *Choreography and Dance* 5(1): 117-27.

———. 1998b. Seeking a feminist pedagogy for children's dance. In *Dance, power, and difference: Critical and feminist perspectives on dance education*, ed. S. Shapiro, 23-47. Champaign, IL: Human Kinetics.

———. 2001. Voices from adolescent males. *DACI in Print* 2:4-6.

———. 2005. The hidden curriculum of gender in dance education. *Journal of Dance Education* 5(2): 51-7.

Stinson, S., D. Blumenfeld-Jones, and J. Van Dyke. 1990. Voices of young women dance students: An interpretive study of meaning in dance. *Dance Research Journal* 22(2): 13-22.

Thomas, H. 1996. Dancing the difference. *Women's Studies International Forum* 19(5): 505-511.

Van Dyke, J. 1992. *Modern dance in a postmodern world: An analysis of federal arts funding and its impact on the field of modern dance.* Reston, VA: American Alliance for Health, Physical Education, Recreation and Dance.

———. 1996. Gender and success in the American dance world. *Women's Studies International Forum* 19(5): 535-43.

Warburton, E., and M. Stanek. 2004. The condition of dance faculty in higher education. In *Merging worlds: Dance, education, society and politics, Conference proceedings of the 6th Annual Meeting of the National Dance Education Organization,* ed. D. Risner and J. Anderson, 420-425. Bethesda, MD: National Dance Education Organization.

Welch, S. 1999. *Sweet dreams in America: Making ethics and spirituality work* New York: Routledge.

chapter 6

Acts of Love Under a Southern Moon. VHS. Choreographer Lliane Loots, Flatfoot Dance Company, recorded in the Elizabeth Sneddon Theatre, University of KwaZulu Natal, May 2005. Available from Flatfoot Dance Company, lootsl@ukzn.ac.za.

The Beautyful Ones Must Be Born. VHS. Choreographer Jay Pather, Siwela Sonke Dance Theatre, recorded on Constitution Hill, Johannesburg, March 2005. Siwela Sonke Dance Theatre, ericshabalala@yahoo.com.

Dudlu Ntombi Interim Report. July 2005. Unpublished. Available from KZN DanceLink; website: www.kzndancelink.co.za.

Epoppée Likelembe Programme. 2004. Unpublished. Available from the African Music Project at the University of KwaZulu-Natal, opondop@ ukzn.ac.za, www.music.ukzn.ac.za.

Flatfoot Dance Company. 2005. *Interim report from Flatfoot Dance Company (July 2005) for KZN DanceLink.* Durban, South Africa: Author.

Gouldie, D. August 2005. African contemporary dance? Proceedings of the JOMBA! Contemporary Dance Conference 2004. Panel discussion, *Creating critical dance work in south Africa.* Conference Papers, coordinated by the Centre for Creative Arts www.cca.ukzn.ac.za.

Hlatshwayo, M. August 2005. African contemporary dance? Proceedings of the JOMBA! Contemporary Dance Conference 2004. Panel discussion, *Young choreographers debate the African dance aesthetic.*

Hoare, Q., and G.N. Smith. 1971. *Selections from the prison notebooks of Antonio Gramsci.* London: Lawrence and Wishart.

KZN DanceLink newsletters, 1,2,3,4.

Maqoma, G. 2005. African contemporary dance? Proceedings of the JOMBA! Contemporary Dance Conference 2004. Keynote Address, *Beyond ethnicity*.

Maree, L. 2004. *The state of the art(s) in* State of the Nation 2004-2005. Cape Town, South Africa: HSRC Press.

Pather, J. August 2005, African contemporary dance? Proceedings of the JOMBA! Contemporary Dance Conference 2004. Keynote address, *Rape is not a cliché*.

Pather, J. 2004. Interview in *Personal affects, power and poetics in contemporary South African art*, New York: Museum for African Art; Cape Town, South Africa: Spier.

chapter 7

Beardall, N. 2005. Dance the dream: Reflections on an eighth grade dance class. In *The arts, education, and social change: Little signs of hope*, ed. M.C. Powell and V.M. Speiser, 7–24. New York: Peter Lang.

Bowles, S. & Gintis, H. In Beyer, L.E. 2000. *The arts, popular culture, and social change*. New York: Peter Lang.

Eisner, E. W. 1996. *Cognition and curriculum reconsidered*. 2nd ed. New York: Paul Chapman.

Horan Jr., R.A. 2000. *Teacher talk: A post-formal inquiry into educational change*. New York: Peter Lang.

Hart, T. 2001. *From information to transformation: Education for the evolution of consciousness*. New York: Peter Lang.

Hinchey, P.H. 2006. *Becoming a critical educator: Defining a classroom identity, designing a critical pedagogy*. New York: Peter Lang.

Ritenburg, H.M. 2001. Relationships in learning: Arts Education at the University of Regina—An interview with Dr. Norman C. Yakel. *McGill Journal of Education* 36(3): 261-70.

Scholte, J. 2000. *Globalization. A critical introduction*. Houndsmills, United Kingdom: Macmillan.

Sklar, D. 1991. On dance ethnography. *Dance Research Journal* 23/1(Spring): 6–10.

Singh, M., Kenway, J., and Apple, M.W. 2005. Globalization education: Policies, pedagogies, & politics. New York: Peter Lang.

Wiki Books. 2007. *SA NCS: Dance Studies.* http://en.wikibooks.org/wiki/SA_NCS:Dance_Studies.

chapter 8

Anttila, E. 2004. Dance learning as practice of freedom. In *The same difference? Ethical and political perspectives on dance,* ed. E. Anttila, S. Hämäläinen, L. Rouhiainen, and T. Löytönen, 19-62. *Acta Scenica* 17. Finland: Theatre Academy.

Anttila, E. 2003a. A dream journey to the unknown: Searching for dialogue in dance education. PhD diss., *Acta Scenica* 14. Finland: Theatre Academy.

Anttila, E. 2003b. Lectio Praecursoria. Theatre Academy. www2.teak. fi/viikkis/vko36-37_03Liite1.htm.

Boal, A. 2000. *Theatre of the oppressed.* London: Pluto Press.

Boal, A. 1992. *Games for actors and non-actors.* London: Routledge.

Bond, K.E. 2000. Revisioning purpose: Children, dance and the culture of caring. Keynote address. In *Proceeding—Extensions and extremities: Points of departure,* ed. J.E. LeDrew and H. Rittenberg, 3-14. Regina, Saskatchewan: Dance and the Child International.

Bruner, J. 1996. *The culture of education.* Cambridge: Harvard University Press.

Buber, M. 1947. *Between man and man.* Trans. R.G. Smith. London: Kegan Paul.

Buber, M. 1937/1970. *I and thou.* Trans. W. Kaufman. Edinburgh: Clark.

Crowther, P. 1993. *Art and embodiment: From aesthetics to self-consciousness.* New York: Oxford University Press.

Damasio, A. 1999. *The feeling of what happens: Body and emotion in the making of consciousness.* New York: Harcourt Brace.

Damasio, A. 1994. *Descartes' error: Emotion, reason, and the human brain.* New York: Putnam.

Eisner, E. 2004. What can education learn from the arts about the practice of education? *International Journal of Education and the Arts.* 5(4). www. ijea.org/v5n4/index.html.

Ellsworth, E. 1992. Why doesn't this feel empowering? Working through the repressive myths of critical pedagogy. In *Feminisms and critical pedagogy,* ed. C. Luke and J. Gore, 90-119. New York: Routledge.

Fraleigh, S. 2000. Consciousness matters. *Dance Research Journal* 32(1): 54-62.

Freire, P. 1998a. Pedagogy of the heart. Trans. D. Macedo and A. Oliveira New York: Continuum.

Freire, P. 1998b. *Pedagogy of freedom: Ethics, democracy and civic courage.* Trans. P. Clarke. Lanham, MD: Rowman & Littlefield.

Freire, P. 1996. Pedagogy of hope. Reliving pedagogy of the oppressed Trans. R.R. Barr New York: Continuum.

Freire, P. 1972. Pedagogy of the oppressed (M.B. Ramos, Trans.). Harmondsworth: Penguin Education.

Gergen, K.J. 1999. *An invitation to social construction.* London: Sage.

Glaser, Daniel. *The Dancer's Brain.* www.youramazingbrain.org/Brainbody/dancers.htm.

Green, J. 2002. Somatic knowledge: The body as content and methodology in dance education. *Journal of Dance Education* 2(4): 114-8.

Greene, M. 1995. *Releasing the imagination: Essays on education, the arts, and social change.* San Francisco: Jossey-Bass.

Hanna, T. 1985. *Bodies in revolt: A primer in somatic thinking.* Novato, CA: Freeperson Press.

Kenway, J., and H. Modra. 1992. Feminist pedagogy and emancipatory possibilities. In *Feminisms and critical pedagogy,* ed. C. Luke and J. Gore, 138-66. New York: Routledge.

Lakoff, G., and M. Johnson. 1999. *Philosophy in the flesh: The embodied mind and its challenge to Western thought.* New York: Basic Books.

Lakoff, G. and M. Johnson. 1980. *Metaphors we live by.* Chicago: Chicago University Press.

Lexova, I. 2000. *Ancient Egyptian dances.* Mineola, NY: Dover.

Marques, I. 1998. Dance education in/and the postmodern. In *Dance, power and difference,* ed. S. Shapiro, 171-85. Champaign, IL: Human Kinetics.

Marques, I. A. 1997. Context-based dance education. Proceedings of the 7th International Conference of Dance and the Child International: The call of forests and lakes. Kuopio, Finland: Dance and the Child International, 240-247.

Merleau-Ponty, M. 1945/1995. *Phenomenology of perception.* London: Routledge.

Oddey, A. 1994. *Devising: A practical and theoretical handbook.* London: Routledge.

Parviainen, J. 2002. Bodily knowledge: Epistemological reflections on dance. *Dance Research Journal* 34(1): 11-26.

Shapiro, S.B. 1999. *Pedagogy and the politics of the body: A critical praxis.* New York: Garland.

Shapiro, S.B. 1998. Toward transformative teachers. In *Dance, power and difference,* ed. S. Shapiro, 7-21. Champaign, IL: Human Kinetics.

Stinson, S.W. 2004. My body/myself: Lessons from dance education. In *Knowing bodies, feeling minds: Embodied knowledge in arts education and schooling,* ed. L. Bresler, 153-68. Dordrecht, Netherlands: Kluwer.

Stinson, S.W. 2001. Choreographing a life: Reflections on curriculum design, consciousness and possibility. *Journal of Dance Education* 1(1): 26-33.

Stinson, S.W. 1998. Seeking a feminist pedagogy for children's dance. In *Dance, power and difference,* ed. S. Shapiro, 23-47. Champaign, IL: Human Kinetics.

Stinson, S.W. 1995. Body of knowledge. *Educational Theory* 45(1): 43-54.

The Great Hymn to the Aten. http://katherinestange.com/egypt/hymn. htm. Retrieved on November 8, 2007.

Thomas, H. 2003. *The body, dance and cultural theory.* New York: Palgrave Macmillan.

Varela, F. 1991. *Embodied mind: Cognitive science and human experience.* Chicago: MIT Press.

Waltari, M. 1949/2002. *The Egyptian: The novel.* Trans. N. Walford New York: G.P. Putnam. (Original published in 1945.)

chapter 9

Bruce, T. 2004. Developing learning in early childhood. London: Sage.

Chang, C.-S. 1991. A creative dance curriculum model for elementary children in Taiwan, Republic of China. PhD dissertation, Columbia University.

Chang, C.-S. 1997. Research into integrated dance curriculum. Taipei: Cloud Gate.

Davies, M. 1995. Helping children to learn through a movement perspective. London: Hodder & Stoughton.

Davies, M. 2003. Movement and dance in early childhood. 2nd ed. London: Chapman.

Elliott, J. 1991. Action research for educational change. Milton Keynes: Open University Press.

Humphrey, D. 1959/1987. The art of making dances. London: Dance Books.

Kapsch, L.A., and A.C. Kruger. 2004. Change in figure drawing following kinesthetic experience. *Visual Arts Research* 30:62-74.

Krechevsky, M., and B. Mardell. 2001. Four features of learning in groups. In *Making learning visible: Children as individual and group learners*, ed. Project Zero and Reggio Children, 284-94. Reggio Emilia: Reggio Children.

Laban, R., and L. Ullmann. 1988. *Modern educational dance*. 3rd ed. London: Northcote House.

Liu, S.-Y. 1998. Reflection on dance education in primary schools in Taiwan. *Kang Hsuan Educational Magazine* 34:9.

Matthews, J. 2003. *Drawing and painting: Children and visual representation*. 2nd ed. London: Chapman.

National Dance Education Organization. 2006. National Dance Education Organization, USA. www.ndeo.org/education.asp.

National Dance Teachers Association. 2006. National Dance Teachers Association, UK. www.ndta.org.uk.

Project Zero. 2006. Project Zero at the Harvard Graduate School of Education. www.pz.harvard.edu.

Sahasrabudhe, P. 2005. *Transmissions and transformations: Learning though the arts in Asia* (an issues paper). New Delhi: India International Center and UNESCO.

Smith-Autard, J. 1994. *The art of dance in education*. London: Black.

Stinson, S. 1991. Transforming movement into dance for young children. In *Early childhood creative arts* ed. L.Y. Overby, pp. 134-139 . Reston, VA: American Alliance for Health, Physical Education, Recreation and Dance.

Taiwanese Ministry of Education. 1998. The guidelines for nine-year integrated curricula. Taipei: Taiwanese Ministry of Education.

Vygotsky, L. 1978. *Mind in society: The development of higher psychological processes*. Cambridge, MA: Harvard University Press.

Whitebread, D. 1996. Young children learning and early years teaching. In *Teaching and learning in the early years*, ed. D. Whitebread, 1-20. London: Routledge.

Zelazo, P., and S. Lourenco. 2003. Imitation and the dialectic of representation. *Developmental Reviews* 23:55-78.

chapter 10

Cruz, C., and P. McLaren. 2002. Queer bodies and configurations: Toward a critical pedagogy of the body. In *Body movements*, ed. S. Shapiro and S. Shapiro, 187-207. Cresskill, NJ: Hampton Press.

Dewey, J. 1934. *Art as experience*. New York: Penguin Books.

Freire, P. 1988. *Pedagogy of the oppressed*. New York: Continuum.

Greene, M. 1973. *Teacher as stranger: Educational philosophy for the modern age*. Belmont, CA: Wadsworth.

Greene, M. 1988. *The dialectic of freedom*. New York: Teachers College Press.

Greene, M. 1995. *Releasing the imagination: Essays on education, the arts, and social change*. San Francisco: Jossey-Bass.

Greene, M. 2001. *Exclusions and awakenings: The life of Maxine Greene*. VHS. Hancock Productions.

Greenwood, J. 2001. Within a third space. *Research in Drama Education* 6(2): 193-205.

McLaren, P. 1999. *Schooling as a ritual performance: Toward a political economy of educational symbols and gestures*. Lanham, MD: Rowman & Littlefield.

Ministry of Education. 2000. *The arts in the New Zealand curriculum*. Wellington, New Zealand: Learning Media.

Shapiro, S. B. 1994. Re-membering the body in critical pedagogy. *Education and Society* 12(1): 61-79.

Shapiro, S.B. 1998. Toward transformative teachers: Critical and feminist perspectives in dance education. In *Dance, power and difference: Critical and feminist perspectives of dance education*, ed. S. Shapiro, 7-21. Champaign, IL: Human Kinetics.

Shapiro, S., and S. Shapiro. 2002. Silent voices, bodies of knowledge: Towards a critical pedagogy of the body. In *Body movements: Pedagogy, politics, and social change*, ed. S. Shapiro and S. Shapiro, 25-43. Cresskill, NJ: Hampton Press.

Zandy, J. 2000. Decloaking class: Why class identity and consciousness count. In *The Institute of Education*, 5th ed., ed. H. S. Shapiro, K. Latham, and S. Ross, 175-185. Boston: Pearson Custom.

chapter 11

Arendt, H. 1958. *The human condition*. Chicago: University of Chicago Press.

Arendt, H. 1976. *The life of the mind: Willing*. Vol. 2. London: Secker & Warburg.

Armstrong, K. 2005. *A short history of myth*. Edinburgh: Canongate Books.

Cavarero, A. 2000. *Relating narratives: Storytelling and selfhood.* London: Routledge.

Fortunoff, D. 2002 Ancient philosophy dialogue, dialectic, and maieutic: Plato's dialogues as educational models. www.bu.edu/wcp/papers/Anci/AnciFort.htm.

Gubernatis, R., and L. Bentiviglio. 1986. *Pina Bausch.* Paris: Theatre de la Ville et Centre International des Lettres.

Hoghe, R. 1980. The theatre of Pina Bausch. *Drama Review* 24(1): 63-74.

Lilja, E. 2003. *Words on dance.* Trans. Frank Perry. Stockholm: ELD.

Lilja, E. 2004. *Dance: For better, for worse.* Trans. Frank Perry. Stockholm: ELD.

Markard, A. 1985. *Jooss.* Cologne: Ballet Bühnen Verlag.

Melrose, S. August 23, 2002. Please adjust your set. Keynote address presented at Goat Island/Bristol University Summer School and Symposium, Arnolfini/University of Bristol. www.sfmelrose.u-net.com/adjustyourset.

Platón. *Obras Selectas.* Trans. Francisco Márquez. Madrid: Edimat Libros.

Sánchez-Colberg, A. 1992. *Traditions and contradictions: A choreological documentation of Tanztheater from its roots in Ausdruckstanz to the present.* PhD dissertation, Laban Centre, London.

Sánchez-Colberg, A. 1993. You can see it like this or like that. In *Parallel lines,* ed. S. Jordan and D. Allen. London: Arts Council.

Sánchez-Colberg, A. 1993. You put your left foot in . . . then you shake it all about: Excursions and incursions into feminism and Bausch's Tanztheater. In *Dance, culture and gender,* ed. H. Thomas, 151-63. London: MacMillan.

Sánchez-Colberg, A. 1996. Altered states and subliminal places: Charting the road toward a physical theatre. *Performance Research* 1(2). 40-56.

Sánchez-Colberg, A. 1998. By independent means. *Animated* Summer. 9-10.

Sánchez-Colberg, A. 2000. On dance, cities and the globe: Futur/Perfekt. *Animated* December www.communitydance.org.uk/metadot/index.pl?id=22231&isa=DBRow&op=show&dbview_id=17860

Sánchez-Colberg, A., and E. Robson. 2000. Becoming space: Futur/Perfekt. *Dance Theatre Journal* December. 36-40.

Sánchez-Colberg, A. 2004. "An(n)a annotated: A critical journey" in *The same difference: Ethical and political issues in dance. Acta Scenica* 17. 193-233.

Storey, A.M. 1940. The art of Kurt Jooss. *Dancing Times* 596-7.

chapter 12

Bauman, Z. 1998. *Globalization: The human consequences.* New York: Columbia Press.

Berman, M. 1989. Coming to our senses: Body and spirit in the hidden history of the west. New York: Bantam

Burn, S. 2005. *Women across cultures: A global perspective.* New York: McGraw-Hill.

Devine, J. 1996. *Maximum security: The culture of violence in inner-city schools.* Chicago: University of Chicago Press.

Eagleton, T. 1990. *The ideology of the aesthetic.* Cambridge, MA: Blackwell.

Eagleton, T. 1996. *The illusions of postmodernism.* Cambridge, MA: Blackwell.

Farley, W. 1985. *Eros for other: Retaining truth in a pluralistic world.* University Park, PA: Pennsylvania State University Press.

Ferdman B.M., 1995. Cultural identity and diversity in organisations: Bridging the gap between group differences and individual uniqueness. In *Diversity in organisations: New perspectives for a changing workplace.* MM Chemers. S Oskamp and MA Costanzo (eds). Thousand Oaks, CA: Sage.

Freire, P., and A.M. Araújo Freire. 1994. Pedagogy of hope : reliving pedagogy of the oppressed. New York: Continuum.

Giroux, H.A., and R.I. Simon. 1988. Schooling, popular culture, and a pedagogy of possibility. *Journal of Education,* 170(1), 9-26.

Greene, M. 1986. In search of a critical pedagogy. *Harvard Educational Review,* 56(4), 427-441.

Greene, M. 1988. *The dialectic of freedom.* New York: Teachers College Press.

Heidegger, M. 1968. *What is called thinking.* Trans. F. Wieck and J. Gray. New York: Harper & Row.

Martin, E. 1989. The cultural construction of gendered bodies: Biology and metaphors of production and destruction. *Ethnos* 54(3-4): 143-60.

MacDonald, J. 2005. *Theory as a prayerful act: The collected essays of James B. MacDonald* Ed: Bradley MacDonald. New York. Peter Lang.

McDade, L. 1987. Sex, pregnancy, and schooling: Obstacles to a critical teaching of the body. *Journal of Education* 169(3): 58-79.

McWilliam, E., and P. Taylor, eds. 1996. Pedagogy, technology, and the body. New York: Peter Lang.

Paris, C. 2001. Defining the African American presence in postmodern dance from the Judson Church Era to the 1990s. *CORD* 2001; Transmigratory Moves Dance in Global Circulation, 234-243.

Schrader, C. 2005. *A sense of dance: Exploring your movement potential.* Champaign, IL: Human Kinetics.

Shapiro, S., and S. Shapiro. 2002. *Body movement: Pedagogy, politics, and social change.* New Jersey: Hampton Press

Shapiro, S. 1999. *Pedagogy and the politics of the body: A critical praxis.* New York: Garland.

Shapiro, S., and S. Shapiro. 1995. Silent voices, bodies of knowledge: Towards a critical pedagogy of the body. *Journal of Curriculum Theorizing* 1:49-72.

Shaw, B.D. 1996. Body/power/identity: Passions of the martyrs. *Journal of Early Christian Studies* 4(3): 269-312.

Smith, D. 1999. *Zygmunt Bauman: Prophet of postmodernity.* Oxford, UK: Blackwell.

Venable, E. 1999. Inventing tradition: Innovation and survival. *CORD* 2000: *Transmigratory Moves Dance in Global Circulation,* 281-290.

index

Note: The italicized *f* or *t* after page references indicate information contained in figures or tables, respectively.

about the editor

Sherry Shapiro, EdD, is a professor of dance and director of women's studies at Meredith College in Raleigh, North Carolina. She earned her EdD in curriculum and teaching (specialization in cultural studies) at the University of North Carolina at Greensboro, her MA in leadership and higher education (specialization in community education), and her BA in interdisciplinary studies at Appalachian State University in North Carolina.

Shapiro has served in state, national, and international organizations; presented nationally and internationally; and is the author or editor of three books: *Body Movements: Pedagogy, Politics and Social Change* (2002); *Pedagogy and the Politics of the Body: A Critical Praxis* (1999); and *Dance, Power and Difference: Critical and Feminist Perspectives in Dance Education* (1998). Chapters in books and articles have been published and reviewed in the United States, Australia, the United Kingdom, and Brazil. She has received awards for research and artistic work as well as her work as a dance educator. Shapiro has served as a project coordinator for a program in peace education research developed as a joint effort between North Carolina and the University of Haifa, Israel, and as the research officer for Dance and the Child International (daCi). Dr. Shapiro is now serving as one of the cochairs of program administration and development for the National Women's Studies Association. Her research interests include examining the notion of embodied pedagogy, aesthetic education and its connections to personal and social transformation, and the relationship of dance to feminist and cultural studies. She attempts to interrogate what it means to become a dancer and the phenomenon of being in dance through the use of critical theory, phenomenological description, and gender studies. Her choreographic work has provided a rich context for exploring the ways in which women's identities are constructed in the context of culture, power, and difference.

about the contributors

Eeva Anttila, PhD, has taught dance since 1980, specializing in children's dance education and dance in public schools. Her doctoral dissertation (2003) focuses on dialogue in dance education. Currently she works as a professor of dance pedagogy and department head in the Theatre Academy department of dance and theatre pedagogy in Finland. Her current interests include feminist and critical pedagogy, dialogical philosophy and its application in dance pedagogy, issues of power and emancipation in dance education, and the notions of body memories and embodied knowledge. She has been involved with daCi (Dance and the Child International) since 1988 and is currently a member and chair-elect of the executive board of daCi. Her publications include *Tanssin Aika* (*Time for Dance*), a handbook of dance education (1994); *Tanssi: Kehon Leikkiä* (*Dance: Body Play*, 2001); *Kaikuja Salista* (*Echoes From the Studio*, 2003); *A Dream Journey to the Unknown: Searching for Dialogue in Dance Education* (2003); and *Dance Learning as Practice of Freedom* (2004).

Ann Kipling Brown, PhD, is currently a professor of dance education in the arts education program in the faculty of education at the University of Regina in Saskatchewan. She works extensively with youth and adults and leads classes in technique, composition, and notation. Her research and publications focus on dance pedagogy, the integration of notation in dance programs, the application of technology in dance education, and the role of dance in children's and adults' worlds. In her professional and community service, Ann has served for several years on the advisory committee and the reference committee for Arts Education for Saskatchewan Education. She has been actively involved in the cultural community, serving on the Regina Arts Commission, Dance Saskatchewan Inc., and SaskCulture Inc. as a committee member and as president. She has also served on several international committees: Congress on Research in Dance, Dance and the Child International (daCi), and International Council of Kinetography Laban. She was the chairperson for the daCi conference 2000 held in Regina and is currently chair for the international organization.

Ana Sánchez-Colberg, PhD, MFA, completed a BA in theater studies and English drama literature at the University of Pennsylvania. She then pursued an MFA in choreography at Temple University in Philadelphia. Under the tutelage of Helmut Gottschild, a former assistant to Mary Wigman, she trained in Wigman, Jooss, and Tanztheater techniques. In 1992 she received her PhD for her research on German Tanztheater.

Since 1989 Sánchez-Colberg has been the artistic director and choreographer for Theatre enCorps, with whom she tours nationally and internationally. The work has received various awards, including the Bonnie Bird Choreography Award in 1995 and, most recently, the Creative Collaborations in Music Award in 2004 for the piece *Mahler's Fifths*. She has won an award from the Swedish Research Council to research and produce the work *We: Implicated and Complicated*, in collaboration with the Danshogskolan and Theatre enCorps. The work will be premiered in Stockholm in April 2007.

Dr. Sánchez-Colberg has also worked with various international companies. She has, among numerous other productions, produced four commissioned pieces for Ballet Concierto de Puerto Rico and for the Ballett des Staatstheaters Cottbus.

Apart from a number of master classes and seminars held around the globe, she contributes regularly to publications such as *Performance Research*, *Total Theatre Magazine*, *Animated*, and *Dance Theatre Journal*. She coedited, with Valerie Preston-Dunlop, *Dance and the Performative*. She contributed a chapter in *The Same Difference: Ethical and Political Issues in Contemporary Dance and Education* (2004).

Ivančica Janković, BA, was born in Zagreb, Croatia. She graduated from the Ana Maletić School of Contemporary Dance in Zagreb and from the Zagreb Faculty of Philosophy, where she earned a BA degree in English language and literature and Spanish language. She started her professional career as a dancer with the Zagreb Dance Company and subsequently became interested in dance education. Since 1974 she has been teaching Laban's theory and practice as well as rhythmics and choreography at the Ana Maletić School of Contemporary Dance. In 2001 she received the Annual Teaching Award. Her students have been awarded numerous first prizes at state dance competitions and at an international competition in Hungary. Apart from teaching, she is expanding her professional interests by writing on issues in dance education, translating movement and dance textbooks from English into Croatian, and giving lectures and workshops at home and abroad. Currently she is serving her second term as a member at large on the executive committee of Dance and the Child International (daCi).

Shu-Ying Liu, PhD, MFA, is an associate professor of dance education in the early childhood education department at the National Hsinchu University of Education in Taiwan. She has also taught in the United States, the United Kingdom, Portugal, and Macao. In 2005 she was a committee member and conference performance organizer at the Art in Early Childhood International conference at Roehampton University in London. In Taiwan she has led projects writing handbooks for creative dance in early childhood and elementary education for Taiwanese teachers and edited the Chinese translations of Willis' *Dance Education From the Trenches* (2004) and Overby's *Interdisciplinary Learning Through Dance: 101 Moventures* (2005). She has presented papers and articles related to her research on the integration of dance and visual arts in the kindergarten curriculum in Taiwan at several international conferences and in both English and Chinese publications. She also contributed "Commentary: A Taiwanese Perspective on Assessment and Evaluation in Dance" in Bresler's *International Handbook for Research in Arts Education* (2006).

Lynn Maree is an educator whose life became caught up in dance when she became the education lecturer at London College of Dance and Drama, where dance teachers were trained. Born in South Africa, she returned there in time for the first democratic elections in 1994 to be the dance director at the Playhouse Company in Durban, a post she left in 1999. She is currently running KZN DanceLink, an umbrella organization for dance in KwaZulu Natal, South Africa. She serves as an advisor for dance to the National Arts Council of South Africa and facilitates antiracism workshops for organizations across the country. Publications related to dance and the arts include "State of the Art(s)," *State of the Nation,* HSRC (October 2004) and "Let the People Dance" in *Africa Is Calling: South African Arts and Culture Manifestation Germany 2006.*

Lúcia Matos, PhD, is a professor of dance theory and practice and research methodology at Faculdade Social da Bahia in Brazil, where she coordinates the scenic arts course. Her doctoral thesis (2006) addresses the construction of bodies in Brazilian contemporary dance groups that include disabled members. She teaches contemporary dance to deaf children and youth in the special education program of the public school system. In 1999 she wrote the dance standards for public schools in the city of Salvador. She is a research associate at GIPE-CIT, an interdisciplinary research group of the Federal University of Bahia, whose focus is education, the arts, and diversity. In 2005 she was nominated representative of the State of Bahia for the Funarte advisory board (sectorial dance chamber) of the Ministry of Culture, working on proposals for public policies on dance in Brazil. She was the chair of the Ninth daCi conference in 2003 (Salvador, Bahia, Brazil) and nominated member at large of daCi's advisory board (2003-2006). She published an article in the book *Temas em Contemporaneidade* (*Contemporary Topics,* 2000) as well as articles in journals and conference proceedings in Brazil and abroad.

Doug Risner, PhD, MFA, is chair and associate professor of dance, Maggie Allesee department of dance at Wayne State University, Detroit, Michigan. His research focuses on critical social issues in dance education. Risner is editor of the *Journal of Dance Education* and serves on the board of directors for the National Dance Education Organization (NDEO). His work has been funded by the Pennsylvania Council on the Arts, the H. George and Jutta F. Anderson Endowment, the North Carolina Department of Public Education, Iowa Arts Council, McNair Scholars Program, and DanceUSA/National Endowment for the Arts. Risner contributes to *Research in Dance Education, Arts Education Policy Review, Dance Research Journal, Journal of Dance Education,* and *Chronicle of Higher Education.* Publications include "Critical Social Issues in Dance Education Research" in Bresler's *International Handbook for Research in Arts Education* (2007) and "Gender Equity in the Visual Arts and Dance Education" in Klein's *Handbook for Achieving Gender Equity Through Education* (2007).

Adrienne Sansom, PhD, is a senior lecturer in dance and drama for early childhood and primary teacher education at the University of Auckland, incorporating the Auckland College of Education, Te Kura Akoranga o Tamaki Makaurau, in Aotearoa/New Zealand. In 2005 she completed her PhD at the University of North Carolina at Greensboro, where her focus was on dance education as critical pedagogy. Adrienne's pedagogy and thus philosophical beliefs are embedded in principles and practices of early childhood education, and her research and writing focus on the body (its presence or absence) and embodied knowing in education. Since 1978 Adrienne has been a member of Dance and the Child International (daCi), and she currently holds the position of research officer on the international committee.

Michael Seaver is a critic and writer with the *Irish Times, Ballet Tanz* magazine, and other publications. He is also a publisher with Kinetic Reflex and has written a study on Irish dance development titled *Weft and Weave* and contributed to *Dancing on the Edge of Europe* and *The Word Life of Dances*. Prior to his dance writing, he worked as a composer, performer, and educator with dance companies in Europe and Mexico. He has curated events on kinesthetic intelligence and criticism for the Irish Arts Council's Critical Voices program and is a cofounder of Dance Research Forum Ireland.

Christopher A. Walker, MFA, is a dancer and choreographer with the National Dance Theatre Company of Jamaica (NDTC). He is also the founder and artistic director of Voices, a dance company exploring the fusion of Caribbean dance and contemporary styles using the traditional stage, alternative spaces, and multimedia as a medium. With Voices, he performed on university campuses in Western New York. With the NDTC, Mr. Walker toured the United Kingdom, the United States, Canada, and the Caribbean. His choreography has been performed in Jamaica, New York, and England, where he has presented solo work for the HIP Dance Festival. In addition, he taught Caribbean dance workshops in Jamaica, England, and the United States and conducted several successful artistic residencies at universities, including Hobart and Williams Smith Colleges, Wayne State University, and Temple University. Mr. Walker is a graduate of the Edna Manley College of the Visual and Performing Arts (EMCVPA) in Kingston, Jamaica, where he received awards for excellence in choreography and dance theater production. He also holds MFA and BFA degrees from the State University of New York College at Brockport, where he taught for over two years. In 2004 Walker received the highest award in the Thayer Fellowship in the Arts Competition in New York and a certificate of merit from the American Theatre Festival Association for his choreography of "Once on This Island" for Brockport's department of theatre. He has since returned to Jamaica to work with the NDTC and his alma mater, the EMCVPA, where he serves as a researcher and lecturer in folk and traditional dance studies. Most recently he received a nomination for best choreography in a musical for Jamaica's Annual National Pantomime and continues to tour and conduct artistic residencies at schools and colleges throughout the United States. Walker is currently a visiting lecturer at the University of Wisconsin at Madison.